From reviews of
The Politics of the Judiciary:

'In his soberly ordered, authoritative exposition and in his telling selection of examples, he has rendered sterling service to all – academic, practitioner and sober citizen alike' – Andrew Currie, *TES*

'The argument of J. A. G. Griffith's book is short, clear and irrefutable' – *Tribune*

'Brilliant little book, which is all the more powerful for being closely and soberly argued and is no mere polemic' – Antony Grey, *Freethinker*

'Informative, accurate, lucid, succinct, lively and provocative, without being extreme. John Griffith has satisfied all of these criteria. The work can be recommended with confidence to sixth formers and beginning law students as well as to a wider audience . . . a substantial contribution to public debate' – William Twining, *Public Law*

'The whole work is a magnificent survey of what is becoming a communal anxiety. All the relevant authorities are paraded and intelligently interpreted' – *Justice of the Peace*

J. A. G. GRIFFITH was born in 1918 and educated at Taunton School and the London School of Economics and Political Science (LSE). He has been on the staff of LSE since 1948, becoming Professor of English Law in 1959 and of Public Law from 1970 until his retirement in 1984. From 1956 to 1981 he edited *Public Law*. His books include *Principles of Administrative Law* (with H. Street), *Central Departments and Local Authorities*, *Government and Law* (with T. C. Hartley), *Parliamentary Scrutiny of Government Bills*, and *Public Rights and Private Interests*. He is the general editor of Understanding Law, the six-volume Fontana Press series of introductory law books.

J. A. G. Griffith

The Politics
of the Judiciary

Third edition

Fontana Press

First published by Fontana Paperbacks
in the series 'Political Issues of
Modern Britain' edited by Bernard Crick
and Patrick Seyd, 1977
Reprinted in June 1978 and March 1979
Second edition, October 1981
Third edition, in Fontana Press, May 1985
Reprinted in September 1987

Set in 10 on 11.2 Linotron Times
Made and printed in Great Britain by
Robert Hartnoll (1985) Ltd., Bodmin, Cornwall

To BEN
who helped

Juger l'administration, c'est aussi administrer
J.-E.-M. Portalis, 1745–1807

*The vanity of appearing as model employers of labour
had not then, apparently, taken possession of the council,
nor had the council become such ardent feminists as to
bring about, at the expense of the ratepayers whose
money they administered, sex equality in the labour
market . . . The council would, in my view, fail in their
duty if, in administering funds which did not belong to
their members alone, they put aside all these aims to the
ascertainment of what was just and reasonable
remuneration to give for the services rendered to them,
and allowed themselves to be guided in preference by
some eccentric principles of socialistic philanthropy, or
by a feminist ambition to secure the equality of the sexes
in the matter of wages in the world of labour.*

Lord Atkinson in *Roberts v. Hopwood* [1925] AC 578

Contents

Preface to the third edition

In my preface to the first edition I said I hoped this was a controversial book. The reviews seemed to suggest it was, varying as they did from shock horror by way of serious criticism to amused condescension. I confess to being somewhat disappointed that so few, not even those from the most eminent in the most respectable periodicals, sought to assess the validity or otherwise of the simple thesis that the judiciary cannot, under our system, act neutrally but must act politically. Some of the more antagonistic reviewers became unusually excited by what they apparently found subversive in a book which I had thought to be a modest analysis, free of political commitment. But there we are. We build both better and worse than we know.

Since the second edition was published much ʌas happened, particularly concerning race relations, immigration policy, contempt of court, the Greater London Council, and industrial relations, which seems to me, biased as ever, abundantly to justify that simple thesis. Towards the end of this edition, I have taken the argument a little further and have tried to show, by examining three recent groups of cases, how the senior judiciary, constrained by their own self-imposed limitations, frequently fail sensibly to interpret the public interest; and to suggest possible lines of development. In other ways also I have tried to bring the book up to date and to correct some errors of fact and judgment. And I have deleted or reduced some sections to keep the book short. But I fear that those who disapproved of the earlier editions are unlikely to conclude that I have repented of heresy. I am grateful to all, friend and foe alike, who were moved to tell me what they thought of my theology.

I am again greatly indebted to my secretary Miss Colleen Etheridge not only (as I have said before) for her fortitude but also for her continued forbearance.

London School of Economics
   and Political Science
October 1984

John Griffith

Part One

The Judiciary

There is one matter which I ought to mention. All the judges, without exception, are members of the Athenaeum, and I presume you will wish to be a member. If so, may I have the pleasure of proposing you? There is a meeting of the Committee early next week.

Lord Cozens-Hardy, MR to Lord Buckmaster – as he became – on the latter's appointment to the Lord Chancellorship, in a letter dated 26 May 1915, quoted by R. F. V. Heuston, *The Lives of the Lord Chancellors 1885–1940*, p. 269.

The most politically influential of the judges, however, has been the Master of the Rolls, Lord Denning . . . With his own modest roots he dismisses the attacks on a class-based judiciary: 'The youngsters believe that we come from a narrow background – it's all nonsense – they get it from that man Griffith.'

Anthony Sampson, *The Changing Anatomy of Britain* (1981), p. 159.

1. Courts and judges

Introduction

This book is concerned with the relationship between the judiciary and politics. In the courts political questions may come before the judges because the matter is already in public controversy, like race or industrial relations; or because the matter concerns some form of protest or demonstration against established authority, as with students or minority groups; or because the matter concerns the exercise of powers by the police; or because the matter impinges on the individual rights of citizens, affecting their freedom or their property.

The laws relating to civil and criminal wrongs are made either by Parliament in the form of Acts of Parliament (also called statutes) or by the judges themselves (called the common law). The common law is made as judges decide cases and state the principles on which they are basing their decisions, this accumulation of principles building into a body of law. Some parts of this common law have long fallen into disuse as having no contemporary relevance. Other parts have evolved to meet social changes. Statute law, however, predominates over common law wherever there is conflict, and much statute law is made to change and to replace parts of the common law.

Statute law itself cannot be a perfect instrument. A statute or one section of a statute may be made to deal with some particular subject – perhaps with immigration, or drugs, or housing or education – but a situation arises where doubt is cast on the meaning of the words of the statute. Does the situation fall within these words or not? For example, do the words 'national origins' include 'nationality'? (See below, p. 95). The judges then must decide how to interpret the statute and by so doing they define its meaning. Not only therefore do the judges 'make law' through the development of the common law. They also do so by this process of statutory interpretation.

Judges are employed to decide disputes. Sometimes these

disputes are between private individuals as when neighbours disagree or one person is injured by another in an accident. Sometimes these disputes may be between large private organizations as when companies argue about the terms of a commercial contract. But public bodies – government departments, local authorities, nationalized industries, and others – are also legal persons and also become involved in disputes which lead to judicial activity. The fact that one of the parties is a public body does not necessarily affect the nature of the dispute or the law applicable to it. If a government department or the Greater London Council or the Post Office enters into a contract with a building company for the construction of a block of offices, and a dispute arises, the law which governs the matter is essentially the same as it would be if the contract were between two private persons.

Such disputes are dealt with by the civil law and in the civil courts. The judgment given will say where the rights and wrongs lie and the court may award damages to one party or even order a party to take certain positive steps or to refrain from certain action.

In criminal law, the dispute is with the State. Over the years laws have been made and amended declaring certain kinds of action to be criminal and punishable with imprisonment or fines. This has been done because it is believed that the State has an interest in seeking to prevent those actions and to punish those who so act. So we have crimes called murder, manslaughter, rape, conspiracy, theft, fraud, assault, and hundreds of others, some of them quite trivial. They are dealt with in the criminal courts.[1]

If the judicial function were wholly automatic, then not only would the making of decisions in the courts be of little interest but it would also not be necessary to recruit highly trained and intellectually able men and women to serve as judges and to pay them handsome salaries.

It is the creative function of judges (see further, below, chapter 8) that makes their job important and makes worthwhile some assessment of the way they behave, especially in political cases. It must be remembered that in most cases for most of the time the function of the judge (with the help of the jury if there is one) is to ascertain the facts. But when questions of law do arise, their determination may be of the greatest importance because of the effect that will have on subsequent cases.

1.   The structure of the civil and criminal courts is summarized on pp. 31–3.

Appointment

The most remarkable fact about the appointment of judges is that it is wholly in the hands of politicians.[2] High Court and Circuit judges, Recorders, stipendiary and lay magistrates are appointed by or on the advice of the Lord Chancellor who is a member of the cabinet. Appointments to the Court of Appeal, to the Judicial Committee of the House of Lords,[3] and to the offices of Lord Chief Justice and President of the Family Division are made on the advice of the Prime Minister after consultation with the Lord Chancellor, who himself consults with senior members of the judiciary before making his choice or consulting with the Prime Minister. The Lord Chancellor has his own department headed, since the 1880s, by a permanent secretary. The department is the centre for the collection of information about the activity, the legal practice, and the reputation of members of the bar including those more senior, almost always Queen's Counsel (the conferment of which status is in the gift of the Lord Chancellor), from whom senior judicial appointments will be made. Inevitably the officials in the department exercise some influence but the extent of this varies and is difficult to assess.[4]

How far the Prime Minister uses his power of appointment or, to put this another way, how far he merely accepts the Lord Chancellor's advice on senior appointments varies with different Prime Ministers and differing circumstances. It seems to be unusual for the Prime Minister or the Lord Chancellor to consult other ministers (except that the Lord Chancellor may discuss the matter with the Attorney-General and the Solicitor-General) unless any such minister happens to be also a distinguished member of the bar, as was Sir Stafford Cripps in Mr Attlee's administration from 1945. But it would be a mistake to assume that Prime Ministers are necessarily mouth-pieces of their Lord Chancellors when making these appointments.

Lord Simon of Glaisdale has written: 'In 1951 Sir Winston [Churchill] particularly wanted [Sir Walter Monckton] in the

2. For a general account see S. Shetreet, *Judges on Trial* (1976).
3. Referred to hereafter simply as the House of Lords.
4. According to *The Times* (19 April 1982) the Lord Chancellor's Department has agreed to include the Society of Black Lawyers in its consultations over judicial appointments.

unenviable post of Minister of Labour, and (presumably by way of compensation) undertook in writing that he should be appointed Lord Chief Justice on the next vacancy.'[5]

Such an undertaking must have been of very little value. Lord Goddard was then in only his sixth year as Lord Chief Justice, never looked like someone about to retire, and indeed continued in office for three years after Sir Winston gave way as Prime Minister in 1955. But the story shows that Sir Winston had no doubt that the office was solely in his gift.

Although Prime Ministers may from time to time use words which suggest that they are not unwilling to exercise their power of appointment, in recent times there is no direct evidence that they have done so. The likelihood is that a modern Prime Minister would depart from the recommendations of the Lord Chancellor only in the most exceptional case.

Solicitors and barristers may be appointed as Recorders or stipendiary magistrates. A Recorder who has served for five years may be appointed as a Circuit judge. Otherwise judges are appointed from the ranks of barristers of at least ten or fifteen years' standing and are likely to have had at least twenty years' practice at the bar. Judges in the Court of Appeal are usually appointed from amongst High Court judges and Law Lords from amongst Appeal Court judges.[6]

In 1985 Lords of Appeal in Ordinary (Law Lords) and the Master of the Rolls were paid £58,500; Lords Justices of Appeal (in the Court of Appeal) £55,000; judges of the High Court were paid £51,250; Circuit judges £33,000.

From these figures it will be seen that High Court judges gain little financially from promotion. And at present Circuit judges are not often promoted to the High Court. Judges of the High Court and above, with the exception of the Lord Chancellor, hold office during good behaviour subject to a power of removal by Her Majesty on an address presented by both Houses of Parliament, but no English judge has been removed under this provision which derives from the Act of Settlement 1701. Circuit judges and Recorders, however, may be removed from office by the Lord Chancellor on the ground of incapacity or misbehaviour. Magistrates are removable by the Lord Chancellor for good cause.

5. 81 *Law Quarterly Review* 295 (1965).
6. The Lord Chancellor need have no legal qualifications whatever, but in practice is appointed from the ranks of those senior barristers who are members of the political party of the government.

Senior judges must retire at seventy-five years of age, Circuit judges at seventy-two with possible extension to seventy-five, Justices of the Peace and stipendiaries at seventy.

In 1977 a full-time salaried judge in Scotland was removed from his office for misbehaviour because he was deemed to have engaged in public political activity. Sheriff Peter Thomson published a pamphlet advocating the holding of a plebiscite on Scottish home rule. In accordance with the Sheriff Courts (Scotland) Act 1971, the Secretary of State for Scotland asked two senior Scottish judges (the Lord President of the Court of Session and the Lord Justice Clerk) to investigate and they reported their finding of misbehaviour which, as for Circuit judges and Recorders in England and Wales, was a ground for dismissal. The Secretary of State, having taken into account that Sheriff Thomson had been previously warned, at the time of a similar offence in 1974, made an Order for his dismissal. Such an Order had to be laid before Parliament and was there debated on 6 December 1977. The case caused much discussion especially as it could scarcely be said that his activity was directly connected with his duties as a judge.[7] Thomson asked for permission to make a statement at the bar of the House of Commons but this was denied.[8]

In December 1983, the Lord Chancellor dismissed for misbehaviour an Old Bailey Circuit judge who had been fined £2000 on two charges of smuggling whisky and cigarettes.

Judges of the superior courts may not be sued for anything done or said while acting in their judicial capacity even if they act from some malicious or corrupt motive. The law does permit judges to be prosecuted for crimes they may commit but proof of criminal intent would be extremely difficult even if an appropriate charge could be devised.[9]

The dangers of criticizing the appointment of particular judges was shown when in June 1980 a Belfast jury awarded £50,000 damages to a Northern Ireland county court judge for a libel contained in an article in the *Economist* suggesting that his appointment had been based, as *The Times* put it in a leading article, not so much on his ability but on the fact that he was a Roman Catholic. One of the principal witnesses for the judge was

7. See 940 HC Deb. col. 1288–1332; also 939 HC Deb. col. 922–5.

8. A summary of the statement was contained in a letter from Mr Thomson to *The Times* on 16 December 1977.

9. For recent authority see *Sirros v. Moore* [1975] QB 118, and Margaret Brazier, 'Judicial Immunity and the Independence of the Judiciary' in [1976] *Public Law* 397.

the Lord Chief Justice of Northern Ireland. The Lord Chancellor refused to disclose any of the correspondence concerning the judge's appointment on the ground that it was not in the public interest to reveal confidences about judicial appointments and this was accepted by the court. Yet the Lord Chief Justice, giving oral evidence, said that he and the Lord Chancellor were at one in their belief that religious affinity should not take precedence over ability in the appointment of judges and, said *The Times*, he gave the impression that his positive feelings towards the judge were shared by the Lord Chancellor. So oral evidence was admitted on the kind of matter for which privilege from disclosure of documents was claimed by the Crown. The *Economist* appealed and the matter was settled on undisclosed terms, the damages being 'adjusted' and the editor expressing himself as being extremely satisfied'.[10]

To what extent, if at all, do the Lord Chancellor and the Prime Minister take into account the political allegiance of those whom they appoint or promote to judicial office?

First, there is one special case. The Attorney-General and the Solicitor-General (the law officers of the Crown) are ministers, not in the cabinet, appointed by the Prime Minister from the ranks of Members of the House of Commons who are barristers. It is often said that by tradition they have a right to judicial appointment when vacancies occur and that this is particularly true of appointment to the office of Lord Chief Justice. In a famous essay, H. J. Laski recorded that between 1832 and 1906, out of 139 judges appointed, 80 were Members of the House of Commons at the time of their nomination and 11 others had been candidates for Parliament; that, of the 80, 63 were appointed by their own party while in office; and 33 of them had been either Attorney-General or Solicitor-General.[11] Laski suggested that it was 'probably undesirable' for law officers to be suddenly made judges and so required to act impartially. Laski treads very daintily here. 'It is not necessary to suggest that there will be conscious unfairness; but it is, I submit, possible that such judges will, particularly in cases where the liberty of the subject is concerned, find themselves unconsciously biased through over-appreciation of executive difficulty . . . Nothing is more disastrous than that any suspicion of the complete impartiality of the judges should be possible.'

In 1937 a Member of Parliament said in the House of Commons that every government took it for granted that the law officers had

10. *The Times*, 1 July and 9 December 1980.
11. H. J. Laski, *Studies in Law and Politics*, pp. 164–80.

the right to 'certain high positions in the State regardless whether they happen to be the most suitable persons' and he instanced the offices of Master of the Rolls and Lord Chancellor. But a government spokesman denied this saying that the law officers had never put forward such a proposition and that there was 'no foundation' for it.[12]

The tradition is certainly weaker today but by no means dead. In 1962, the Solicitor-General was appointed to the Presidency of what was then the Probate, Divorce and Admiralty Division of the High Court. And Attorneys-General, then or previously in that office, may be strong candidates for appointment as Lord Chancellor though the political nature of that office distinguishes it from appointment to purely judicial office. It is perhaps significant that none of the last four Lord Chief Justices – Lords Goddard, Parker, Widgery and Lane – had been law officers. It may be that, today, law officers have greater expectations of political promotion and prefer to pursue that ambition. Nevertheless if they wished to become judges and vacancies occurred appropriately, it must be supposed they would always be strong candidates.

The wider question, also raised by Laski's figures, is the extent to which an active political life, and particularly Membership of the House of Commons, is regarded by the Lord Chancellor as a positive qualification for appointment to a judgeship. Practice has differed over the years.

Lord Halsbury was Lord Chancellor for far longer than any other during the last hundred years. He had three periods in that office which he held, in all, for over seventeen years between 1885 and 1905. His judicial appointments were much criticized on the ground in effect that 'Halsbury appointed to the High Court, and to a lesser extent to the county court, men of little or no legal learning whose previous career in public life had been largely in the service of the Conservative Party or else were relations of his own'.[13] Professor Heuston has examined such criticisms. Of the judges appointed by Halsbury to the High Court, eight were MPs at the date of their appointment and of these six were Conservatives. Five others had been unsuccessful Parliamentary candidates, three of them being Conservatives. One other had been a Conservative MP nearly twenty years before. So fourteen out of the thirty appointments

---

12. 324 HC Deb. col. 1202. See J. Ll. J. Edwards, *The Law Officers of the Crown* (1977), especially chapter 15.
13. R. F. V. Heuston, *The Lives of the Lord Chancellors, 1885–1940* (1964), p. 36.

were, in those senses, of politicians – and ten were Conservatives. Heuston concludes that of Halsbury's thirty appointments to the High Court, four or five were men of real distinction, eighteen or nineteen were men of competent professional attainments, leaving no more than seven 'whose appointments seem dubious'. Four of these seven were Conservative MPs at the date of the appointment, one had been a Conservative MP, and another had twice been an unsuccessful Conservative candidate. We may say, therefore (this is my conclusion not Heuston's), that of the ten Conservative politicians whom Halsbury appointed, six were bad appointments. Every Lord Chancellor, especially if he holds office as long as did Halsbury, will make some mistakes (and Heuston suggests that as many as three of the six were 'unlucky' appointments) but Halsbury's experience may suggest that the proportion of bad appointments is likely to be statistically higher amongst appointments made from the Lord Chancellor's political associates.

Certainly at that time it was accepted that a political career was likely to be an advantage for a barrister aspiring to a judgeship, though it was important that his seat should be safe, as no government would wish to run the possibility of diminishing its strength in the House. Heuston tells us how Lord Halsbury when he was a Parliamentary candidate was congratulated by Sir Edward Clarke on his election defeat by nine votes in 1874. Clarke explained that if Halsbury had won by such a majority he could not have expected elevation to a judgeship. But, as it was, he could expect to be made Solicitor-General and found a safe seat. This is indeed what happened although he held the office for over a year until the seat was found for him in 1877. (During the interval he was in fact offered a judgeship, which he declined, but it was made clear that the government could not long countenance a Solicitor-General without a seat in the House of Commons.)

In August 1895, arising out of argument about the fees payable to the law officers, Lord Salisbury, as Prime Minister, promised Sir Edward Clarke that he would be appointed Attorney-General if a vacancy occurred within two years. In 1897, a new Master of the Rolls had to be appointed. If the Attorney-General (Sir Richard Webster) took the post, Clarke would have to be appointed Attorney-General. Lord Salisbury, who had a poor opinion of Clarke's abilities (as had Halsbury) wrote in much perplexity to the Lord Chancellor but saying that the Rolls should be offered to Clarke 'on party grounds' because he would do less harm as a judge than as Attorney-General. Salisbury continued:

There remains the third course, to throw Clarke over altogether and tell him that the highest point of his career has been reached. I confess that the more I consider this alternative, the more I dislike it. It is at variance with the unwritten law of our party system; and there is no clearer statute in that unwritten law than the rule that party claims should always weigh very heavily in the disposal of the highest appointments . . . It would be a breach of the tacit convention on which politicians and lawyers have worked the British Constitution together for the last 200 years. Perhaps it is not an ideal system – some day no doubt the MR will be appointed by competitive examination in Law Reports, but it is our system for the present; and we should give our party arrangements a wrench if we throw it aside.

Lord Salisbury did offer the Rolls to Clarke who declined it on the ground that it would put an end to his political career, though he added that he would accept being a Law Lord. But that offer did not come.[14]

The change in the attitude to the appointment of barrister-politicians as judges is said to date from Lord Haldane's Chancellorship (1912–15) when legal and professional qualifications became the criteria, though at first the change was not extended to the most senior appointments. Lord Haldane himself expressed his 'strong conviction that, at all events for a judge who is to sit in the Supreme Tribunals of the Empire, a House of Commons training is a real advantage. One learns there the nuances of the Constitution, and phases of individual and social political life which are invaluable in checking the danger of abstractedness in mental outlook.'[15]

But a little later Lord Sankey, who was Lord Chancellor from 1929 to 1935, when resignations occurred, replaced five Law Lords who had had political backgrounds by others whose reputations rested on their professionalism as lawyers.[16]

In recent years Lord Chancellors have differed in their opinions about the value of judges having had experience as politicians. During the 1950s, being an MP came once again to be regarded as a qualification for appointment to a judgeship. In 1964, Lord Gardiner, who shortly afterwards became Lord Chancellor himself,

14. On all this see Heuston, *op. cit.*, pp. 52–4, 323–4.
15. Quoted in Heuston, *op. cit.*, p. 39.
16. Abel-Smith and Stevens, *Lawyers and the Courts* (1967).

said that since 1951 'one or two' Lord Chancellors (there had been only three) 'felt that the standard of members of the bar going into the House of Commons has fallen noticeably since the war, and if you want the right men in the House of Commons then you must reward the man who votes the right way with a judgeship'.[17] Lord Gardiner himself thought that political views ought not to affect judicial appointments at all, and he pursued this policy during his period of office as Lord Chancellor (1964–70).

Today, being an active member of a political party seems to be neither a qualification nor a disqualification for appointment.

It must be remembered that Lord Chancellors in making their appointments to the High Court have a relatively small group to select from. Effectively, the group consists of experienced barristers between the ages of forty-five and sixty and the number of genuine possibilities – the short list – may be as small as half a dozen.

Personal characteristics must be taken into account. A man or woman whose social or personal habits are unconventional or uncertain is not likely to be risked. On the other hand, it is obvious from the appointments made that the strength of a candidate's convictions, including his political opinions, is not considered a disadvantage. But those opinions should fall within the ordinary range represented in the House of Commons.

Politically the most important judicial appointment is that of Master of the Rolls. As president of the Court of Appeal his view on the proper relationship between the Executive government and the individual including powerful private organizations, is crucial. When Sir John Donaldson was appointed to succeed Lord Denning in July 1982, this was seen as a strongly political appointment and one which the Prime Minister favoured. Sir John had been a Conservative councillor and had presided over the National Industrial Relations Court for the two and a half years of its existence during the Heath administration. On its demise he reverted to his position as a judge of the High Court and was not promoted during the years of the Labour Government 1974–9. From the beginning of 1984 when it seemed probable that Lord Hailsham would soon resign as Lord Chancellor, Sir John was widely discussed as his probable successor in the Thatcher cabinet. This highlighted his political characteristics and qualifications and may have led to his decision not to preside over the Court of Appeal when it considered the appeal by the Government against the decision of Glidewell J rejecting the decision to ban trade union membership at GCHQ.[18]

Social and political position

From time to time in recent years, analyses have been made, based on information in reference books, of the social background of the more senior judiciary.

The most comprehensive in terms of social class origins[19] covers the period from 1820 to 1968.

Period of Appointment	1820–1875	1876–1920	1921–1950	1951–1968	1820–1968	Number
Social class	%	%	%	%	%	
I Traditional landed upper class	17·9	16·4	15·4	10·5	15·3	59
II Professional, commercial and administrative upper class	8·5	14·6	14·3	14·0	12·7	49
III Upper middle class	40·6	50·5	47·3	52·3	47·4	183
IV Lower middle class	11·3	9·7	8·8	8·1	9·6	37
V Working class	2·8	1·0	1·1	1·2	1·3	6
Not known	18·9	7·8	13·2	14·0	13·5	52
	100	100	100	100	100	
Number	106	103	91	86	386	386

18. See below, p. 86.
19. Class assignment is according to father's occupation or rank. The judges in this table are those of the High Court, the Court of Appeal and the House of Lords or of their equivalents.

Over the whole period the dominance of the upper and upper middle classes is overwhelming. They account for 75·4 per cent to which may be added, proportionately, 10 per cent from those 'not known'. Moreover the total percentage of these first three groups in the most recent period is 76·8, which is higher than the overall percentage. Over the whole period covered by this analysis the dominance of the first three classes is unchanged.[20]

Another survey, published in 1975, covers the period 1876–1972 and, with a few omissions, analyses the 317 judges who sat in the High Court, the Court of Appeal and the House of Lords during that period. The author does not, however, break down these ninety-six years into shorter periods so trends within the whole are not apparent. He considers school background and finds that 33 per cent attended one of the so-called Clarendon Schools (Charterhouse, Eton, Harrow, Merchant Taylors, Rugby, St Paul's, Shrewsbury, Westminster, Winchester), while 70 per cent attended Oxford or Cambridge Universities.[21]

School education is a good indicator of social and economic class background, particularly as the relative cost of attendance at one of the independent 'public' schools has changed little, until very recently. It must also be remembered that university education at Oxford and Cambridge before 1945 (when those who are now judges attended) was also very largely a middle-class activity, within the first three groups of the table set out above.

In 1956 the *Economist*[22] published a short survey. This covered 69 judges of the Supreme Court, House of Lords and Judicial Committee of the Privy Council and showed that 76 per cent had attended 'major public schools' (not further defined) and the same percentage had been to Oxford or Cambridge. In May 1970 *New Society*[23] looked at 359 judges including those offices surveyed by the *Economist* but also, amongst others, county court judgeships and metropolitan magistrates. This found that 81 per cent had attended public schools and 76 per cent had attended Oxford or Cambridge. In 1969, Henry Cecil investigated the background of 117 out of 235 judges of the House of Lords, the Supreme Court, county courts and stipendiary magistrates. From a random group

20. From an unpublished M. Phil. dissertation by Jenny Brock quoted in *The Judiciary*, the report of a Justice subcommittee (1972).
21. C. Neal Tate, 'Paths to the Bench in Britain', 28 *Western Political Quarterly* 108.
22. 12 December 1956, pp. 946–7.
23. 14 May 1970 (by Kevin Goldstein-Jackson).

of 36 judges of the Court of Appeal and the High Court, he found
that 31 had been to public schools (86 per cent) and 33 to Oxford
or Cambridge (92 per cent). From a random group of 45 (out of 90)
county court judges and 24 (out of 48) stipendiaries, he found that
52 had attended public schools (75 per cent) and 56 Oxford or
Cambridge (81 per cent). In 1975 Hugo Young analysed the
educational background of 31 appointees to the High Court during
the previous five years. He found that 68 per cent went to public
schools and 74 per cent to Oxford or Cambridge.[24]

These figures have changed very little over the last thirty or
more years. In 1940 about 80 per cent of the judges of the Supreme
Court had attended public schools. In 1969, this was true of 79
per cent of Henry Cecil's group of 117. A higher proportion of
the earlier generation did not attend university at all – 8 out of
35 in 1940 but only 8 out of 135 in 1970. Of those who did attend,
the bias in favour of Oxford and Cambridge has remained
effectively unchanged.[25] The *New Society* survey compared county
court judges in three recent years. In 1947, in 1957 and in 1967,
seven county court judges were appointed. Of these 21 judges, all
but one in 1947, two in 1957 and one in 1967 had attended public
schools; all but three in 1947, two in 1957 and three in 1967 had
attended Oxford or Cambridge. In 1978, of 74 High Court judges
listed, over 75 per cent had attended public schools and, of these,
41 per cent had attended one of the Clarendon Schools.[26] Of the 17
High Court judges appointed between 1 January 1980 and 1 May
1982, 76 per cent attended public schools and 88 per cent Oxford
or Cambridge.[27]

The decline in the number of 'political' judges is also shown. The
Economist's survey of 1956 recorded that 23 per cent of their 69
judges had been MPs or Parliamentary candidates. But fourteen
years later, Henry Cecil could find only 10 MPs and 5 candidates
out of his 117 judges (13 per cent).

The age of the full-time judiciary has remained constant over
many years: the average on appointment has been about fifty-two
or -three and the average of all those in office has been about sixty.
Inevitably, given the system of promotion, the average age is

24. *The Sunday Times*, 5 October 1975.
25. Henry Cecil, *The English Judge* (2nd edn, 1972). For a survey of judges sitting
on 1 January 1970, see Fred L. Morrison, *Courts and the Political Process in England*
(1974), ch. 3; the findings are very similar to those in the surveys quoted above.
26. HC Deb. 16 May 1978, col. 107–10.
27. *LAG Bulletin*, August 1982 (Phil Cohen).

highest in the Court of Appeal and the House of Lords, at about sixty-five and sixty-eight years respectively.

Between 1876 and 1972 there were 63 Lords of Appeal in Ordinary (Law Lords). An analysis of 49 of these showed that 18 had fathers who were lawyers, 16 had fathers of other professions (churchmen, doctors, teachers, architects, soldiers); 12 fathers were in business (of whom one was working-class), and 3 fathers were farmers or land-owners. Forty-six Law Lords had been to Oxford or Cambridge, seven to Scottish universities, four to Trinity College Dublin, two to London University (one of whom had also been to Cambridge) and one to Queen's Belfast. These facts and figures added relatively little to what was already known in outline. More interesting is the analysis of political background. The authors[28] divided their period into three groups. Group A included twenty Law Lords appointed in the period 1876–1914; group B had twenty-one appointed between 1918 and 1948; group C had twenty-two appointed in 1948–69. Of the twenty Law Lords in group A, eleven had been MPs and three Parliamentary candidates; of the twenty-one in group B, five had been MPs; of the twenty-two in group C, four had been MPs and two Parliamentary candidates. While these figures show the decline since the late nineteenth and early twentieth century of appointments of such politicians, they also show little change since 1918. It is, however, unwise to base generalizations on such figures. What matters more than prior political involvement is how far Law Lords consciously or otherwise are influenced in their judgments by their own political opinions, how far this is avoidable and how far it is undesirable. One highly 'political' Lord Chancellor – like Lord Hailsham of St Marylebone – can, if he chooses, make a considerable impact on judicial law-making at the highest level but, for this to be so, it is not necessary that he should have held political office or have been a Member of Parliament or a law officer.

All these figures show that, in broad terms, four out of five full-time professional judges are products of public schools, and of Oxford or Cambridge. Occasionally the brilliant lower-middle-class or working-class boy has won his place in this distinguised gathering. With very few exceptions, judges are required to be selected from amongst practising barristers and it is very difficult indeed for anyone without a private income to survive the first years of practice. To become a successful barrister, therefore, it is

28. L. Blom-Cooper and G. Drewry, *Final Appeal* (1972).

necessary to have financial support and so the background has to be that of the reasonably well-do-do family which, as a matter of course, sends its sons to public schools and then either straight to the bar or first to Oxford or Cambridge.

Nevertheless, some men and women have, since the middle 1960s, benefited from the expansion of university education, from the growth of law faculties in universities, and from the wider availability of this education and, with little private income, have been able (largely because of the increase in publicly financed legal aid) to make a living at the bar. By the mid-1980s some of these will move into the ranks of successful barristers from whom judicial appointments are made. Only then shall we be able to assess how far the dominance of the public schools and (what is of much less significance) of Oxford and Cambridge has begun to lessen. And not until the 1990s shall we know whether (as seems most unlikely) judicial attitudes have changed as a result.

Judicial independence means that judges are not dependent on governments in any ways which might influence them in coming to decisions in individual cases. Formally, this independence is preserved by their not being dismissible by the government of the day. This does not affect their promotion, which, like their appointment, is effectively in the hands of the Lord Chancellor with, nowadays, a measure of Prime Ministerial intervention. In financial terms, such promotion is not of much significance. But life in the Court of Appeal and, even more, in the House of Lords is not so strenuous as in the High Court (or below), personal prestige and status are higher among the fewer, with a life peerage at the top. These are not inconsiderable rewards for promotion, and the question is whether there are pressures on, particularly, High Court judges to act and to speak in court in certain ways rather than others. Are there decisions which could be classified as popular or unpopular in the eyes of the most important senior judges or the Lord Chancellor? Is a judge ever conscious that his reputation as a judge is likely to be adversely affected in their eyes if he decides one way, and favourably affected if he decides another way?

The answer is that such pressures do exist. For example, a judge who acquires a reputation among his seniors for being 'soft' in certain types of cases where the Lord Chancellor, the Lord Chief Justice, the Master of the Rolls and other senior judges favour a hard line is as likely to damage his promotion prospects as he would if his appointment were found to be unfortunate on other more obvious grounds. But this does not amount to dependence on the political wishes of governments or ministers as such. In no real sense does such direct dependence or influence exist. How far judges consciously or unconsciously subserve the wider interests of governments is another and more important question.

What is meant by saying that judges must be impartial and seen to be so? Judges themselves claim this as their great virtue and only occasionally is it seen to be departed from. Lord Haldane was a practising barrister in 1901 when he recorded:

> I fought my hardest for the Dutch prisoners before the Privy Council this morning, but the tribunal was hopelessly divided, and the anti-Boers prevailed over the pro-Boers. It is bad that so much bias should be shewn, but it is, I suppose, inevitable.[29]

D. N. Pritt in his autobiography told of his many political cases and of one which 'came before a judge of great experience and knowledge, so bitterly opposed to anything left-wing that he could scarcely have given a fair trial if he had tried'.[30]

Are such phrases applicable today? Every practising barrister knows before which judges he would prefer not to appear in a political case because he believes, and his colleagues at the bar believe, that certain judges are much more likely than others to be biased against certain groups, like demonstrators or students, or certain kinds of action, like occupations of property by trade unionists or the homeless. Sometimes counsel for one of the parties in a case will make objection to a particular judge hearing the case. And the judge may then decide not to sit. In 1978 Lord Denning MR acceded to such a request when told that the Church of Scientology of California felt that in his court there was an unconscious influence operating adversely to the church.[31] In January 1978, the Lord Chancellor announced that Judge Neil McKinnon had said that he wished not to preside in future over cases involving racial questions; and that this wish would be given effect to. Judge McKinnon had been widely criticized for comments made during his hearing of a case of inciting racial hatred. Occasionally the Lord Chancellor will publicly reprimand a judge, as happened in 1978 when Mr Justice Melford-Stevenson was rebuked for describing an Act of Parliament as a 'buggers' charter'.

29. Quoted by Heuston, *op. cit.*, p. 195.
30. *From Right to Left* (1965), p. 142.
31. See *The Times*, 21 February 1978.

In January 1982, Lord Hailsham repudiated the comment of a judge that a rape victim who hitch-hiked a lift was guilty of contributory negligence and that the rapist's penalty should accordingly be reduced. In January 1984, Lord Hailsham reprimanded a Recorder who attacked as an affront to British justice a decision by Woolworths to prosecute a widow aged seventy-seven for shoplifting.

This however is to say little more than that, as we have already remarked, judges are human with human prejudices. And that some are more human than others. But if that were all we would expect to find a wide spectrum of judicial opinion about political cases. Instead, we find a remarkable consistency of approach in these cases concentrated in a fairly narrow part of the spectrum of political opinion. It spreads from that part of the centre which is shared by right-wing Labour, Liberal and 'progressive' Conservative opinion to that part of the right which is associated with traditional Toryism – but not beyond into the reaches of the far right.

A note on the structure of courts

Civil cases are first heard either in county courts by Circuit judges (of whom there are some 350); or in the High Court by judges of the High Court[32] (of whom there are about 70). Each case is heard by a single judge (very occasionally with a jury).[33] The High Court is divided into the Queen's Bench, Chancery, and Family Divisions. The head of the Queen's Bench is the Lord Chief Justice, of the Chancery is the Vice-Chancellor, and of the Family Division is its President. For certain cases two or three judges of the Queen's Bench sit together and are then called the Divisional Court of the Queen's Bench Division.[34]

Appeal from county courts and the High Court lies to the Court of Appeal (civil division) which is presided over by the Master of the Rolls and where the other judges are called Lords Justices of Appeal (of whom there are eighteen). Two or three judges sit on each case. From the Court of Appeal, appeal may lie to the House

32. The numbers of judges etc. are taken from the Bar List 1983. At any time there may be a few more or less.
33. Also, registrars (who are solicitors) frequently try small cases in county courts.
34. Very occasionally the other Divisions also adopt this device.

CIVIL JURISDICTION

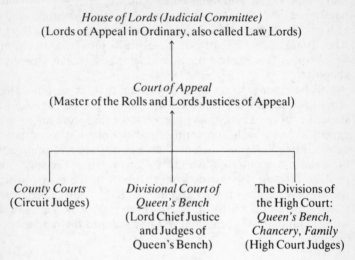

House of Lords (Judicial Committee)
(Lords of Appeal in Ordinary, also called Law Lords)

↑

Court of Appeal
(Master of the Rolls and Lords Justices of Appeal)

↑

| *County Courts*
(Circuit Judges) | *Divisional Court of*
Queen's Bench
(Lord Chief Justice
and Judges of
Queen's Bench) | The Divisions of
the High Court:
Queen's Bench,
Chancery, Family
(High Court Judges) |

of Lords in important cases. The House of Lords for this purpose consists of the Lord Chancellor (who sits infrequently) and the Lords of Appeal in Ordinary (Law Lords, of whom there are not more than eleven). Other peers who hold or have held high judicial office (presently seventeen in number) may sit but rarely do so. Five usually sit on each case. For an appeal to the House of Lords, either the Court of Appeal or the House of Lords must give leave. It is possible, in certain circumstances, again if leave is obtained, to appeal direct from the High Court to the House of Lords, leapfrogging the Court of Appeal.

Less serious *criminal* cases are tried summarily (without a jury) by magistrates' courts where sit either two or more lay Justices of the Peace (of whom there are some 20,000) or a legally qualified stipendiary magistrate (of whom there are about fifty, mostly sitting in London). More serious criminal cases are first enquired into by magistrates' courts to see if there is sufficient evidence for the case to go further. If there is, the case goes to the Crown Court (sitting with a jury and in many different places) where it is heard by a Queen's Bench or Circuit judge or by a Recorder (in certain circumstances joined by two to four Justices of the Peace). Recorders (of whom there are some 460) are practising barristers or solicitors who are required to sit for a few weeks each year.

CRIMINAL JURISDICTION

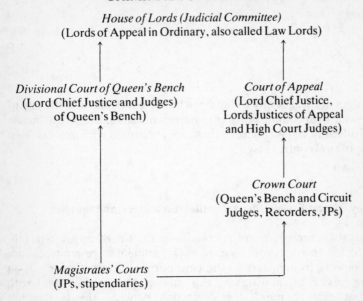

House of Lords (Judicial Committee)
(Lords of Appeal in Ordinary, also called Law Lords)

Divisional Court of Queen's Bench
(Lord Chief Justice and Judges)
of Queen's Bench)

Court of Appeal
(Lord Chief Justice,
Lords Justices of Appeal
and High Court Judges)

Crown Court
(Queen's Bench and Circuit
Judges, Recorders, JPs)

Magistrates' Courts
(JPs, stipendiaries)

Appeals from decisions of magistrates' courts on less serious cases go either, if only a question of law is disputed, to the Divisional Court of the Queen's Bench Division or, where the appeal is on questions of fact and/or law, to the Crown Court. Appeals from decisions in more serious cases (heard originally by the Crown Court) go to the Court of Appeal (criminal division) which draws its members from the Lord Chief Justice, the Lords Justices of Appeal and the judges of the High Court. Normally, three sit on each case. From the Divisional Court and the Court of Appeal, further appeal lies to the House of Lords if leave is obtained.

The Court of Appeal, the High Court and the Crown Court are together known as the Supreme Court of Judicature.

Finally, the Judicial Committee of the Privy Council hears appeals from a very limited number of overseas territories. It is composed of Law Lords, and others who hold or have held judicial office in the United Kingdom or the Commonwealth.

2. Extrajudicial activity

Judges are frequently called upon by the government of the day to preside over commissions, committees and administrative tribunals of different kinds. Some of these are concerned with matters deep in political controversy.

Royal Commissions, departmental committees, and the like

Royal Commissions are appointed by the Crown to enquire into selected matters of concern.[1] Departmental committees are appointed by ministers for the same purpose. As the Crown acts on the advice of ministers in this matter, and as they deal with comparable matters, the distinction between the two is not substantial. Royal Commissions have more prestige but nothing of real consequence flows from this, and the matters which these bodies investigate vary greatly in importance.

Dr T. J. Cartwright has recorded that 640 such bodies were appointed between 1945 and 1969 and he examined 358. These included 24 Royal Commissions; and 334 'major' departmental committees which he defined as those dealing with matters of direct concern to the government of Britain and whose reports were published as command papers.

The mean size of the twenty-four Royal Commissions was thirteen members, but when departmental committees are added the mean size falls to eight members. Of the twenty-four Royal Commissions, judges chaired seven. Only academics equalled them in number of Royal Commission chairs and no one group[2] of

1. See T. J. Cartwright, *Royal Commissions & Departmental Committees in Britain* (1975); see also G. Rhodes, *Committees of Inquiry* (1975).
2. See Cartwright, *op. cit.*, p. 72. His other groups are civil service; retired central government; other government (active or retired); legal profession; business, finance, industry; medical profession; trade unions; other; no information.

persons held half as many chairs of departmental committees.

Judges chaired commissions or committees concerned with, among other things, Justices of the Peace (1946–8), medical partnerships (1948), police conditions of service (1948–9), the industrial health services (1949–50), State immunities (1949–51), taxation of profits and income (1951–5), marriage and divorce (1951), dock workers (1955–6), the interception of communications (1957), prison conditions (1957–8), the working of the monetary system (1957–9), legal education for African students (1960), security in the public service (1961), the security service and Mr Profumo (1963), children and young persons in Scotland (1961–4), jury service (1963–5), the port transport industry (1964–5), pay for dock workers (1966), tribunals of enquiry (1966), 'D' notices (1967), the age of majority (1965–7), trade unions and employers' associations (1965–8), Scottish inshore fisheries (1967–70), the constitution (1969–73), one-parent families (1969–74), the adoption of children (1969–72), and the Brixton disorders (1981). Many of these were highly political, some also highly controversial. Since 1969, important departmental committees chaired by judges have included those on the interrogation of terrorists (1971–2), crowd safety (1971–2) legal procedures to deal with terrorists (1972), the working of the Abortion Act (1971–4), the Red Lion Square disorders (1974–5), standards of conduct in public life (1974–6), and police pay (1977–8).

All those related to affairs within the United Kingdom. In addition, judges have frequently been employed on overseas matters. One of the most famous of these in post-war years was the Nyasaland Commission of Enquiry of 1959 led by Mr Justice Devlin who reported in terms of which the government of the day did not wholly approve. More recently Lord Pearce chaired a Commission on Rhodesian Opinion (in 1972) appointed to ascertain directly from all sections of the population of Rhodesia whether or not certain proposals for the government of that country were acceptable. The number of such judicial appointments for overseas territories is considerable.

Judges are therefore overwhelmingly the persons most frequently chosen to chair Royal Commissions and departmental committees, totalling 118 out of Dr Cartwright's 358 bodies. Academics come second with 60 chairmen, followed by businessmen with 55. The job is time-consuming and unpaid and this no doubt helps to limit the field of choice.

In addition (and excluded from the examples listed above) judges are normally appointed as chairmen of those numerous committees which are concerned with reform of substantive law or legal procedure. Specifically a judge is chairman of the Law Commission which is the permanent body concerned with law reform. Judges are therefore constantly involved in the process of making recommendations for improvement in the law and this includes not only technical legal subjects but also those on the boundaries of law and politics, like conspiracy. The Scottish Law Commission, also chaired by a judge, became deeply involved in the debate on devolution, submitting memoranda particularly dealing with the distribution of powers between the United Kingdom Parliament and the proposed Scottish Assembly.[3] These memoranda, although generally avoiding comment that might be regarded as politically partisan on the question of the desirability or otherwise of devolution, contain passages which were bluntly, even scathingly, critical of the statements of the means by which the government hoped to achieve their objectives.

One of the Scottish Law Commission's proposals was that if the area of devolution was sufficiently extensive, responsibility for the courts should also be transferred to the Scottish Assembly. A few months earlier Lord Wheatley spoke on behalf of all the High Court judges in Scotland. He accepted that a judge, as a member of a Royal Commission or a departmental Committee of Enquiry, might have to explain publicly the recommendations arrived at. However, he continued:

> When the subject enters the political arena and becomes politically controversial, we assume an elective silence on the political issues and confine ourselves, if we intervene at all, to constitutional or legal questions or views on practical matters affecting the law and its administration where our views may naturally be expected and sought.[4]

He went on to say that the unanimous view of the High Court judges in Scotland was that the Scottish courts should remain the responsibility of the United Kingdom and not become the responsibility of the Scottish Assembly.

It is difficult to see how this disagreement between the Scottish Law Commission and the Scottish High Court judge could be thought of as other than political.

3. See Scottish Law Commission: memorandum no. 32 incorporating also an earlier memorandum.
4. 367 HL Deb. col. 837 (27 January 1976).

It is of course a matter of debate how far chairmen, whether judges or not, influence their committees, and no consistent answer is possible. But it is the tradition of chairmen in the United Kingdom to be active. For this reason who is appointed is regarded as being as important as the terms of reference. For many important commissions and committees, those terms are announced first and this is followed some time later by the name of the chairman. Many interests will typically have to be consulted before the chairman is decided on and thereafter his views on the membership will be sought. Far more than any other member, the chairman is privy to the government's hopes and intentions, and contact between him and the minister or ministers concerned will often be close and may well be continuous.

Judges also preside over enquiries set up under the Tribunals of Enquiry (Evidence) Act 1921. These enquiries are nowadays reserved for investigations into matters which may involve the reputation of ministers or public officials. Between 1945 and 1970 there were five: in 1948–9 into questions of possible bribery of ministers, chaired by Mr Justice Lynskey;[5] in 1957–8 into leakage of bank rate, chaired by Lord Justice Parker;[6] in 1959 into allegations of police assault on a boy, chaired by Lord Sorn;[7] in 1962–3 into a case of spying in which a minister's moral behaviour might have been involved, chaired by Lord Radcliffe;[8] and in 1966–7 into the responsibility for the Aberfan disaster, chaired by Lord Justice Edmund Davies.[9] Since 1970, this procedure has been used twice in Northern Ireland, as we shall see.[10] In 1972 a Tribunal of Enquiry presided over by Mr Justice James enquired into the collapse of the Vehicle and General Insurance Company and reported in terms which were critical in particular of one civil servant.[11] In 1978 a Tribunal was appointed, under the chairmanship of Mr Justice Croom-Johnson, to investigate the activities of the Crown Agents.

Three outstanding examples of the use of the judiciary in politics are to be found in the control of restrictive practices, industrial relations, and Northern Ireland.

5. Cmnd 7616.
6. Cmnd 350.
7. Cmnd 718.
8. Cmnd 2009.
9. HC 553 of 1966–7.
10. See below, pp. 43–5; see generally Cmnd 3121.
11. HC 133 of 1971–2.

The Restrictive Practices Court

The Restrictive Practices Court was established under an Act of 1956 and consisted of five judges and not more than ten other members qualified by virtue of their knowledge of or experience in industry, commerce or public affairs. The function of the court is to decide whether restrictive agreements made between businessmen may continue. A restriction is deemed to be contrary to the public interest unless the court is satisfied that it is reasonably necessary or that its removal would be more harmful to the public than its retention. The first President of the court was Mr Justice Devlin. For a hearing the court is composed of one, two or three judges and two or more other members, and is therefore a mixed court of judges and laymen. As the minister said when introducing the Bill in 1956, the decisions to be made were decisions not only of fact and law but of economic and social judgment. And so it proved to be. During the first six years of its hearings, the court decided twenty-six major English cases ranging widely over different industries. During the first sixteen months, only one out of seven restrictions was upheld; during the next eighteen months, two out of nine were upheld; during the next two years, six out of ten were upheld.[12]

The second case decided by the court was one of its most significant. In *Re Yarn Spinners Agreement*[13] the court consisted of three High Court judges and four laymen and it was asked to consider an agreement under which the Yarn Spinners' Association asked its members to adopt prescribed minimum prices. The cotton industry for many years had been in recession because of competition from India, Pakistan, Japan and Hong Kong. The court concluded that the effect of ending the agreement and so creating a free market would be to raise the general level of unemployment in eleven areas, in which about 100,000 employees (or about 70 per cent of the industry) were situated, from 4·3 per cent to 5·9 per cent; and in four of those areas from 5·2 per cent to 7·8 per cent. Put simply, the court had to choose between this rise in the level of unemployment on the one hand, and the disadvantage of the higher price, the damage to the export trade, and the waste of national resources on the other. The court decided that the agreement was contrary to the public interest and so

12. See R. B. Stevens and B. S Yamey, *The Restrictive Practices Court* (1965). (See now the the Restrictive Practices Court Act 1976.)

13. [1959] 1 WLR 154.

accepted the consequence of a rise in unemployment.

Obviously that is a political judgment, and the court said things like: 'We are satisfied that the industry can and ought to be made smaller and more compact . . . We cannot see why price invasion is a bad thing or something which ought to be prevented; it is only one form of normal trade competition . . . Competition in quality is no doubt a benefit, but the removal of the restrictions would not prevent it.' And in a curious sentence the court, having noted that the unemployment might cause great hardship, added: 'But we are clear that once we have reached a conclusion of fact, it is our duty to disregard the consequences of our findings.'

The use of judges in this way to make political and economic decisions was widely criticized in 1956. But by 1964 the court was generally thought to have been succesful. The Resale Prices Act of 1964 extended the court's jurisdiction but during the debates in that year Lord Gardiner who was to become Lord Chancellor later that year expressed doubts about 'the increasing practice in the last ten years of employing Her Majesty's judges to perform tasks other than their ordinary tasks.' He added, 'I am not quite clear whether Her Majesty's judges have any special qualifications to determine what are really socio-economic questions, but they have done well.'[14] Lord Gardiner did not explain what he meant by this last phrase. Nevertheless doubts continued to be expressed about the wisdom of involving judges in the making of political decisions of this kind and his view was supported by those who believed that judicial purity, as they saw it, should be preserved. On the other hand it could be argued that the control of monopolies and restrictive practices by the courts has a long history. It may be that the operation of the Restrictive Practices Court provided some sort of precedent for the involvement of the judiciary in the highly political field of industrial relations.

Industrial relations

Under the Industrial Courts Act of 1919[15] the minister may set up a court of enquiry into a trade dispute. Since 1954, fourteen of such courts have been presided over by judges, normally with two experienced non-lawyers. Lord Pearson leads the field with five enquiries into disputes in the electricity supply, seamen's, civil air

14. 258 HL Deb. col. 835, 836.
15. I was helped by being able to read an unpublished thesis for MSc (Econ.) by David Cockburn (1972).

transport, steel, and port industries.[16] Lord Cameron follows with four: Ford's, port transport, printing, and building sites.[17] Lord Wilberforce presided over two enquiries into disputes in the electricity supply and coal industries;[18] Lord Morris into a shipbuilding and engineering dispute;[19] Lord Evershed into a London docks dispute;[20] and Lord Justice Scarman into the Grunwick dispute.[21]

These are far from being solely fact-finding enquiries. The terms of reference frequently require the court to have regard to the public interest or the national interest or the national economy or considerations like 'the need for an efficient and competitive' industry.[22] In one recent enquiry[23] into the electricity supply industry, Lord Wilberforce asked the Treasury to submit a memorandum on the significance of the dispute to the interests of the national economy and the Treasury responded with a document that argued for a progressive and substantial reduction in the levels of settlements.[24] This request from the court caused some difficulties as it was argued that the government was seeking to impose its views and even a favoured solution of the dispute upon the court. Lord Wilberforce sought to rebut this but the request clearly, in the minds of some, showed that the court was not independent or impartial.

The status and function of these courts came into question during one of the most critical of these enquiries, that presided over by Lord Wilberforce in 1972 into the dispute about miners' pay[25] which had led to a widespread stoppage of work. The extent to which the courts could become involved in the politics of such disputes had been shown a few years earlier when Lord Cameron presided over an enquiry into a dispute on London building sites.[26] The report then expressed the opinion that certain workmen should be eligible for re-employment if they sought it but not in any circumstances for election as shop stewards; and that other workmen should not be offered re-employment.

16. Cmnd 2361, 3025, 3211, 3551, 3754, 4429.
17. Cmnd 131, 510, 3184, 3396.
18. Cmnd 4954, 4903.
19. Cmnd 9084, 9085.
20. Cmnd 9302, 9310.
21. Cmnd 6922.
22. See Cmnd 3025 – the industry was shipping.
23. See Cmnd 4594.
24. See Cmnd 4579.
25. See Cmnd 4903.
26. Cmnd 3396.

In the miners' dispute Lord Wilberforce became deeply enmeshed in job evaluation, the social and physical conditions in the pits and, above all, the need to produce a settlement under which the miners would go back to work. Lord Wilberforce discovered that there were two factors in any possible wage increase. One was the periodic factor – that wages did increase from time to time, and the other was what he called the adjustment factor which meant that a time might come in any industry when a distortion or trend had to be recognized as such for correction. 'The existence of these two quite separate factors,' said the report, 'appears to have been overlooked until the present Enquiry brought it to light.' If a large increase could not be paid for by the National Coal Board then the government should meet it.

The *Economist* referred to the device of 'calling in a High Court judge to write incredible economic nonsense',[27] but whatever view is taken of the justice or the wisdom of the report which recommended a considerable wage increase and which formed the basis of the settlement, the impression given was that the government had set up this enquiry to produce a report which would enable them to yield to the miners' claim without total loss of face.

Under other legislation, less formal committees may be set up to enquire into trade disputes, and in the 1960s Lord Devlin produced three reports on the port industry[28] and Lord Cameron reported on a dispute concerning bank employees.[29]

In 1962, the Royal Commission on the Press recommended that there should be set up a Press Amalgamations Court, like the Restrictive Practices Court, consisting of judges of the High Court and lay members appointed on the recommendation of the Lord Chancellor after consultation with the Trades Union Congress and the Press Council.[30] Lord Hailsham, then a minister, was doubtful about the value of the idea as he thought that the question of the public interest in a proposed amalgamation (which the court would have to consider) was 'not justiciable'. He went on to point out 'the danger of getting the judiciary into politics' especially as newspapers were often linked to political parties. The primary concern of the judiciary, said Lord Hailsham, must be 'to retain the

27. 26 February 1972.
28. Cmnd 2523, 2734, 3104.
29. Cmnd 2202.
30. Cmnd 1811 paras 337–49.

respect of the public for their independence – which involves not merely their real independence of mind, but also the belief which the public can have that they are seen to be independent in every respect.'[31] Eight years later these considerations did not apparently deter Lord Hailsham (then Lord Chancellor) from supporting the setting up of the National Industrial Relations Court (NIRC).

When in 1970 the minister was introducing in the Commons legislation which created the NIRC, he said that the NIRC's existence showed 'in fact as well as in symbol' that the provisions of the Bill[32] would not be arbitrarily implemented by the Secretary of State of the day but would 'depend on the rule of the law'. The court, he said (inaccurately), would be 'something new in British justice' and would consist of judges and laymen sitting together.[33]

Many kinds of dispute arising out of industrial relations could find their way to the NIRC which, because of its status as a superior court of record and the powers given it by statute, was able to order the payment of fines and, if that or any other of its orders was disregarded, could imprison for contempt. The application of that sanction led to the involvement of the ordinary courts. Here I am concerned to emphasize that the NIRC was required by the legislation under which it operated to make decisions which were likely to lead, and did in fact lead, to considerable and widespread political protest.

Whether the NIRC always acted with the greatest wisdom may be debatable. But its failure was due not primarily to the way it performed its functions, but to the nature of those functions. Many people doubted whether the issues before the Restrictive Practices Court were justiciable. What the NIRC was required to do was to make binding decisions, and to see that they were enforced, in the context of dispute between trade unions, individual workmen, employers, and employers' federations. This, as many said at the time, was not a function which judges and courts could perform successfully.

Now under the Employment Protection Act of 1975 an Appeal Tribunal has been set up consisting of judges, and of others having special knowledge or experience of industrial relations, either as representatives of employers or as representatives of workers. So in structure, if not in other ways, this tribunal is similar to the NIRC.

31. 250 HL Deb. col. 938–9.
32. This became the Industrial Relations Act 1971.
33. 808 HC Deb. col. 982.

It can hear appeals from tribunals under or by virtue of the Equal Pay Act 1970, the Sex Discrimination Act 1975 and others, as well as the Employment Protection Act itself. It is a somewhat curious body in that much of its jurisdiction is to hear appeals on questions of law, for which the lay members might appear unfitted. Perhaps we are seeing, as an evolution (the origins of which can be traced to the nineteenth century), the emergence of a genuine hybrid tribunal, in which case to suggest that this body is a further example of the use of judges for extrajudicial activities is only one way to describe it. It could also be said to be an example of the developed use of experienced laymen to assist in the determination of disputes.

Northern Ireland

The first involvement of judges, acting outside their courts, in Northern Ireland was in 1969 when the Governor appointed Lord Cameron to lead a commission of enquiry into disturbances.[34] Then in 1971 Sir Edmund Compton (not a judge but the former Parliamentary Commissioner for Administration) chaired an enquiry into allegations of physical brutality by the security forces. Sir Edmund found there had been cases of physical ill-treatment such as wall-standing, hooding, noise, deprivation of sleep, and diets of bread and water. The Home Secretary rejected any suggestion that the methods authorized for interrogation contained any element of cruelty but he appointed three Privy Councillors to consider those methods. One was Lord Parker (who had just retired as Lord Chief Justice) and another was Lord Gardiner (who had been Lord Chancellor from 1964 to 1970). Lord Parker and the third Privy Councillor (Mr J. A. Boyd-Carpenter) concluded that these methods, subject to proper safeguards, and limiting the occasions on which and the degree to which they could be applied, conformed to the authority given. Lord Gardiner said that they were secret, illegal, not morally justifiable and alien to the traditions of what he believed still to be the greatest democracy in the world. The disagreement was wide.[35]

In April 1972, two reports were published. Lord Widgery (who had succeeded Lord Parker as Lord Chief Justice) had been appointed as a one-man tribunal of enquiry to enquire into the

34. Cmd (N.I.) 532.
35. Cmnd 4901 (March 1972).

events of 'Bloody Sunday' which led to thirteen civilian deaths in Londonderry. This tribunal was set up under the Tribunals of Enquiry (Evidence) Act 1921 the procedure of which is designed to elicit facts. The line between matters of fact and opinions deduced from facts is not always easy to draw. Lord Widgery spoke about the justifiability of decisions taken by army commanders and soldiers, about actions which, he concluded, did 'not require censure', and in using such language caused dispute and argument about the nature of his findings.[36]

In the meantime Mr Justice Scarman had since 1969 been enquiring with two others into the violence and civil disturbances of that year. This tribunal also operated under the Act of 1921 and its report was substantial. It investigated a large number of incidents and drew conclusions about fault and responsibility. It assessed the social cost in terms of deaths, personal injuries, damage to property, damage to licensed premises, intimidation and displacement of persons.[37]

At the end of 1972 a commission under the chairmanship of Lord Diplock reported on the legal procedures to deal with terrorist activities in Northern Ireland. It concluded that the main obstacle to dealing efficiently with terrorist crime in the regular courts of justice was intimidation of would-be prosecution witnesses. It recommended that trials of scheduled terrorist offences should be conducted without a jury; that members of the armed services should be given power to arrest and to detain for up to four hours to establish identity; that bail should not normally be granted; that the onus of proof as to the possession of firearms and explosives should in certain circumstances be shifted to the accused; and that the rules about the admissibility as evidence of confessions and signed statements should be relaxed.[38]

That commission led to the passing of the Northern Ireland (Emergency Provisions) Act 1973. In 1974 Lord Gardiner was appointed chairman of a committee to consider what provisions and powers, consistent to the maximum extent practicable in the circumstances with the preservation of civil liberties and human rights, were required to deal with terrorism and subversion in Northern Ireland, including provisions for the administration of justice; and to examine the working of the Act of 1973. The

36. HC 220 of 1971–2.
37. Cmd (N.I.) 566.
38. Cmnd 5185.

committee reported early in 1975,[39] and made a large number of recommendations, some endorsing the Diplock Commission and the Act, others being critical and proposing amendments to the law. In particular, it proposed the ending of detention without trial as soon as was politically possible, and it condemned as a serious mistake the establishment of a 'special category' for convicted prisoners claiming political motivation.

So from the beginning of 1972 there have been involved in five major enquiries relating to Northern Ireland a former Lord Chancellor (twice), a present and a former Lord Chief Justice, a Lord of Appeal, and a High Court judge. On one occasion, two of these were seen to be in open disagreement about the legitimacy and desirability of actions taken by the authorities; on another occasion, one of these was set up, in effect, to review recommendations made by another. It may be that a judge is well qualified to conduct enquiries to establish what took place on particular occasions. But it is impossible for him in his findings not to interpret events. He must draw deductions about what he thinks took place from the evidence that is presented to him. And so he will be involved in political controversy and, in circumstances like those prevailing in Northern Ireland, inevitably accused of bias, of whitewashing, of serving certain political masters. These accusations may be wholly untrue but they will be made to an extent not paralleled by criticism of any judgment he may make from the bench of the regular courts.

Legislative process

Finally, the most senior judges sit in the House of Lords[40] and may take part in its legislative and other activities. Lords of Appeal in Ordinary – Law Lords – receive life baronies on appointment unless they are already ennobled. A survey has been made[41] of the twenty-six judges who were active Law Lords during the period 1952–68 together with two Lord Chief Justices, two Masters of the Rolls and one president of what was then the Probate, Divorce and Admiralty Division. The authors of the survey say that there was very little 'in the way of political activism' on the part of the Law Lords whose contribution to debates on bills was largely that of acting as

39. Cmnd 5847.
40. I.e., the Upper House of Parliament.
41. L. Blom-Cooper and G. Drewry, *Final Appeal* (1972), ch. 10.

'resident technical consultants to the legislature on legal points' and it seems that those with records of overt political affiliation did not speak more than others.

While participating Law Lords agreed with one another more frequently than they disagreed, the authors of the survey list thirteen items between 1956 and 1967 where there was a substantial measure of disagreement and of these several were not matters of technical law. They included capital punishment, artificial insemination, adultery, the minimum age for the death penalty, corporal punishment of young offenders, and disputes concerning majority verdicts, suspended sentences and parole. In one recent debate, five Law Lords, in an unprecedented way, spoke against a legislative proposal which provided that in assessing damages payable to a widow on the death of her husband, her remarriage or prospects of remarriage should not be taken into account. Two other Law Lords participated and all the Law Lords with two exceptions attended the debate on 6 May 1971. 'In the face of almost certain defeat in the Lobby,' say Blom-Cooper and Drewry, 'the Law Lords, as decorously as they were able, withdrew their amendment and retired once more into their judicial shells.'[42]

Where technical law ends and political controversy begins is not always easy to determine. It is clear, however, that Law Lords while for the most part restricting themselves to the obviously technical are not averse from speaking on social questions like capital punishment, the treatment of offenders and adultery. They do occasionally assume the role of 'self-appointed guardians of the nation's conscience'.[43]

A well-known example from earlier in this century of a Law Lord speaking on a political matter in the House of Lords arose when Lord Carson in 1921 strongly attacked the proposal to establish an Irish Free State. His right to do so was challenged by Lord Chancellor Birkenhead and defended by former Lord Chancellor Finlay during a debate in 1922 on Law Lords and party politics.[44]

In 1963, Lord Hodson, already well known for his judicial views on matrimonial matters, strongly opposed provisions in Mr Leo Abse's Matrimonial Causes and Reconciliation Bill. He spoke once during the second reading debate, spoke or intervened thirteen

42. Ibid., p. 215.
43. Ibid., p. 204.
44. 49 HL Deb. col. 931–73.

times in committee, once on report, and once on third reading.[45] And Lord Hodson was concerned primarily with the substantive merits and demerits of the Bill, not with its legal technicalities.

But more dramatic and more political was Lord Salmon's contribution in 1975 to the debates on the government's controversial Trade Union and Labour Relations (Amendment) Bill. He said:

> We cannot shut our eyes to the fact that there are groups, very small numerically but extremely cohesive and tenacious, who have infiltrated the unions with the intention of seizing power if they can. Their objects and ideas are entirely different from those of the trade unions, which we all know and respect. Their avowed purpose is to wreck the Social Contract and the democratic system under which we live. Their ethos derives from foreign lands where individual liberty is dead, and where the courts and trade unions are mere tools of the Executive, to do its will.[46]

The argument is familiar – Lord Gordon-Walker said he had heard it for forty years – but, even more, it is a political argument. Lord Salmon clearly felt strongly and spoke in the name of freedom and democracy. He posed the question whether the disadvantage of a judge speaking on matters which in one form or another – such as unfair dismissal from employment or from a trade union – might well come before him when he was on the bench was outweighed by the advantage of hearing his views or by the argument that he should not be prevented, by convention or otherwise, from speaking in Parliament on such a matter.[47]

Nor is it uncommon for judges to be consulted from time to time by members of the Executive on matters within their expertise. One recent example was the desirability of introducing automatic parole for short-term prisoners; another was the possibility of dividing every sentence of three years or under into three parts: imprisonment, supervised release, and remission (which the Lord Justices on the criminal side of the Court of Appeal made clear they did not like). In November 1983 it was revealed that Sir John Donaldson MR had advised a senior civil servant on the extent to

45. 250 HL Deb. col. 401–5, 1537, 1538–43; vol. 251 col. 1553–5, 1560, 1561, 1564, 1578–9, 1591–4, 1595, 1596, 1597, 1600; vol. 252 col. 419–20, 430.

46. 358 HL Deb. col. 27.

47. For other, earlier, examples (mostly on more legal questions) see Shetreet, *op. cit.*, pp. 257–8, 345–7.

which the judiciary could play a greater role in industrial relations. Lord Hailsham made a statement emphasizing the importance of the Lord Chancellor being informed when such consultations took place.

If one believes that judges can and should be politically neutral when they are on the judicial bench, then their involvement in such highly political questions as restrictive practices, industrial relations and Northern Ireland, is to be regretted. But if one does not believe that the pure doctrine of political neutrality can be or is applicable to judges in their courts, then their involvement in outside political affairs appears less regrettable. If it is accepted that judges on the bench already display common characteristics and common attitudes when they are dealing with political cases (see below, p. 198) then it is difficult to argue that their judgments are seriously contaminated by their extrajudicial activities. If we swallow the camel, we should not strain at the gnat.

The falseness arises when judges are put forward to preside over enquiries which are inherently political in character (such as any dispute connected with the disorders and killings in Northern Ireland or with large-scale industrial disputes) on the ground that their participation will ensure neutrality. When this is done and when subsequently it comes to be perceived by large numbers of people that the neutrality is a sham, then damage is done to the judicial system.

To say that the neutrality is a sham does not mean that judges act dishonestly. It means that if a judge is sent to preside over an enquiry in Northern Ireland or into a nationwide strike by power workers, he can do no more than any other intelligent man. He will try to make allowance for his own prejudices to the extent that he knows them and he will try to produce a report which will leave matters nearer to an agreed solution than they were before he arrived. But if the myth of his neutrality and objectivity, *because he is a judge*, is paraded, its exploding will make more difficult the proper performance on the bench of all members of the judiciary.

According to a press report in 1980, a spokesman for the Home Office, justifying the Home Secretary's refusal to appoint a public enquiry into the death of Blair Peach during the disturbances at Southall in 1979, said that one reason was the reluctance of judges to chair such enquiries because to do so might have the eventual effect of prejudicing the public's view of their impartiality. And a spokesman for the Lord Chancellor's office is reported to have said: 'Judges feel at home when they are asked to take factual matters, apply the law to them and come to conclusions. They feel that their training just does not fit them to decide really controversial issues.'[48]

Nevertheless, in April 1980 the Home Secretary announced that a judge would be appointed to review on a continuing basis the purposes, procedures, conditions and safeguards governing the interception of communications on behalf of the police, Customs and Excise and the security service. He would report to the Prime Minister. His first, but not any subsequent, report would be published and Parliament would be informed of any findings of a general nature and of any changes in the arrangements.[49] Lord Diplock was the appointed judge and Robin Cook MP objected to his suitability on the ground that he had been chairman of the Permanent Security Commission since 1971 and that he had not formerly indicated any understanding of the concern of civil liberties and privacy which had given rise to public and press anxiety about the procedures of the security services. Cook also referred to Lord Diplock's 'evident distaste for trade unions' and said it was well known that 'taps' were frequently placed on trade unionists involved in trade disputes. The Home Secretary refused to make a statement on the criteria he applied in selecting Lord Diplock and rejected the criticism.[50] Lord Diplock's first report of five pages was published in March 1981. It was not regarded generally as being informative and provoked some press comment unfavourable to the use of judges for such purposes.[51] And the Speaker ruled in the House of Commons that it was offensive even in relation to these extrajudicial activities to refer to Lord Diplock as 'a Tory judge'.[52]

The purpose of this book is to look at the ways in which judges of the High Court, the Court of Appeal, and the House of Lords have in recent years dealt with political cases which have come before them. By political I mean those cases which arise out of controversial legislation or controversial action initiated by public authorities, or which touch important moral or social issues.

When people like the members of the judiciary, broadly homogeneous in character, are faced with such political situations, they act in broadly similar ways. It will be part of my argument to suggest that behind these actions lies a unifying attitude of mind, a political position, which is primarily concerned to protect and

48. *The Guardian*, 26 July 1980.
49. 982 HC Deb. col. 205–20.
50. 987 HC Deb. col. 651 and *The Times*, 11 July 1980.
51. See Cmnd 8191 and *The Sunday Times*, 8 March 1981.
52. 996 HC Deb. col. 824–6 (18 December 1980).

conserve certain values and institutions. This does not mean that the judiciary inevitably and invariably supports what governments do, or even what Conservative governments do, though that is the natural inclination. Individually, judges may support the Conservative or the Labour or the Liberal parties. Collectively, in their function and by their nature, they are neither Tories nor Socialists nor Liberals. They are protectors and conservators of what has been, of the relationships and interests on which, *in their view*, our society is founded. It is as difficult to imagine the judiciary in the United Kingdom handing down judgments like those sometimes handed down by the Supreme Court of the United States, based on radical and reforming principles, as it would be to imagine such judgments being handed down by the Supreme Court of the Soviet Union.

Part Two

Cases

The Court's position had not been made any easier by suggestions that it was possible for the Government to influence its decisions. The Court was surprised that those suggestions should have been made, and the Court owed it to its members and to all concerned to make it clear that no attempt had been made by anyone directly or indirectly, otherwise than in open court, to influence its decision.

Sir John Donaldson, President of the National Industrial Relations Court in *Midland Cold Storage Ltd v. Turner and Others* as reported in *The Times*, 28 July 1972.

It was a matter of real concern that the divisional court, exercising the power of judicial review, was increasingly . . . being used for political purposes superficially dressed up as points of law. The proper remedy was the ballot box and not the court. If a rating or precepting authority over-rated or over-precepted, the remedy was in the hands of the electorate . . . The impropriety of coming to the court when political capital was sought to be made could not be overstressed. It was perhaps even worse when public servants were or felt constrained to file affidavits which demonstrated a political purpose.

McNeill, J. in *R.v. Greater London Council ex parte Kensington and Chelsea BC* dismissing an application for judicial review of a precept issued by the GLC, as reported in *The Times*, 7 April 1982.

The intellectual isolation of appellate judges, who resolve 'hard cases' with reference to notions of social justice and public policy which they are singularly (and collectively) ill-equipped to understand . . . remains a deeply worrying feature of our judicial process.

Mr Gavin Drewry in 47 *Modern Law Review* (1984), p. 380.

3. Industrial relations

The early cases

From the middle ages, Parliament has been concerned with the problems, central to the national economy, of productivity and the control of wages. And, for hundreds of years, workers who were thought to be failing in their duties were subjected to imprisonment and other penalties.

The use of the penal law against workers, especially when it involves imprisonment, or the possibility of imprisonment, is one of the most persistent sources of conflict between labour and management, and between labour and governments. Parliament legislated extensively against the combination of workers but the judges also, through their power of interpreting statutes and of making and extending the common law, were a powerful source of constraint on the emerging trade union movement in the industrial society of the nineteenth century. Two outstanding characteristics of labour law during the second half of that century were the intermittent recognition by politicians in government and Parliament that control of trade unionism by the imposition of penalties was of doubtful efficacy; and the recurrent attempts by the courts to preserve the penal method.[1]

Statutes of 1859, 1871 and 1875 were designed to relieve trade unions of criminal liability, especially for conspiracy. Specifically, the Conspiracy and Protection of Property Act 1875 provided that an agreement by two or more persons to do or procure to be done any act in contemplation or furtherance of a trade dispute should not be a criminal conspiracy unless the act itself was punishable as a crime. So to strike ceased to be a crime.

The last decade of the nineteenth century saw the development of a considerable antipathy to trade unionism among influential public opinion. This was in part due to the emergence of New Unionism which sought to organize unskilled workers. Professor

1. I am much indebted to Lord Wedderburn on whose writings and advice I have freely drawn in preparing and revising this chapter.

Saville has written that the old unions 'were able to rely upon the skill of their members as a crucial bargaining weapon' but 'the new unionists were at all times, even in years of good trade, subject to the pressures of an over-stocked labour market'. So 'the employers, too, in the semi- and unskilled trades were more uncompromising than their fellows in industries where unionism had long been established.' The industrial offensive against the trade unions in the early years of the 1890s was 'most successful against the dockers, the seamen and the casual trades' but all the New Unions lost heavily in membership.[2]

It is against the background of this offensive that the judicial decisions[3] of 1896–1901 must be seen. Although the right to strike had been established, some of the judges were not to be so easily defeated. In addition to the crime of conspiracy, there was the civil wrong (or tort) of conspiracy, consisting of an agreement which has been acted on and which is made in order to attain either an unlawful object or a lawful object by unlawful means. It was to this that some judges turned their attention.

In *Allen v. Flood*[4] a dispute arose between the ironworkers' union and woodworkers, the former objecting to certain work being done by the latter. Ironworkers told one of their officials that they would stop working if the woodworkers were continued in employment. The official informed the employers accordingly and the employers lawfully dismissed the woodworkers who then brought an action against the official.

The case was first argued in December 1895 before seven members of the House of Lords[5] including Lord Chancellor Halsbury, and a former Lord Chancellor, Herschell. 'From the very beginning,' says Professor Heuston, 'Lord Halsbury took a view strongly adverse to the position of the trade union and expressed his firm opinion that the plaintiffs . . . were entitled to damages for an interference with their right to work. It was also clear, however, that on this point he would be unable to carry with him a majority of his colleagues.' Apparently, Halsbury then 'conceived the idea that the case should be re-argued before an enlarged body of Law Lords and that, in addition, the House should adopt once more the

2. John Saville, 'Trade Unions and Free Labour: the Background to the Taff Vale Decision' in *Essays in Labour History* (ed. Asa Briggs and John Saville, 1960) vol. 1, p. 317.
3. Including *Lyons v. Wilkins* (see below, p. 60).
4. [1898] AC 1.
5. Here and elsewhere this means the House in its judicial capacity.

practice of summoning the High Court judges to advise', a practice generally thought to be obsolete. Lord Herschell was angered by this idea and, says Professor Heuston, 'the High Court judges at that time, many of whom were Halsbury's own appointments, were not on the whole notable for progressive views on social or industrial matters.'[6]

Between 25 March and 2 April 1897 the case was re-argued before the original seven Law Lords and two others. Of the eight High Court judges who attended, and gave their 'opinions', six agreed with Lord Halsbury and two disagreed. But when the nine Law Lords delivered their judgments in December 1897, Lord Halsbury's views were supported by only two of his colleagues, with Lord Herschell and five others in the opposing majority. So the trade unions remained protected.

Then in 1901, in *Quinn v. Leathem*,[7] the effect of that decision was reversed. For many years, L supplied a butcher with meat. The trade union sought to persuade L not to employ non-union men. When this failed, the union instructed their members working for the butcher that, if he continued to buy L's meat, they were to cease work. So the butcher took no more meat from L who brought an action against the union officials for conspiracy fo injure him. The House of Lords decided in his favour.

In *Quinn v. Leathem* five Law Lords delivered judgments and they were unanimous in deciding against the union officials. In addition to Lord Halsbury, two of them had taken part in *Allen v. Flood* where they had been in the majority. Now they supported the Lord Chancellor. The distinctions drawn between the two cases were primarily that in *Allen v. Flood* there was no conspiring between two or more persons (as there was in *Quinn v. Leathem*) and that in *Allen v. Flood* the purpose of the defendant was to promote his own trade interest whereas in *Quinn v. Leathem* the purpose of the defendants was to injure the plaintiff in his trade rather than legitimately to advance their own interests. From the trade unionists' viewpoint the effect of *Quinn v. Leathem* was seriously to curtail their power to operate in ways which would strengthen the working-class movement against employers. This was thought by trade unionists to be inconsistent with the leading decision of ten years before which had protected employers' associations from conspiracy on the ground that the acts had been

6. R. F. V. Heuston, *The Lives of the Lord Chancellors 1885–1940*, pp. 119–20.
7. [1901] AC 495.

done 'with the lawful object of protecting and extending their trade and increasing their profits' without employing unlawful means, although the consequence had been to injure their competitors.[8]

These judicial decisions caused great political upheaval and resulted in the passing of the Trade Disputes Act 1906 which followed the same pattern as the Act of 1875, protecting trade unions from actions for civil conspiracy if the acts were done in furtherance or contemplation of a trade dispute.

Another struggle centred on trade union funds. In law, property may be held either by a natural person, or by a number of such persons, or by an incorporated body such as a company. Trade unions fell into the second of these groups, but, because of their large and fluctuating membership and because of certain provisions in the Trade Union Act 1871, it was assumed that it was impracticable to bring actions against them so as to make their funds liable. In 1900 a dispute arose because it was said that the Taff Vale Railway Company had victimized a trade unionist who led a wage demand. The House of Lords held that trade unions could be sued, in effect, for losses sustained by employers as a consequence of strike action.[9] Lord Halsbury gave one of the five unanimous judgments. As Professor Heuston says, the decision left 'a legacy of suspicion and mistrust . . . to poison relations between the courts and the unions for many years'. He adds: 'One of Baldwin's favourite themes was the folly of this *Taff Vale* decision: "The Conservatives can't talk of class-war: they started it," he would remark to G. M. Young.'[10]

But it is not clear that Baldwin was referring to the House of Lords' decision. G. M. Young said that Baldwin's theme was 'the gross and almost irreparable error which, under the vehement guidance of Lord Chancellor Halsbury, the Conservative government had made in 1901',[11] and Young goes on to say that in Baldwin's view the Tory party (that is, the government) should at once, by passing an Act of Parliament, have restored the position intended by the Tory legislation of 1875.[12] Baldwin's comment

8. *Mogul Steamship Co. v. McGregor Gow & Co.* [1892] AC 25.

9. *Taff Vale Railway Co. v. Amalgamated Society of Railway Servants* [1901] AC 426.

10. Heuston, *op. cit.*, p. 76; G. M. Young, *Stanley Baldwin* (1952), p. 31.

11. G. M. Young, ibid.

12. Ibid, p. 32.

seems therefore to refer to the political failure of the Tory government to reverse the *Taff Vale* decision rather than to the decision itself and we are left to wonder whether Halsbury's 'vehement guidance' was exercised over his fellow judges or over his colleagues in the cabinet. Certainly his judgment in the Lords was the reverse of vehement and consisted of one substantive sentence of fifty moderate words. So perhaps we have here an example of a Lord Chancellor publicly delivering judgment in a case and then privately urging his political colleagues not to reverse it by legislation.

The *Taff Vale* decision was a serious blow to trade unionism. The law had seemed 'so clearly settled to the contrary', wrote Lord Asquith, that 'public opinion was unprepared for any such decision'.[13] Liberal opinion strongly favoured its reversal. This was effectively carried through by the strong Liberal government elected in 1906 in the Trade Disputes Act of that year.

A few years later, the judiciary again intervened, this time by invoking the doctrine of *ultra vires*. This doctrine applies mainly to public authorities exercising statutory powers and to companies registered under the Companies Acts to pursue certain objects described in their constitutions. If powers or objects are exceeded, action can be brought to restrain those authorities or companies. Trade unions had for some time been supporting candidates for the House of Commons and spending union funds for this purpose. In 1909, a member of the Amalgamated Society of Railway Servants successfully challenged this practice.[14] This of course was also a severe blow to the emerging Labour Party and again the politicians had to try to restore what had been understood to be the position by passing the Trade Union Act 1913.[15]

For much of the interwar period, the judges seemed to withdraw from the conflict or, when asked to intervene, tended to adopt a neutral position. Indeed, such decisions as were made were markedly more generous in their recognition of the legitimacy of the purposes of trade unions. Moreover, during the 1930s, employers did not need to seek the help of the courts, the unions being in a weak condition. As we shall see, judicial intervention was not noticeably restrained at this time in other political cockpits.

13. Quoted by Wedderburn, *The Worker and the Law* (2nd edn, 1971), p. 317.
14. *Amalgamated Society of Railway Servants v. Osborne* [1910] AC 87.
15. See S. and B. Webb, *The History of Trade Unionism* (1920 edition), pp. 608–11.

The general strike

Nevertheless the general strike of 1926 gave rise to one case in the courts and a group of incidents seemed to show some curious connections between the courts and the politicians. On Thursday 6 May 1926 (the third day of the strike) Sir John Simon MP spoke in the House of Commons. Then known as a former Attorney-General and a former Home Secretary, Sir John was a Liberal MP who still perhaps had hopes of leading his party in the future. He argued that the general strike was not a strike at all because it was unlawful as the workmen had 'terminated their engagements' without giving due notice to their employers. The decision of the General Council of the Trades Union Congress to call out everybody was not, he said, a lawful act and every workman who obeyed it had broken the law. The general strike was 'a novel and an utterly illegal proceeding'. Thus every railwayman on strike was 'personally liable to be sued in the County Court for damages'. Sir John went further and said that every trade union leader who had advised and promoted the strike was 'liable in damages to the uttermost farthing of his personal possessions'. He then emphasized in what he called 'a perfectly dogmatic statement' that no trade unionist who refused to obey the order of his union to strike would lose any benefits payable under a rule of the union because the order would be unlawful. 'It cannot be too widely and plainly known', said Sir John, 'that there is no court in this country which would ever construe such a rule as meaning that the man would forfeit his benefits if he is asked to do that which is wrong and illegal.'[16]

The following Monday (10th) the cabinet met at 4.30 p.m. and agreed that the Prime Minister (Mr Baldwin) should arrange for a question and answer in the House of Commons the next day to the following effect:

Question Does the Government intend to deal with the position of the Trades Unions?
Answer The Government are not now contemplating any modification in existing trades union legislature, but they are considering the desirability of making clear what they believe to be now the law, namely, that a general strike is illegal.

That Monday evening Sir Henry Slesser, who had been Solicitor-

16.   195 HC Deb. col. 584–6.

General in the Labour Government of 1924, replied in the House (against the wishes of his leader Ramsay MacDonald) to correct what he believed to be 'an erroneous view of the law'. He deplored Simon's introduction of 'highly debatable' questions of law which, he said, should be discussed in the Law Courts and not in Parliament.[17] Sir John responded at 6 p.m. the next afternoon[18] and was able strongly to buttress his arguments with quotations from a judgment delivered that very morning by Mr Justice Astbury in the Chancery Division of the High Court. When the cabinet met (also at 6 p.m.), their attention was drawn to this judgment. The Prime Minister informed his colleagues that, as a result of a consultation with the Earl of Birkenhead, a cabinet colleague, 'following the receipt of certain information'[19] he had earlier decided not to implement the cabinet decision to arrange for a question and answer in the House of Commons.

The case arose because the National Sailors' and Firemen's Union did not support the strike but their Tower Hill branch passed a resolution calling out their members in support of the TUC. The union asked for a declaration that the secretary and delegates of the branch were not entitled to call out their members and for an injunction to restrain them from doing so. In the course of his judgment, Mr Justice Astbury said:

> The so-called general strike called by the Trades Union Congress Council is illegal, and persons inciting or taking part in it are not protected by the Trade Disputes Act 1906. No trade dispute has been alleged or shown to exist in any of the unions affected, except in the miners' case, and no trade dispute does or can exist between the Trades Union Congress on the one hand and the Government and the nation on the other.

Astbury went on to say that no member of the union could lose his trade union benefits by refusing to obey unlawful orders. An injunction was issued.[20]

It seems that the case was first heard by Astbury on 6 May, on the evening of which day Sir John Simon made his first speech, declared the general strike illegal, argued that strikers were liable to pay damages, and referred to the protection of non-strikers' benefits. Then, the day after Sir Henry Slesser's attack, Astbury

17. Ibid. col. 787.
18. Ibid. col. 862–4.
19. Was this perhaps what Astbury J. was going to say?
20. *National Sailors and Firemen's Union of Great Britain v. Reed* [1926] Ch. 536.

delivered his judgment which strongly supported Sir John's position and provided judicial authority for Sir John's second speech that same evening. It is difficult to believe that the judge and the politician were not sharing their thoughts on this matter. It seems likely that they knew one another well. Astbury had been a fellow Liberal MP for four years having been first returned at the same time as Simon during the Liberal victory of 1906; and he was made a judge in 1913 during Simon's five-year period as Solicitor-General and then Attorney-General.

Opinions differ greatly about the importance of Simon's speeches and Astbury's judgment.[21] It is said that Astbury claimed more than once that his contribution had saved the nation. And, on one view, the TUC leaders were genuinely alarmed at the prospect of imprisonment. But there were undoubtedly more important factors affecting the decision of the TUC to call off the general strike on 12 May.

As I have said, the courts were not much involved in disputes affecting trade unions during the 1930s or for some years after 1945. But the 1960s gave rise to certain assumptions about the nature and the power of trade unions which, true or false, have coloured and affected the attitudes of the middle classes and, in consequence, the policies of the Conservative, Labour and Liberal parties. Once again, the judges have become central figures in these political issues.

Picketing

Picketing is a practice which stands uneasily across the boundary, as variously interpreted, of legal and illegal action. It can become conduct likely to cause a breach of the peace, or obstruction, or even assault. The Conspiracy and Protection of Property Act 1875 restated the criminal offence of 'watching or besetting' but excluded from that activity 'attending at or near the house or place where a person resides, or works, or carries on business, or happens to be . . . in order merely to obtain or communicate information'. But in *Lyons v. Wilkins*[22] the Court of Appeal had decided against the officers of a trade union who, having ordered a strike against the plaintiffs and against S (who made goods for the plaintiffs only), organized pickets to seek to persuade work-people not to work for

21. For a powerful argument that Astbury J was wrong in law, see A. L. Goodhart in 36 *Yale Law Journal* (1926–7) p. 464.
22. [1896] 1 Ch. 811; [1899] 1 Ch. 255.

the plaintiffs. That, said Lindley LJ, was not merely obtaining or communicating information. It was putting pressure on the plaintiffs by persuading people not to enter their employment. And that was illegal. It was further decided that such watching and besetting might be a nuisance at common law and illegal on that ground also. Once again the legislature reversed the courts and by the Trade Disputes Act 1906 made picketing lawful if in contemplation or furtherance of a trade dispute and if the purpose was peacefully obtaining or communicating information or 'peacefully persuading any person to work or abstain from working'.

The interpretation of the law remained contentious. During a trade dispute in 1960, a police officer found two pickets standing at the front entrance of a factory, four standing at the back entrance and ten or twelve outside the back entrance. The officer told the defendant three times that he considered two pickets at each entrance were sufficient but the defendant, persisting in his intention to join the pickets, 'pushed gently past' the police officer, 'was gently arrested', and was charged with obstructing the police in execution of their duty. The Divisional Court held that he was properly convicted on the ground that the police officer had reasonable grounds for anticipating that a breach of the peace was a real possibility.[23] In *Tynan v. Balmer*[24] (1966) forty pickets in a continuous circle around a factory (which had the effect of sealing off the highway) were held not to be legalized by the Act of 1906 because their action was a nuisance at common law and an unreasonable use of the highway. In 1972, a strike picket held a placard in front of a vehicle on a highway, urging the driver not to work at a site nearby and preventing him from proceeding along the highway. The picket was charged with obstruction of the highway although the whole incident lasted for not more than nine minutes. The House of Lords upheld the prosecution.[25] The following year, a police cordon prevented pickets from approaching a coach carrying workers out of a site. The defendant was involved in a scuffle with a constable and was successfully charged with obstructing him in the execution of his duty.[26] The result of these cases was greatly to limit the right to picket. They enlarged the scope within which the police could prevent picketing and they

23. *Piddington v. Bates* [1960] 3 All ER 660.
24. [1967] 1 QB 91.
25. *Hunt v. Broome* [1974] AC 587.
26. *Kavanagh v. Hiscock* [1974] 2 WLR 421; see also *Hubbard v. Pitt* [1975] 3 WLR 201 (see below, pp. 159–60).

greatly narrowed the scope within which picketing could lawfully be undertaken.[27]

Moreover, the use by the courts of these common law devices of obstruction, breach of the peace and nuisance is difficult to legislate against as the essential purpose (which before the 1960s had been more or less achieved with police co-operation) is to permit 'reasonable' picketing, including the right to accost for a short period within which arguments can be advanced, without putting persons in fear or to immoderate inconvenience.

'The attendance', said counsel for the defendant in *Hunt v. Broome*, 'is for the purpose of peacefully persuading a man not to work so the attendance must be in a position where the persuasion can be carried out; otherwise its purpose is frustrated . . . Attendance for the purpose of peaceful persuasion is what is protected by the Act . . . not mere attendance, standing with banners; the attendance is for oral communication.'[28]

As the courts presently interpret the law this purpose is often difficult and sometimes impossible to achieve. It is also true that the right to picket may be abused.

The right to strike

In 1964 the House of Lords in *Rookes v. Barnard*[29] delivered a judgment which seemed like a return to the early heady days of the century. R worked for BOAC with whom his union had an agreement that all workers should be union members. In 1955 R left the union after a disagreement with union members. Two local union members, and a district union official employed by the union, threatened BOAC that labour would be withdrawn if R were not removed within three days as required by a resolution passed at a members' meeting. Such a strike would have been a breach of contract by each member. BOAC gave R long notice and lawfully discharged him. R sued the two members and the official for conspiracy.

Under the Trade Disputes Act 1906 no action for conspiracy would lie unless the act would be unlawful if done by a person alone. So the Law Lords considered whether a threat to strike could be 'unlawful' in this sense. And they held it could be.

This decision was seen by trade unionists as a direct attack on the

27. For the *Shrewsbury* case, see below, p. 151.
28. Mr John Mortimer, QC.
29. [1964] AC 1129.

right to strike. The Law Lords certainly seemed to stretch themselves to arrive at their conclusion. Lord Devlin, for example, could find 'nothing to differentiate a threat of a breach of contract from a threat of physical violence'. It was a time when strikes were being blamed for most of the country's ills, and Lord Hodson said: 'The injury and suffering caused by strike action is very often widespread as well as devastating and a threat to strike would be expected to be certainly no less serious than a threat of violence.' Once again the politicians had to seek to reverse their Lordships' decision and passed the Trade Disputes Act 1965.

Inducing breach of contract

In 1952, certain drivers and loaders told Bowaters Ltd, the paper suppliers, that they might not be prepared to deliver paper to the plaintiffs who were printers and publishers. Bowaters told the plaintiffs and they brought an action against officers of the unions to which the drivers and loaders belonged. The Court of Appeal held that the evidence did not establish that there had been any direct procurement by the defendants of any wrongful acts by the drivers or loaders or that the latter had committed any wrongful acts; also that there was no evidence of any actual knowledge by the defendants of any contract between Bowaters and the plaintiffs. So the plaintiffs lost their action.[30]

In 1964, the House of Lords considered a case in which a union were met by a refusal of a company to negotiate with them on terms and conditions of service although they organized the majority of the men concerned, being watermen in the Port of London. Another union organized the minority. So the first union issued instructions that none of their men would man, service or tow empty barges belonging to the company. The company owned and hired out barges but did not employ any of the union men, but their action meant that barges were not returned and so the company's business came to a standstill. The company brought an action against the union officials. The House of Lords found for the company on the ground that the union had knowingly induced breaches of the hiring contract and their members' contracts of employment. Most importantly, their Lordships decided that there was, on the facts, no trade dispute within the meaning of the Trade

30. *Thomson & Co. v. Deakin* [1952] 1 Ch. 646.

Disputes Act 1906 because the basis of the embargo was trade union rivalry.[31]

This attitude of the courts was strengthened by the decision of the Court of Appeal in *Torquay Hotel v. Cousins*.[32] Union members picketed the Torbay Hotel, cutting off fuel oil supplies, and later, when the manager of the plaintiff hotel was reported as having called for a stand against the union, picketed that hotel with the same result. The union also told an alternative oil supplier not to supply the plaintiff hotel. The Court of Appeal held that as the plaintiffs employed no union members the union's actions were not in furtherance of a trade dispute and injunctions were issued against the union. As Professor Wedderburn has observed, the result of this decision could be that where an association of employers is fighting off a trade union, it may be able to 'keep its smaller members in the front line and avoid any of its bigger members being parties to the dispute'.[33] The trade unions' 'golden formula' of action 'in furtherance of a trade dispute' looks weaker as a protection than it did.

No wonder that, in 1968, a member of the Royal Commission on Trade Unions and Employers' Associations wrote:[34]

A thing that worried me all through the deliberations . . . was this: supposing we made all the right recommendations and supposing the Government gave effect to them in legislation, how long would it be before the judges turned everything upside down?

Industrial Relations Act 1971

But the most dramatic judicial intervention was yet to come. In 1971 was passed the Industrial Relations Act. This measure of a Conservative government was strongly opposed, in and out of Parliament, by the trade union movement and the Labour Party. It established the National Industrial Relations Court (NIRC) presided over by Sir John Donaldson, formerly a judge of the High Court. The NIRC had wide jurisdiction to consider complaints arising under the Act, to impose penalties, and to punish those who disregarded its orders.

31. *Stratford v. Lindley* [1965] AC 269.
32. [1969] 2 Ch. 106.
33. Wedderburn, *op. cit.*, p. 336.
34. Quoted by Wedderburn, *op. cit.*, p. 8.

In recent years, the amount of work available for dock-workers has drastically declined because of the growing practice of loading and unloading goods in containers at depots outside the port areas. From mid-1971, the Transport and General Workers' Union authorized the practice of selective 'blacking' of the goods carried by certain road haulier firms to ports. When the Act of 1971 came into force in February 1972, the union became liable to complaints and penalties for this blacking. The first complaint was made on 23 March 1972 and the NIRC ordered the union, its officers, servants and agents to refrain from certain specific blacking. The union's officers advised their shop stewards to obey this order but the advice was rejected. On 29 March the NIRC found the union in wilful contempt of the order and, following subsequent complaints, imposed fines totalling £55,000.[35]

On 13 June the Court of Appeal decided that the union was not accountable for its shop stewards and set aside the fines.[36] But the next day the NIRC ordered three London dockers who had defied an order against blacking made on 12 June to be committed to prison for contempt of court. The warrants for their arrest were to be issued on 16 June, and widespread strikes became imminent. However, as the result of a curious intervention by the Official Solicitor (an officer of the court), the Court of Appeal was able to review the decision to imprison, although the three dockers did not ask for it to be reviewed; and the decision was set aside. So the dockers did not go to prison and the strikes were avoided.[37]

For a fortnight there was a breathing space. Then on 3 July another complaint was lodged with the NIRC against seven dockers including two of the original three. On 7 July, the NIRC ordered them to refrain from their actions and, after further proceedings, on 21 July committed five of the seven to prison for contempt. Unofficial dock strikes began at once and the threat of widespread stoppages of work became very real.

On 24 July the General Secretary of the Trades Union Congress went to see the Prime Minister who said, according to *The Times*, that he would not intervene. On 25 July, the Official Solicitor visited the dockers in prison but they made clear that they did not intend to give any undertakings of obedience to the NIRC or to apologize – which is normally essential before those in contempt are released. Nevertheless the Official Solicitor on that day tried to

35. *Heaton's Transport (St Helens) Ltd v TGWU* [1972] 1 ICR 285.
36. Ibid. 308; [1973] AC 15.
37. *The Times*, 12 and 14 June 1972.

persuade the NIRC to convene immediately so that he could apply for the committal orders to be discharged. But he was told to come back not later than the afternoon of the next day.

On 25 July the situation seemed to have reached an impasse. Sir John Donaldson, president of the NIRC, had said in June, 'By their conduct these men are saying they are above the rule of law. No court should ignore such a challenge. To do so would imperil all law and order.' On 21 July he said: 'These breaches are serious and were deliberately committed, quite literally in contempt of this court . . . The issue is whether these men are to be allowed to opt out of the rule of law . . . It is a very simple issue but vastly important for our whole way of life is based upon acceptance of the rule of law.' The NIRC had committed the men to prison. The men showed no intention of modifying their position. Dock strikes were occurring and a general strike was clearly impending. How could industrial action on a wide scale be avoided and the face of the NIRC be saved?

We have seen that on 13 June the Court of Appeal had decided in *Heaton*'s case that the Transport and General Workers' Union was not accountable for the action of its shop stewards. From that decision, leave was given to appeal to the House of Lords. That appeal was heard between the 10th and 19th of July. Their Lordships reserved judgment and then, with almost unprecedented speed (at least eight weeks normally elapse), Lord Wilberforce delivered their joint opinion, on the morning of 26 July – that 'next day', intimated to the Official Solicitor. And the House of Lords reversed the Court of Appeal and decided that the union was responsible for its shop stewards.[38] Immediately the NIRC convened and, avowedly because of that decision, released the dockers from prison.[39]

The difficulty is finding any necessary connection between two cases. The House of Lords' decision determined an important question of law concerning the liability of trade unions for the actions of their shop stewards. But the five dockers' case was about the 'very simple issue' of punishment for men who had defied the order of the NIRC and had expressed their intention to continue in that defiance. In releasing the dockers, the president of the NIRC said that, because of the House of Lords' decision, the situation was

38. [1972] 1 ICR 308; [1973] AC 15. Subsequently, however, it appeared that this was not a proposition of general application: see *General Aviation Services v. TGWU* [1976] IRLR 224, a decision which seemed to indicate a desire by the House of Lords (Lord Salmon dissenting) to put the decision in *Heaton*'s case behind them.
39. *The Times*, 27 July 1972.

'entirely changed'. The unions were accountable and the burden of their task would be 'immeasurably increased' if the dockers remained in prison. 'The cause of the rule of law will not be advanced by placing an avoidable burden upon the unions.' Nevertheless five men, who had been imprisoned because they deliberately and flagrantly disobeyed the orders of the NIRC, and so imperilled the rule of law and 'our whole way of life', were released although they had not asked to be released and had made clear that they had no intention of apologizing to the court for their behaviour or of desisting from that behaviour.

A political and economic crisis of possibly considerable dimensions was avoided by two actions. First, the speeding-up of the delivery of the House of Lords' decision; and secondly, the discovery by the NIRC that, because of that decision, they could release the dockers. It appeared very much as if the judicial system had bent itself to the needs of the politicians and that, in particular, the principles of the rule of law to which the NIRC earlier paid such respect had been sacrificed to the expediency of the political and economic situation.

This last example of judicial activism in political affairs differs from the others. The latter have shown a conservative judiciary interpreting legislation and developing the common law in ways which government and Parliament sought to reverse. The establishment of the NIRC was a political act aimed at trying to contain trade union power within particular rules prescribed by the Industrial Relations Act 1971. The experiment failed and the NIRC was abolished in 1974. But the apparent willingness of the House of Lords to expedite the delivery of their judgment coupled with the highly eccentric use made of that judgment by the NIRC to release the five dockers was so convenient for the government of the day that it aroused the strong suspicion of judicial compliance with political expediency.

A later industrial dispute was a pretty example of the intermingling of the exercise of powers in the high places of government in the United Kingdom. In October 1973, the NIRC fined the Amalgamated Union of Engineering Workers £100,000 for contempt of court when they refused to obey the court's order to call off a strike.[40]

To obtain payment of the fine the court sequestrated against assets held in the political fund of the union. Labour MPs put down a motion in the House of Commons calling for the removal from

40. *Con-Mech (Engineers) Ltd v. AUEW* [1973] ICR 620.

office of the president of the NIRC for 'political prejudice and partiality'. Sir John Donaldson defended himself in a public speech saying that the court had not known that the assets had been earmarked for a political or any other purpose. At this point Lord Hailsham, then Lord Chancellor, in a public speech and as head of the judiciary, attacked those who had signed the motion and said that the public should note the identity and party of the Members concerned. Whereupon Labour Members tabled another motion condemning the Lord Chancellor and alleging 'a gross contempt of the House of Commons'.[41]

In the event neither of the motions was debated and the matter lapsed.

The conflict between the courts and trade unions showed itself in the second half of the nineteenth century and the first decade of the twentieth as an expression of class conflict. The trade unions were growing in militancy, especially during the years after 1890, and were displaying powers which dismayed a large part of middle-class society. The dismay was in part because of the anticipated economic consequences of this militancy, but also because it threatened the existing social order of late Victorian England.

Many politicians, from Disraeli onwards, had realized that trade union power was an economic factor which had to be taken seriously into account and certainly was not capable of being overcome by crude shows of force. Her Majesty's judges, however, were less prescient and less capable of adjusting legal principles and traditions to the new pressures. So, under men like Halsbury, they reacted to the legislation of the later nineteenth century with all the inflexibility of those who are determined that what was good enough for their fathers' social and economic structures was good enough for them. And in the more general upheaval of political beliefs which accompanied 'the strange death of liberal England', influential judges were more often to be found towards the right of the spectrum of opinion.

The most recent developments may prove to be of the utmost importance and to have the most lasting consequences. What litigation might have been promoted by the Labour government's aborted proposals in the late 1960s[42] we shall never know. But the much more rigorous policy embodied in the Conservatives' Industrial Relations Act of 1971 was a revolution in the long story. For this Act deliberately sought to use the courts and the judges to

41. See 865 HC Deb. col. 1089–91, 1291–7.
42. See *In Place of Strife* (Cmnd 3888).

achieve political ends. The institution of the NIRC reflected the new techniques and reintroduced the old arguments. The identification of 'law' and 'policy' made almost impossible the continuance of the interplay between the judges and politicians which had provided a valuable tolerance. Had the Act succeeded, the damage to the reputation of judicial institutions would have been considerable; but it was always highly probable that this attempt to use the judges for these political purposes would fail. The failure was forecast by almost all those with the greatest knowledge of the working of industrial relations in this country and, more particularly, abroad. But the circumstances of its failure, and the manoeuvrings of politicians and judges which accompanied that failure, combined to produce a calamity which went far beyond the collapse of a doomed policy, for the failure directly resulted in a deep distrust of the judicial system. Trade unionists, as we have seen, had little cause to look to the judiciary for the protection of their statutory rights. Now the suspected subservience of the judiciary to the politicians seemed to be made manifest. There is no evidence that the judges at any time protested to Her Majesty's government in or out of Parliament against the proposals to involve them directly and indirectly in the administration of the act of 1971. Their failure to do so rests with the Lord Chancellor (Lord Hailsham), the Master of the Rolls (Lord Denning), and, to a lesser extent, the Lord Chief Justice (Lord Widgery).

The events of 1972 finally persuaded the leaders of organized labour (and the great mass of trade union members) that the judges were not to be trusted. Today the relations between the trade unions and the judiciary are worse than they were in the period immediately following the *Taff Vale* decision in 1901. Mr Heath deliberately employed the judges as instruments of his policy, enmeshed trade unionists in new legal rules, and then, in chorus with the judges, condemned them, in the name of the rule of law, for seeking to extricate themselves.

Less easy to understand is the apparent willingness of the judiciary to lend themselves to this manoeuvring. It is difficult to believe in the political naïveté of judges, but Sir John Donaldson, president of the NIRC, looking back on the short history of that court, has expressed views which are bewildering in their ingenuousness. He emphasized the need for guidelines in all aspects of industrial relations and continued:

With such guidelines, the courts could be given their traditional role of investigating the merits of disputes and helping the party who is right . . . The public suffers from every industrial dispute. Ought they not to know who is right? Adopting this new approach they *would* know, for the court which investigated the dispute would tell them. Those who suffered injustice would then be supported by the courts.[43]

On this evidence it seems possible that a large part of the conflict that arose in the administration of the NIRC was the result of a belief of its president that, in industrial conflicts, one side can be discovered, after proper examination by judges, to be 'right' and the other side 'wrong'. But industrial conflicts are not of this kind. They can be solved only by compromise and by the exercise of economic and political strength, not by the application of legal principles or guidelines. This may be unfortunate but it is the reason why the NIRC was bound to fail.

The Law Lords restrain Denning

In a group of cases in 1978 and 1979 the Court of Appeal sought considerably to limit the immunities of trade unionists from criminal and civil liabilities for acts done 'in contemplation or furtherance of a trade dispute'.[44] Then, in three cases decided between July 1979 and February 1980, the House of Lords reversed this development. Both the substance and the manner in which this was done throw further light on the politics of the judiciary in dealing with industrial relations.

The first of these cases was *NWL Ltd v. Woods*.[45] The International Transport Workers' Federation blacked a ship in an attempt to force its owners to pay wages in accordance with the Federation's scales. Since the crew of the ship were not directly involved, the owners argued that there was no trade dispute. Two years before, in *BBC v. Hearn* (1977),[46] trade union officials had threatened that their workers would refuse to allow the BBC to televise the cup final so that it could be seen in South Africa,

43. *Lessons from the Industrial Court* (1975) 91 LQR at 191–2.
44. *Beaverbrook v. Keys* [1978] ICR 582; *Star Sea Transport of Monrovia v. Slater 'The Camilla M'* [1978] IRLR 507; *Associated Newspapers Group Ltd v. Wade* [1979] ICR 664.
45. [1979] 1 WLR 1294.
46. [1977] 1 WLR 1004.

because of the union's disapproval of the racial policies of the government of that country. The Court of Appeal had held that there was no trade dispute and so no protection for the trade union officials. In *NWL* the House of Lords did not question that decision. But in 1978, the Court of Appeal had decided, in '*The Camilla M*',[47] where the facts were similar to those in *NWL*, that the presence of an 'extraneous motive' for trade union action was sufficient to prevent that action being a 'trade dispute'.[48]

In *NWL* the House of Lords rejected this test. Lord Diplock said that even if the predominant motives were 'to bring down the fabric of the present economic system by raising wages to unrealistic levels', that would not make the dispute any less one connected with the terms and conditions of employment and therefore a trade dispute. Similarly Lord Scarman said that if the dispute were connected with one of the matters referred to in the statute (for example, terms and conditions of employment) then 'it is a trade dispute, and it is immaterial whether the dispute also relates to other matters or has an extraneous, e.g. political or personal, motive. The connection is all that has to be shown.' The legislative purpose of the Trade Union and Labour Relations Act 1974, said Lord Scarman, was 'to sweep away not only the structure of industrial relations created by the Industrial Relations Act 1971, which it was passed to repeal, but also the restraints of judicial review which the courts have been fashioning one way or another since the enactment of the Trade Disputes Act 1906 . . . Briefly put, the law is now back to what Parliament had intended when it enacted the Act of 1906 – but stronger and clearer than it was then.'

In *Express Newspapers v. McShane*,[49] there was a dispute over pay between the proprietors of provincial newspapers and members of the National Union of Journalists. The national executive of the union called out on strike all its members on provincial newspapers. These newspapers used news copy supplied by the Press Association and the union called on PA journalists to strike also. This strike affected national newspapers. The union instructed its members on the *Daily Express* and other nationals to refuse to use copy sent out by the PA.

The plaintiffs sought an injunction against the members of the

47. See footnote 44.
48. The Court of Appeal in *NWL* discharged the injunction given in the lower court on the ground that the union had not made 'impossible demands' and so distinguished '*The Camilla M*'.
49. [1979] 2 All ER 360.

national executive of the union to restrain them from inducing or procuring their members not to use PA copy. The defendants claimed that what they were doing was in furtherance of their dispute with the provincial newspapers. The judge at first instance granted the injunction and the Court of Appeal upheld his decision, Lord Denning MR saying that there was no evidence that the blacking at the *Daily Express* had had any effect on the provincial dispute. So the Court of Appeal held that the acts were not done in furtherance of a trade dispute. 'Furtherance' was to be tested objectively by the courts as well as subjectively by reference to the defendants' intentions.

The House of Lords overruled the Court of Appeal,[50] giving its reasons on 13 December 1979. Four of their Lordships held that 'in furtherance' referred only to the subjective state of mind of the defendant and that he so acted if his purpose was to help the parties in the dispute to achieve their objectives and if he honestly and reasonably believed his actions would do so. Lord Wilberforce, while agreeing in the result, said that the test was whether the act done, pursuant to the general intention, was reasonably capable of achieving its objective. Lord Denning, said Lord Wiberforce, 'finally settled, I think, upon practical effect. This, I think, with respect goes too far.'

Six weeks later, on 26 January 1980, the Court of Appeal decided *Dupont Steels v. Sirs.*[51] Steelworkers in the public sector had for some time been in dispute with their employers, the British Steel Corporation, and had come out on strike. Their union, the Iron and Steel Trades Confederation, in order to bring pressure on the government (who, the union hoped, would then put pressure on the BSC to settle the strike), decided to extend the strike to the private sector of the steel industry. Certain private steel companies sought injunctions to prevent this.

The Court of Appeal granted the injunctions on the ground that the extension had generated a second dispute, between the ISTC and the government, which was separate from the union's dispute with the BSC, and not a trade dispute because the government was not the employer. Lord Denning MR added the further reason that the acts done were too remote to be regarded as furtherance. As a leading article in *The Times* put it: 'Undaunted by the superior timidity of the House of Lords the Court of Appeal persevered in

50. [1980] 2 WLR 89.
51. [1980] 1 All ER 529.

its determination to set limits to the scope of the immunities granted to trade unions by statute.'[52]

This 'second dispute' argument was not advanced by counsel for the steelworkers but emanated from the bench. Counsel thought so little of it that he did not seek to sustain it before the House of Lords. On the legal substance of the case, the House of Lords had little to add to the principles on which they had decided *Express Newspapers v. McShane*. The 'connection' between the strike in the private sector and the strike in the public sector was obvious, as was the honest and reasonable belief of the union that that extension would further their dispute with the BSC. So their Lordships again overruled the Court of Appeal.[53]

In another group of cases the courts grappled somewhat variously with a new institution.

The Advisory, Conciliation and Arbitration Service (ACAS) was established by the Employment Protection Act 1975. It is charged with the general duty of promoting the improvement of industrial relations, and in particular of encouraging the extension of collective bargaining and the development and, where necessary, reform of collective bargaining. One of its powers is to make recommendations requiring an employer to recognize a particular trade union as a negotiating body. Its functions were not at first regarded by the courts with much enthusiasm.

It is therefore clear that as a result of the statutory machinery an individual can have a substantial measure of control over his own working life compulsorily delegated to an agent, a trade union, which he has not selected and may even have his own contract of service varied without his consent. These are very large powers, every bit as large as powers of compulsory acquisition of property; and, in my judgment, the court should seek to ensure that, just as in the case of compulsory purchase powers, the conditions for the exercise of the powers conferred by the 1975 Act are strictly observed.[54]

In the case from which that quotation is drawn the court set aside a questionnaire issued by ACAS on the ground that it was an unlawful exercise of discretion. Much more seriously, the House of

52. *The Times*, 28 January 1980.
53. [1980] 1 All ER 529.
54. Browne-Wilkinson J in *G. C. Powley v. ACAS* [1977] IRLR 190.

Lords in *Grunwick Processing Laboratories Ltd v. ACAS* (1978)[55] effectively made the resolution of recognition disputes dependent on the co-operation of employers. This could be seen as an example, from the other side, of the dangers of seeking to impose legal and compulsory arbitration over industrial relations. The union request for recognition was referred to ACAS which sent questionnaires to union members at Grunwick's but not to the rest of the workers because the employers would not supply ACAS with their names and addresses. The duty on ACAS under the statute was to 'ascertain the opinion of the workers to whom the issue relates'. The failure of ACAS to ascertain the opinion of the non-union members (who numbered two-thirds of all those employed) rendered void ACAS's recommendation of recognition for the union.

The next two cases, however, show a broader understanding of what ACAS was supposed to be doing. In *United Kingdom Association of Professional Engineers v. ACAS* (1980)[56] the Association sought recognition from a company already well supplied with trade unions. ACAS refused to recommend recognition partly because to do so would arouse strong opposition from the other unions with a risk of industrial action which would be damaging to the industry. In the Court of Appeal, Lord Denning MR saw this as 'another story of David and Goliath . . . a small union pitted against a great one'. He set aside ACAS's report, saying that the threats of industrial strife should have been ignored. But the House of Lords (Lord Scarman delivering the main opinion) reversed the Court of Appeal and upheld the report. Similarly, in *Engineers' and Managers' Association v. ACAS* (1980)[57] the House of Lords by a majority held that ACAS had not acted unreasonably in postponing its statutory enquiries for the time being because another union was also seeking recognition and the plaintiff Association was also suing the Trades Union Congress. Lord Scarman said: 'ACAS has to form its view as to what is best for the promotion of industrial relations and the extension of collective bargaining. The Court of Appeal erred in substituting its judgment for that of ACAS.'

ACAS has had a short and troubled life and its powers limited and subjected to greater ministerial control by the Employment Act 1980. It remains to be seen how the courts will treat ACAS in its new shape.

55. [1978] AC 655.
56. [1979] 2 All ER 480 (CA); [1980] 1 All ER 612 (HL).
57. [1980] 1 All ER 896.

The Conservative attack

Legislation since 1979 has greatly affected industrial relations, often in line with the expressed views of the Court of Appeal and the House of Lords.

Section 17 of the Employment Act 1980 is designed to limit 'secondary action', that is action taken by workers in support of a trade dispute between other workers and their employers. The section defined secondary action in relation to a trade dispute as arising when a person induces another to break a contract of employment if the employer under the contract of employment is not a party to the trade dispute.

Marina Shipping Ltd v. Laughton (1982)[58] was one in a long line of cases[59] arising out of attempts by the International Transport Workers Federation (ITF) to force ship owners employing cheap labour recruited abroad to pay European standard rates of wages. In this case, ITF officials blacked a ship with the result that lock keepers, in breach of their contract with port authorities at Hull, refused to operate gates and so prevented the ship from sailing. Section 17(3) of the Act permits secondary action if (a) the purpose or principal purpose of the secondary action was directly to prevent or disrupt the supply during the dispute of goods or services between an employer who is a party to the dispute (here the ship owners) and the employer under the contract of employment to which the secondary action relates (here the port authorities); and (b) the secondary action was likely to achieve that purpose. This would seem to cover the action of the lock keepers in this case. But section 17(6) provides that references to the supply of goods and services between two persons are references to the supply by one to the other in pursuance of a contract between them. The Court of Appeal held that there was no contract between the owners and the port authority and so the secondary action was illegal.

Very similar facts were considered by the House of Lords in *Merkur Island Shipping Corporation v. Laughton* (1983).[60] Here the ITF persuaded tugmen, in breach of their contract with their employers, to refuse to operate tugs to enable the ship to leave port. The House of Lords held that since the ship owners were not party to any contract with the tug owners (the arrangements had been

58. [1982] 2 WLR 569.
59. See, for example, *NWL v. Woods* (above, p. 70).
60. [1983] 3 All ER 914.

made by the charterers of the ship) the secondary action was, again, illegal.

The effect of these decisions is to prevent the ITF from pursuing its aim of requiring owners of ships flying 'flags of convenience' to pay wages at levels compatible with collective agreements made by 'bona fide organizations of shipowners and seafarers' in accordance with the recommendations of the International Labour Organisation. It has been strongly argued that the interpretation is mistaken. As the law stands, everything turns on the fortuitous circumstance of the existence or non-existence of a formal contract between two parties even though the reality of the supply of goods and services from one of the principals to another within the meaning of section 17(3) is not in question. If the *purpose* is to interrupt an apparent contract and the secondary action would be likely to achieve that purpose, then the secondary action should be legitimate even if no such contract exists in fact.[61]

In *Cheall v. Association of Professional, Executive, Clerical and Computer Staff*,[62] the House of Lords overruled a majority of the Court of Appeal. Cheall resigned from one trade union (ACTSS) and joined another (APEX). In accepting Cheall, without first enquiring of ACTSS whether it objected, APEX breached the Bridlington principles designed to prevent unions poaching members from one another. As a result the Trades Union Congress Disputes Committee required APEX to dismiss Cheall and advise him to rejoin his former union. This APEX did, in accordance with its own rules, whereupon Cheall sought a declaration that his dismissal was invalid. In the Court of Appeal,[63] Lord Denning MR decided in favour of Cheall, invoking the European Convention on Human Rights, which declared that everyone had a right to join a trade union, which proposition Lord Denning identified with the common law. He also referred to the case of the three railwaymen, dismissed for refusing to join a trade union, who had succeeded before the Court of Human Rights[64] and he reached the conclusion that the relevant article of the Convention was 'part of the law of England or at any rate the same as the law of England'. Had this view been upheld, it would have destroyed the Bridlington principles. Slade LJ also decided in favour of Cheall but on more

61. See Wedderburn, 45 *Modern Law Review* (1982) 317, and 46 *Modern Law Review* (1983) 632.
62. [1983] 2 WLR 679.
63. [1982] 3 WLR 685.
64. *Young v. United Kingdom* [1981] IRLR 408.

modest grounds. Donaldson LJ disagreed. He quoted Lord Atkin that the doctrine of public policy 'should only be invoked in clear cases in which the harm to the public is substantially incontestable, and does not depend upon the idiosyncratic inferences of a few judicial minds'.[65] Donaldson LJ continued:

> Above all I think that judges must beware of confusing political policy with public policy . . . Whether judges are better or less able than others to assess the merits and demerits of political policies is beside the point, because that is not their function.
> . . . We are being invited to apply considerations of political rather than public policy. This I absolutely decline to do.

The Law Lords unanimously rejected Cheall's application on the ground that there was no principle of law which prevented the union from relying on its own rules which also bound Cheall. 'My human sympathies', said Lord Diplock, 'are with Mr Cheall, but I am not in a position to indulge them; for I am left in no doubt that upon all the points that have been so ingeniously argued, the law is against him.' But Lord Diplock suggested that different considerations might apply if the effect of Cheall's expulsion from APEX were to have put his job in jeopardy because of the existence of a closed shop or for some other reason.

In *Carrington v. Therm-A-Stor Ltd*,[66] a group of employees decided to try to introduce a trade union into the factory where they worked. By late April 1980 between sixty and sixty-five of the seventy employees had joined or applied to join. The district secretary of the union wrote to the managing director setting out the union's case for recognition. Two days later the employers' managing committee decided to dismiss twenty of the employees and instructed the chargehands to decide who should be chosen. Four of those chosen brought this action for unfair dismissal. The industrial tribunal found that the reason for the dismissals was that the managing director was strongly anti-union but that none of the four could show that the reason for his dismissal was his own union membership or activities. The Court of Appeal, with regret, rejected their claim on the ground that, although the relevant statutory provision declared a dismissal to be unfair if the reason for it was that the employee proposed to join a trade union or take

65. *Fender v. St John-Mildmay* [1938] AC 1.
66. [1983] 1 WLR 138.

part in union activities, the provision was 'not concerned with an employer's reactions to a trade union's activities, but with his reactions to an individual employee's activities in a trade union context' (Sir John Donaldson MR). The narrowness of this interpretation is self-evident.

The British Telecommunications Act 1981 established BT as a public corporation and transferred telecommunication functions to it from the Post Office. By a government licence under the Act, Mercury Communications, a private company, was authorized to establish a communications system. An agreement between BT and Mercury provided for interconnections between the two systems. The Post Office Engineering Union waged a campaign against the licensing of competitors of BT and against proposals, in a Bill before Parliament, on privatization of BT. The union instructed its members not to make the interconnection, there was a day of action and a series of selective strikes. The union also instructed its members to 'black' BT services at Mercury's premises. There was a threat of industrial action against Mercury's shareholders. Mercury applied to the court for interlocutory injunctions to restrain the union and its members from inducing breach of contract between Mercury and BT.

We have seen that a persistent principle since 1906 had been that an act done by a person in contemplation or furtherance of trade dispute could not be actionable in tort on the ground of inducing another person to break a contract. By the Employment Act 1982 the definition of a trade dispute was narrowed. Disputes between workers and workers – demarcation disputes – are excluded; so are disputes between workers and an employer unless he is their own. Also it is no longer sufficient that the dispute should be 'connected with', in the instant case, termination of employment; now it had to relate 'wholly or mainly' to that. The Court of Appeal readily allowed new evidence to be admitted and held that since the risk to jobs did not appear to be a major factor in the dispute, it seemed unlikely that the union would be able to bring itself within the definition of a trade dispute and so the injunction should be granted.

Sir John Donaldson MR said it was important in such disputes, which gave rise to strong, indeed passionate, feelings, that 'everyone should know where the courts stand. They are on neither side. They have an independent role, akin to that of a referee . . . Parliament makes the law and is solely responsible for what the law is. The duty of the court is neither to make nor to alter nor to pass judgment on the law. Their duty is simply to apply it as they understand it.'[67] The effect of the decision was to make clear that the courts, under the new legislation, will decide in what circumstances industrial action is, in their view, 'political' and when not. And this, far more than in the past, will determine the legality or illegality of the action.

The House of Lords shows every sign of adopting a hard line against trade unions when interpreting the new legislation, as this next case demonstrates.

The Dimbleby newspapers had been printed by an associated company, Dimbleby Printers Ltd, which became engaged in a closed shop dispute with the National Graphical Association. As a result of that dispute, the NGA members were on strike and the Dimbleby newspapers were not being printed. So the Dimbleby company turned to TBF (Printers) Ltd, which was itself a company closely associated with (same shareholdings, same management) T. Bailey Forman Ltd, with whom the NUJ was engaged in a trade dispute and had been since 1979. The NUJ instructed its members employed by Dimbleby newspapers not to supply copy to Dimbleby newspapers and argued that, because of their effective identity, TBF (Printers) Ltd, as well as T. Bailey Foreman Ltd, was an 'employer who is party to the dispute' between the NUJ and T. Bailey Forman Ltd, within the meaning of that phrase in section 17(3) of the Act of 1980. But the House of Lords rejected this argument.[68]

Lord Wedderburn has summarized several of these recent developments thus:

So, workers may picket, but only at their own place of work. Sympathy or solidarity action must be made tortious *because* it is 'secondary', i.e. it transgresses the rule about staying within employment unit boundaries. Access to tribunals for unfair dismissal of strikers is narrowed to victimization in the complainant's own 'establishment'; workers taking part in it elsewhere no longer count as his fellows. And the 'trade dispute' itself – the central concept of the system of immunities – is now confined to disputes with a worker's *own* employer only and to disputes which relate wholly or mainly to the industrial conditions of the workers in that employment unit only. As it faces the power of capital organized in interlocking but legally

67. *Mercury Communications v. Scott-Garner* [1983] 3 WLR 914.
68. *Dimbleby and Sons Ltd v. National Union of Journalists* [1984] 1 WLR 427.

separate corporate entities, labour is now cut up into atomized units of which the boundaries are by law coterminous with the employers' definitions of employment units in both private and public sectors. Trans-enterprise solidarity is no longer acceptable to the law. Any doubtful points are increasingly swept aside by Law Lords who found that the old immunities stuck in their 'judicial gorges'. And if need be, there are always new common law liabilities ready to hand not necessarily protected by immunities.[69]

The last sentence refers particularly to the development of the notion of 'economic duress' as creating liabilities for trade unions.[70]

Finally, an old argument seems to be acquiring increased significance. Actions against trade unions are frequently begun as applications for interlocutory injunctions asking the court to order the unions to desist from action they are taking until the case can come on for trial. Commonly, the granting of such an application effectively ends the dispute and the plaintiffs do not need to pursue the matter. It is for the court to determine where 'the balance of convenience' lies between the parties[71] and this inevitably confers a wide discretion on the judiciary. Moreover, such cases are frequently not properly reported. This has been particularly so in some of the more important litigation arising from the miners' strike in 1984 and in the dispute between the National Graphical Association and Mr Shah. Indeed, during 1983 and 1984, in relation to these disputes, both the use of the law and the failure to use the law have demonstrated how fortuitous can be its application.

The miners' strike in 1984

The litigation arising out of the industrial action taken in 1984 by members of the National Union of Mineworkers has been various and complicated. One common sequence of events was begun by working members applying to the courts for an order that a strike

69. 'Labour Law Now: a Hold and a Nudge' in 13 *Industrial Law Journal* (1984) 73.

70. See *Universe Tankships of Monrovia Inc. v. International Transport Workers Federation* [1982] 2 WLR 803; but note *Hadmor Productions v. Hamilton* [1982] 2 WLR 322.

71. *American Cyanamid Co. v. Ethicon Ltd* [1975] Ac 396.

was unlawful because the rules of an Area of the union (each Area has the status of a union as well as being part of the NUM) required a ballot which had not taken place. When the courts made such an order, leaders of the NUM and some of the Areas defied the courts either by making statements rejecting the order, or by disobeying specific orders to stop 'blacking' particular companies, or to stop organizing pickets, or to stop describing the strike as official. The courts then declared some of the offenders to be in contempt of court and fined them or the NUM or the Area as a punishment. When those fines were not paid, the courts appointed sequestrators to seize the assets of the NUM or Areas.

An important and novel sequel to these events was the appointment of receivers to replace the officials or other union members as the holders and trustees of the union funds. This was the method adopted first in the case of the NUM itself whose trustees were the president (Mr Scargill), the vice-president (Mr McGahey) and the general secretary (Mr Heathfield). The Court of Appeal held that they were not fit persons to remain as trustees because of their continued defiance of the orders of the courts – especially the order not to treat the strike as 'official' – and their refusal to undertake to obey future orders. Where a receiver is appointed, he stands in the shoes of the union's trustees as an agent of the court and becomes the only person or body entitled to deal with their financial affairs. The legal authority derives from section 37 of the Supreme Court Act 1981 which provides that the High Court may by order appoint a receiver in all cases in which it appears to the court to be just and convenient. Any such order may be made either unconditionally or on such terms and conditions as the court thinks just.

From this summary it can be seen that the courts had a discretion whether or not to act, and how to act, in four separate situations. The first situation arose when the court had to decide whether to grant an injunction ordering the union to desist from particular action. If that injunction was not obeyed the second situation arose and the court had to decide whether to fine unions and their officials for contempt of court. Where specific action, forbidden by order of the court, had been deliberately continued, the court had little option. Where the defiance was only verbal, the court could disregard it, but in practice did not do so. The third situation arose when the court had to decide whether officials of the NUM or of an Area were, because of their conduct, unfit to continue as trustees of the funds. Here the choice before the court was much more real.

The allegation against the trustees was that their actions were likely to put the funds in jeopardy and the evidence for this was, in part, based on their moving funds abroad and, in part, on their apparent unwillingness to give firm assurances that they would undertake to obey all orders, past and future, of the courts. It is not self-evident that on this evidence the court was obliged to find the trustees unfit. The fourth situation arose when the court had to decide whether the appointment of a receiver was 'just and convenient'. Here again the courts could have found that so drastic an action was neither just nor convenient, and that the trustees could have been allowed to continue to administer the financial affairs of their union despite the political and legal arguments about the nature and extent of the industrial action.

Over a period of a few months, dozens of writs were issued and actions brought against the NUM, the Areas, individual members of executive committees, and trustees of the unions. Different remedies were sought and obtained (many of them interlocutory), sequestrators and receivers were appointed, the whole amounting to a considerable legal campaign, mostly instituted by working members of the unions, financed by outside sources. The unions' side of the arguments was frequently, especially in the earlier stages, not presented because the unions did not put in an appearance. When the actions, as was common, involved contempt of court, it is perhaps not surprising that the courts were not inclined to exercise their discretionary powers in the unions' favour. Even when contempt was not in issue, the courts almost invariably exercised those powers against the unions.

4. Personal rights

Individual freedom

Traditionally, judges are thought of as the defenders of the rights of individuals from attack by public authorities. In recent years this tradition has been upheld only spasmodically.

In 1939 the government took powers by Defence Regulations to detain persons without trial but these powers were expressed in those regulations to be exercisable only 'if the Secretary of State has reasonable cause to believe' that a person had hostile associations. The use of the limiting adjective, one would have thought, clearly empowered the courts to review the reasonableness of the 'cause'. But the House of Lords in *Liversidge v. Anderson*[1] held otherwise. This was a considerable abdication by the courts, in circumstances of national emergency, of their controlling jurisdiction.

Yet this decision was also a rallying ground for those who believed that, especially where a man's personal freedom was involved, the powers of the executive should be strictly interpreted. For this was the case in which Lord Atkin, alone against such powerful colleagues as Lords Maugham, MacMillan, Wright and Romer, delivered the most highly influential minority opinion in the English courts of the twentieth century. In the course of his judgment he said:

I view with apprehension the attitude of judges who on a mere question of construction when face to face with claims involving the liberty of the subject show themselves more executive minded than the executive. Their function is to give words their natural meaning, not, perhaps, in wartime leaning towards liberty, but following the dictum of Pollock CB in *Bowditch v. Balchin*[2] cited with approval by my noble and learned friend Lord

1. [1942] AC 206. See also *Greene v. The Secretary of State for Home Affairs* [1942] AC 284.
2. (1850) 5 Ex. 378.

Wright in *Barnard v. Gorman*:[3] 'In a case in which the liberty of the subject is concerned, we cannot go beyond the natural construction of the statute.' In this country, amid the clash of arms, the laws are not silent. They may be changed, but they speak the same language in war as in peace. It has always been one of the pillars of freedom, one of the principles of liberty for which on recent authority we are now fighting, that the judges are no respectors of persons and stand between the subject and any attempted encroachments on his liberty by the executive, alert to see that any coercive action is justified in law. In this case I have listened to arguments which might have been addressed acceptably to the Court of King's Bench in the time of Charles I.

Liversidge v. Anderson was a wartime case and the powers of detention without trial (internment) were conferred on the executive under an express statutory provision which authorized the making of regulations 'for the detention of persons whose detention appears to the Secretary of State to be expedient in the interests of public safety or the defence of the realm'.[4] The comparable legislation passed for the purposes of the 1914-18 war contained no express powers authorizing internment but in *R. v. Halliday*[5] the majority in the House of Lords held that general words in the Defence of the Realm Act 1914 were sufficient, a view from which Lord Shaw dissented. In contrast, it was later held by Mr Justice Salter that a similar exercise of powers, this time to take property without payment of full compensation, was illegal.[6] Here, as elsewhere, the courts seemed to be more concerned to protect property rights than rights of personal freedom. In *R. v. Governor of Wormwood Scrubs Prison*[7] it was held by the Divisional Court that the internment powers extended to cover the situation in Ireland even after the war was over.

The decision of the majority in *Liversidge v. Anderson* effectively meant that the minister's order authorizing internment could not be questioned because the minister could not be required to show on what basis his order had been made. The general principle that this is the proper interpretation of the words 'If the minister has

3. [1941] AC 378, 393.
4. Emergency Powers (Defence) Act 1939, section 1(2)(a). See R. J. Sharpe, *The Law of Habeas Corpus* (1976), especially pp. 89-124.
5. [1917] AC 260.
6. *National Breweries v. The King* [1920] 1 KB 854.
7. [1920] 2 KB 305.

reasonable cause to believe' has been doubted[8] and two recent decisions in Northern Ireland courts have suggested that improper arrest or a failure to provide the internee with a statement of the material on which the internment was based is sufficient for the internment order to be set aside.[9]

However the majority decisions in *R. v. Halliday* and *Liversidge v. Anderson* were referred to with approval by Lord Denning in *R. v. Secretary of State for Home Affairs ex parte Hosenball*[10] in 1977 where an American journalist lost his appeal against deportation under the Immigration Act 1971. The decision to deport was challenged in the Court of Appeal on the ground that there had been a breach of the rules of natural justice in that the Home Secretary had refused to tell the appellant any of the details on the basis of which the Home Secretary had decided that the appellant was a security risk.

In a remarkable passage Lord Denning MR seemed to accept that the courts had no part to play because the government never erred. He said:

> There is a conflict between the interests of national security on the one hand and the freedom of the individual on the other. The balance between these two is not for a court of law. It is for the Home Secretary. He is the person entrusted by Parliament with the task. In some parts of the world national security has on occasion been used as an excuse for all sorts of infringements of individual liberty. But not in England. Both during the wars and after them successive ministers have discharged their duties to the complete satisfaction of the people at large. They have set up advisory committees to help them, usually with a chairman who has done everything he can to ensure that justice is done. They have never interfered with the liberty or the freedom of movement of any individual except where it is absolutely necessary for the safety of the state.

It is well known that unlawful detention may be challenged by means of an application for habeas corpus but the courts sometimes withhold that remedy for political reasons.

Dr Sharpe summarizes his extensive examination of the authorities on habeas corpus and other remedies thus:

8. E.g., in *Nakkuda Ali v. Jayaratne* [1951] AC 66 and *Ridge v. Baldwin* [1964] AC 40.
9. *Re McElduff* [1971] 23 NILQ 112; *Re Mackay* [1972] 23 NILQ 113.
10. [1977] 1 WLR 166.

This review of the authorities demonstrates that habeas corpus can be an effective remedy to control the exercise of discretionary power, but that policy considerations may often make the courts reluctant to act. There are several habeas corpus cases which illustrate the ordinary rule of the reviewability of executive action and, most recently, the law of immigration has provided examples. On the other hand it is submitted that the cases which involve emergency powers indicate a reluctance on the part of the courts to use the remedy of habeas corpus to its full potential. Judicial innovation would not have been required to justify intervention in *Halliday* or in *Greene* and *Liversidge v. Anderson*. In each case, accepted principles of constitutional and administrative law were available and applicable. In *Halliday*, and almost certainly in *Greene* and in *Liversidge v. Anderson*, the legal arguments weighed against the result reached, and the judges acted on policy grounds.[11]

When it is remembered that habeas corpus is not a discretionary remedy, this amounts to saying that the judiciary, despite all the rhetoric which they pour out in praise of this ancient writ, are willing to deny it to an imprisoned applicant, who in law should be set free, because they consider that the politics of the situation entitle them to do so. This is not what is generally understood to be the function of the courts.

The great weight attached by the courts to claims of national security was shown in the unanimous decision of the House of Lords in *In re the Council of Civil Service Unions* (1984).[12] This was the GCHQ (Government Communications Headquarters) case where the Government, without consulting the unions, introduced with immediate effect new conditions for civil servants at GCHQ the effect of which was that they were no longer permitted to belong to national trade unions. The Law Lords held that normally the unions had a legitimate expectation that there would be prior consultations before such a change was made but that the requirements of national security overrode this. The argument first advanced by the Crown before Glidewell J was that previous disruptions caused by trade union activity made the change necessary, although there had been no such disruption during the twenty months preceding the change. The judge ruled in favour

11. R. J. Sharpe, *op. cit.*, pp. 123-4.
12. [1984] 3 All ER 935; compare *Secretary of State for Defence v. Guardian Newspapers Ltd* [1984] 3 WLR 986, see below, p. 128.

of the unions. Before the Court of Appeal, however, the Crown claimed that there had been no consultation because to have consulted would have made disruption more likely. The Law Lords were willing to accept that the Crown had to show there was some evidence to support the claim that the interests of national security must prevail. But it was apparent that they were willing also to accept very slight, even contradictory, evidence for this purpose.

The right to a jury selected at random has been under recent judicial scrutiny. In *R. v. Crown Court at Sheffield ex parte Brownlow*[13] two police officers were charged and committed for trial on counts of assault occasioning bodily harm. On an application by the prosecution, the Crown Court judge ordered that a copy of the panel from which the jury for the hearing would be drawn be supplied to the chief constable and that he supply the accused's solicitors and the prosecution with full details of criminal convictions recorded against any member of the panel. This might have included offences which would not normally disqualify a juror from service. In the Court of Appeal, Lord Denning MR strongly condemned this practice of jury vetting, and called it 'unconstitutional'. Shaw LJ echoed this opinion. The majority of the Court of Appeal held, however, that they had no jurisdiction to revoke the judge's order and when the chief constable applied to the judge for revocation, the judge declined to do so but amended his order only so as to exclude spent convictions.

Three months later, in *R. v. Mason*,[14] a differently composed Court of Appeal expressed very different views. Lawton LJ said that if, when a panel was scrutinized, convictions were revealed which did not amount to disqualifications, 'there was no reason why information about such convictions should not be passed to prosecuting counsel' (but not to the defence) who could then ensure that that juror would not be selected to hear the case. 'The practice of the past was founded on common sense. Any juror might be qualified to sit on juries generally but might not be suitable to try a particular case.'

Police powers

Police powers and their exercise frequently result in the judiciary drawing and redrawing the lines of what they consider to be

13. [1980] 2 All ER 444.
14. *The Times*, 4 June 1980.

permissible and impermissible conduct. In a leading case from the 1930s, a public meeting was held to protest against the Incitement to Disaffection Bill then before Parliament and to demand the dismissal of the chief constable of Glamorgan. Between 500 and 700 people were present. James Sawkins, a sergeant of the Glamorgan County Police, sought admission to the meeting, was told at the door that police officers were not to be admitted, but nevertheless (with other policemen) entered and sat in the front row. At one point Alun Thomas 'laid a hand' on one of the policemen (an inspector) and Sergeant Sawkins pushed his hand away saying, 'I won't allow you to interfere with my superior officer.' Neither Alun Thomas nor Sergeant Sawkins used more force than was reasonably necessary to effect their purposes. Alun Thomas charged Sergeant Sawkins with unlawful assault. The Divisional Court held that a police officer was entitled, as part of his duty of preventing crime, to enter private premises when he had reasonable ground for believing that an offence was imminent or likely to be committed and that Sergeant Sawkins was properly acquitted.[15]

At the end of May 1933, Katherine Duncan of the National Unemployed Workers' Movement addressed a street meeting following which 'a disturbance took place'. On 30 July 1934 she began to address a meeting at the same place, although told by a police inspector that she could not, whereupon she was arrested and taken into custody. It was not alleged that she or any of the persons present at the meeting had either committed, incited or provoked any breach of the peace. The Divisional Court held that she had been properly convicted of wilfully obstructing the police who 'reasonably apprehended a breach of the peace'.[16]

The difficulty and danger of such decisions is that so much discretion resides in the police and neither the courts nor the legislature are willing to lay down any guidelines. This gives rise to suspicion that the police will prosecute one person advocating one set of views while not prosecuting another advocating a different set of views. Certainly this was the impression conveyed when Pat Arrowsmith was convicted of obstructing the highway when addressing a meeting at a place where such meetings were frequently held and where previously no prosecutions had followed. 'That,' said the Lord Chief Justice, speaking without

15. *Thomas v. Sawkins* [1935] 2 KB 249.
16. *Duncan v. Jones* [1936] 1 KB 218.

apparent irony, 'of course, has nothing to do with this court. The sole question here is whether the defendant had contravened section 121(1) of the Highways Act 1959.'[17]

The laws relating to arrest, to questioning, to accessibility to lawyers, to search and to seizure of goods, come frequently before the courts for elucidation. And the judges are immediately faced with the constantly recurring dilemma posed by the impossibility of being, at one and the same time, the protectors of personal rights and key performers in the preservation of law and order.

For many years a statement of principles called the Judges' Rules – because made by them – has been made public. These are not rules of law but indicate what the judges consider to be proper practice. They provide for the 'cautions' which the police should put before a person makes a statement to the police, indicating that he is not obliged to say anything but that, if he does so, it will be taken down in writing and may be used in evidence. If a person at his trial gives an account of what took place which he did not give to the police when cautioned, the judge is not permitted to suggest to the jury that this account is false because, if it had been true, he would have told the police. In 1964, the Criminal Law Revision Committee was asked by the Home Secretary to consider these matters and in 1972 they reported. Amongst other things, they proposed that this 'right of silence' should be removed in the sense that the inference of falsity could be drawn to the attention of the jury. The reaction of some members of the judiciary to the proposals of the Criminal Law Revision Committee was strongly adverse and did much to (at least) postpone the implementation of the recommendations, as did a similar reaction from members of the legal profession.[18] There is a commmon law rule, embodied in the introduction to the Judges' Rules, that a person arrested for a suspected offence must be charged or informed that he may be prosecuted as soon as there is sufficient evidence to prefer a charge. In *R. v. Holmes ex parte Sherman and Apps*, this principle was reaffirmed.[19]

In these matters of evidence and proof, the judiciary have a variable record. Recently a defendant who refused to answer police questions was held not to have obstructed the police.[20] On the other

17. *Arrowsmith v. Jenkins* [1963] 2 QB 561.
18. The proposals were debated in the House of Lords on 14 February 1973 (338 HL Deb. col. 1546-1678).
19. [1981] 2 All ER 612.
20. *Rice v. Connolly* [1966] 3 WLR 17.

hand where a confession was obtained without the usual caution having been given, the Court of Appeal held in 1971 that the confession was admissible if the judge decided that it was made voluntarily. [21] And an interrogation in a police station need not, it has been held, be preceded by cautions (even when the person questioned has been arrested) if at the time of the interrogation the police have no information which could be put before the court as the beginnings of a case. [22]

In *R. v. Jones* the Court of Appeal quashed convictions where the accused had forcibly resisted unlawful attempts by the police to take her fingerprints. [23]

It may be of the utmost importance to know whether an arrest is being made. An arrested man who runs away commits an offence; and a charge of unlawful arrest will fail if there was no arrest. So also, a blood specimen may be taken to support a charge of driving while drunk only if the driver has been arrested. If a police constable says, 'I shall have to ask you to come to the police station for further tests', is that a request or an order? Only if it is, in the circumstances, an order, will the words imply an arrest. Local justices in such a case decided it was not an arrest and the higher court refused to disagree with them, the question being so much one of fact. [24]

From time to time the courts find it necessary to remind the police that, save very exceptionally under special statutory provisions, there is no power to arrest anyone so that they can make enquiries about him. [25] Actions lie against the police if an arrest is wrongful. [26]

The House of Lords has recently approved police conduct which looks like a dangerous modification of such principles. The plaintiff was arrested by a detective constable on suspicion of theft and taken to a police station where she was questioned. She was not charged and she brought an action for wrongful arrest. The judge found that the detective had decided not to interview her under caution but to

21. *R. v. Prager* [1972] 1 All ER 1114, *R. v. Gowan* [1982] Crim LR 821; but contrast *R. v. Hudson, The Times*, 29 October 1980, and *Re Sherman and Apps, The Times*, 9 December 1980.
22. *R. v. Osborne* [1973] 1 All ER 649.
23. [1978] 3 All ER 1098; and see *Brazil v. Chief Constable of Surrey* [1983] 1 WLR 1155.
24. *Alderson v. Booth* [1969] 2 WLR 1252.
25. E.g., *R. v. Houghton, The Times*, 23 June 1978.
26. E.g., *Wershof v. Commissioner of Police for the Metropolis* [1978] 3 All ER 540.

subject her to the greater pressure of arrest and detention so as to induce a confession. He awarded her £1000 damages. The House of Lords overruled this decision and held that the interrogation of a suspect in order to dispel or confirm a reasonable suspicion was a legitimate cause for arrest so that the fact that the detective, when exercising his discretion to arrest the plaintiff, took into consideration that she might be more likely to confess if arrested did not render the exercise of the discretion unlawful. In practice that may often be indistinguishable from legalizing an arrest for the purpose of questioning.[27]

Elias v. Pasmore[28] is a leading case on search and seizure. The plaintiffs were the lessees of the headquarters of the National Unemployed Workers' Movement. Walter Hannington (one of the plaintiffs) made a speech in Trafalgar Square in consequence of which a warrant for his arrest was issued. The defendant police inspectors entered the headquarters, arrested Hannington, and seized a number of documents, some of which were used at the trial of the plaintiff Elias on a charge of inciting Hannington to commit the crime of sedition. The plaintiffs claimed the return of those documents, and the question was whether their seizure was lawful, since they had no relevance to the charge against Hannington and no search warrant had or would have been obtained. The court decided that, though the original seizure of the documents was 'improper', it was 'justified' because they were capable of being used, and were used, as evidence in the trial of Elias.

In 1969 police officers enquiring into the disappearance of a woman they believed to have been murdered, searched (without a warrant) the house of her father-in-law. At their request he handed them the passports of himself, his wife and daughter. Subsequently these persons, being Pakistanis and wishing to visit Pakistan, asked for the return of the passports but the police refused. The court ordered their return but in the course of his judgment Lord Denning, summarizing the law where police officers enter a man's home without a warrant, said:

> I take it to be settled law . . . that the officers are entitled to take any goods which they find in his possession or in his house which they reasonably believe to be material evidence in relation to the crime . . . for which they enter. If in the course of their search

27. *Mohammed-Holgate v. Duke* [1984] 2 WLR 666.
28. [1934] 2 KB 164.

they come upon any other goods which show him to be implicated in some other crime, they may take them provided they act reasonably and detain them no longer than is necessary.[29]

Two years later in another case, police officers, armed with a warrant authorizing them to enter premises to search for explosives, found none but seized a large number of leaflets and posters, contending that these were evidence of a crime such as conspiracy to pervert the course of justice or to commit contempt of court. The police claimed further that they needed to retain the documents for comparison with other documents purporting to emanate from a criminal organization responsible for causing explosions. The court held that the police were entitled to seize the documents and that they had established they were acting reasonably and were detaining the documents no longer than necessary.[30]

In 1977, the defendant was arrested by officers of the drug squad for stealing a sandwich from a public house. They then searched his lodgings where they found cannabis, and he was charged with possession of the drug. The court held that the entry and search were unlawful but nevertheless that the evidence was admissible.[31] In another case it was confirmed that, save with regard to admissions and confessions and generally to evidence obtained from the accused after the commission of the offence, judges have no discretion to refuse to admit relevant admissible evidence on the ground that it was obtained by improper or unfair means, for example, through the activities of an *agent provocateur*.[32]

The policy choices which are presented to the judiciary were shown clearly in *R. v. Inland Revenue Commissioners ex parte Rossminster Ltd* (1980).[33] One morning at 7 a.m., at different places, revenue officers armed with search warrants signed, as the empowering statute required, by a Circuit judge, entered offices and private houses and took away masses of documents. The statute was the Taxes Management Act 1970 which provided that if the Circuit judge was satisfied on information on oath given by an

29. *Ghani v. Jones* [1970] 1 QB 693. Cp. *Frank Truman Export v. Commissioner of Police for the Metropolis* [1977] 3 All ER 431.

30. *Garfinkel v. Metropolitan Police Commissioner, The Times*, 4 September 1971.

31. *Jeffrey v. Black* [1977] 3 WLR 895.

32. *R. v. Sang* [1979] 3 WLR 263. Cp. *Morris v. Beardmore* [1980] 2 All ER 753.

33. [1979] 3 All ER 385.

officer of the Inland Revenue that there was reasonable ground for suspecting that an offence involving any form of fraud in connection with, or in relation to, tax had been committed and that evidence of it was to be found on premises specified in the information, the judge might issue a search warrant. The statute further provided that a revenue officer might seize and remove any things whatsoever found there which he had reasonable cause to believe might be required as evidence for the purpose of proceedings in respect of an offence referred to above.

These are very wide powers indeed and the Court of Appeal unanimously held that the warrants were defective in that they did not particularize the specific offences. The court also held that the officers could not have had reasonable cause to believe that all the documents might be required as evidence because documents were removed without being examined.

Lord Scarman described the statutory provisions as a 'breathtaking inroad upon the individual's right of privacy and right of property'. But he was part of the majority of the members of the House of Lords who allowed the appeal by the Inland Revenue on the ground that the warrant was strictly and exactly within the authority of the statute. Lord Salmon dissented because the warrant did not recite the essential fact that the Circuit judge had satisfied himself that there were reasonable grounds for suspecting that a tax fraud had been committed.[34]

Tax frauds are unpopular offences amongst those who have not the means (in both senses) for their committal. And it is in the nature of such frauds that drastic and comprehensive action needs to be taken before allegedly incriminating documents are destroyed. It was probably the intention of Parliament that the powers given should be used as they were in this case. But also the facts in this case were such that the courts could, without perversity, decide either way. As it was, the eight judges in the Court of Appeal and House of Lords split evenly, with those favouring possible tax fraud detection being more strategically placed than those favouring personal rights of privacy and property. Subsequently in *W. T. Ramsay Ltd v. Inland Revenue Commissioners* the House of Lords came down very heavily on artificial tax avoidance schemes of the kind which *Rossminster Ltd* had prepared and sold to clients. Previously the Law Lords had taken a 'legalistic' approach to such

33. [1979] 3 All ER 385.
34. [1980] 2 WLR 1.

schemes but Lord Wilberforce refused to indulge in such 'an excess of judicial abstinence'.[35]

The general trend of these cases is alarming. It comes very close to giving the police a right to search and to seize documents which have nothing to do either with the warrant (if they have one) or with the original purpose of their investigations. It is an old tradition that general warrants to arrest unspecified persons and to search property at large are illegal and are not justifiable on the ground of the public interest. The tradition is beginning to look less strong than it did. The danger of placing so sharp a weapon in the hands of the government and of the police is very obvious. For police powers generally, see now the Police and Criminal Evidence Act 1984

Telephone tapping by the police and the security services has been much debated in recent years. In *Malone v. Commissioner of Police for the Metropolis (No. 2)* the courts were given an opportunity, which they did not take, to lay down some principles to govern the activity which has no statutory or other legal authority. Vice-Chancellor Megarry held that there was in English law neither a general right of privacy nor a particular right in relation to telephone communication. The practice has been that all such interceptions are made only on the express warrant of the Home Secretary though how general a warrant may be, how many separate interceptions a warrant may authorize, over how long a period, has never been made clear. The European Convention for the Protection of Human Rights was cited to the court which observed only that it was not part of English law. The Vice-Chancellor rested his refusal to intervene judicially on the general proposition that: 'If the tapping of telephones by the Post Office at the request of the police can be carried out without any breach of the law, it does not require any statutory or common law power to justify it: it can be lawfully be done simply because there is nothing to make it unlawful.' But he added: 'Telephone tapping is a subject which cries out for legislation.'[36] This judicial encouragement was not welcomed by the Home Secretary who, instead, published in 1980 an uninformative White Paper on the general question of the interception of communications during a debate in the House of Commons in April 1980.[37]

35. [1981] 1 All ER 865.
36. [1979] All ER 620.
37. Cmnd. 7873.

Race relations

The earlier cases

In 1965 the Race Relations Act was passed making discrimination on the ground of colour, race, ethnic or national origins unlawful in certain circumstances. These provisions were expanded by the Race Relations Act 1968. In 1972 came the first of a series of leading cases.

Stanislaw Zesko was born and bred a Polish national and joined the Polish Air Force. In November 1939, after the Nazi invasion of Poland, he escaped to France, came to the United Kingdom, enlisted in the Royal Air Force, and completed three operational tours in Bomber Command. After the war he remained in the United Kingdom, married and for fourteen years lived in the borough of Ealing in conditions of great hardship. He was, said the judge who first heard the case, 'a man of perfect character and integrity and a wholly admirable person'. In 1966, and again in 1968, Mr Zesko applied to be placed on the housing waiting list of Ealing Borough Council. His applications were refused under a council rule that an applicant had to be 'a British subject within the meaning of the British Nationality Act 1948'. A complaint was made to the Race Relations Board which, after investigation, notified the council that its action was one of unlawful discrimination because the Race Relations Act 1968 made unlawful the special treatment of a person on the ground of his national origins. The council applied to the courts for a declaration that its rule was not unlawful. The House of Lords, by a majority of four to one, decided in favour of the council on the ground that 'national origins' did not mean 'nationality' which was what the council's rule was concerned with.[38]

The approach of the majority was linguistic and formalistic.[39] Viscount Dilhorne argued that Parliament could have used the word 'nationality' and the failure to do so indicated that discrimination on the ground of nationality was meant to be excluded from the Act. It was also argued that to interpret national origins so as to include nationality would extend its meaning in a different context and enlarge the scope of the criminal offence of stirring up hatred under the Act of 1965.

---

38. *Ealing London Borough Council v. Race Relations Board* [1972] AC 342.
39. For a discussion of the case see John Hucker, *The House of Lords and the Race Relations Act*, 24 ICLQ 284 (1975).

More serious because affecting more people were two decisions about clubs which the House of Lords decided in 1973 and 1974.

In April 1969 Mr Amarjit Singh Shah, who was employed in the Post Office and was a Conservative (having joined the local association in 1966), applied to join the East Ham South Conservative Club. He was proposed and seconded. When his application was considered by the committee, the chairman indicated in reply to a question that he regarded the colour of Mr Shah's skin as relevant and, on the chairman's casting vote, Mr Shah's application for membership was rejected. Mr Shah complained to the Race Relations Board, who issued a plaint against the club. The county court judge rejected the plaint, the Court of Appeal upheld it, and the House of Lords by a majority of four to one rejected it.[40] The Race Relations Act of 1968 provides that it is unlawful for any person concerned with the provision to the public or a section of the public of any services, etc., to discriminate. The majority decided that the club members were not 'a section of the public'.

In the second case [41] a member of a dockers' club in Preston took in as his guest Mr Sherrington, a coloured man. Mr Sherrington was told by the secretary to leave ('We do not serve coloured people'). Mr Sherrington was a member of another club in Preston which had no colour bar. Both these clubs, and some 4000 others, were banded together in a union and each member of one club was an associate member of all others in the union. The question was whether associates were 'a section of the public'. The county court judge and the Court of Appeal found for the Race Relations Board. But the House of Lords unanimously found for the club.

How did it come about that the judges who sat in the Court of Appeal and the House of Lords in these two cases differed so markedly? The answer seems to be that they took one of two different 'political' views.

The conservative view is that Parliament should intervene as little as possible in matters about which people differ in large numbers and that statutes should be so interpreted. No doubt motives are mixed when intervention to control racial discrimination is discouraged. But Lord Diplock in the *Dockers' Club* case put it thus, referring to the Race Relations Act:

40. *Charter v. Race Relations Board* [1973] AC 868.
41. *Dockers' Labour Club v. Race Relations Board* [1974] 3 WLR 533; in *Race Relations Board v. Applin* [1975] AC 2598 the House of Lords held that foster parents were concerned with the provision of facilities or services to a section of the public, i.e. the children.

This is a statute which, however admirable its motives, restricts the liberty which the citizen has previously enjoyed at common law to differentiate between one person and another in entering or declining to enter into transactions with them . . . The arrival in this country within recent years of many immigrants from disparate and distant lands has brought a new dimension to the problem of the legal right to discriminate against the stranger. If everyone were rational and humane – or, for that matter, Christian – no legal sanctions would be needed to prevent one man being treated by his fellow men less favourably than another *simply upon the ground of his colour, race or ethnic or national origins*. But in the field of domestic or social intercourse differentiation in treatment of individuals is unavoidable . . . Thus, in discouraging the intrusion of coercion by legal process in the fields of domestic or social intercourse, the principle of effectiveness joins force with the broader principle of freedom to order one's private life as one chooses. [Italics in the original.]

This view begins with the private rights of the individual, including the right to discriminate on the ground of the colour of a man's skin. In interpreting an Act of Parliament, it assumes that those rights are to be diminished to the extent necessary to make sense of the legislation but no further. Therefore within the spectrum of happenings which range from the way a family makes provision for its friends within the home to the conduct of an open market, the definition of 'a section of the public' must be restricted as tightly as possible.

The alternative view does not found itself on this individualist position, does not think primarily of private rights. It makes other assumptions. It seeks to interpret the Race Relations Act in a way which will extend its operation and not restrict it, while recognizing that the Act clearly means to avoid intervention in the domestic sphere and in other private gatherings (certainly including some clubs). It regards racial discrimination not as an individual right but as a social wrong.[42]

One of the most remarkable decisions of the Court of Appeal since 1965 was in *R. v. Race Relations Board ex parte Selvarajan*.[43] The applicant, a graduate of Madras and London Universities, was appointed in 1961 to the City of Westminster (now Walbrook)

42. On the 'club' cases, see now Race Relations Act 1976.
43. [1975] 1 WLR 1686.

College as a lecturer grade 1. Most lecturers are promoted to grade 2 within a few years. S was never promoted during fourteen years. He felt this was because of his colour or race and he complained to the Race Relations Board. The case was referred to a conciliation committee under the Race Relations Act 1968. A subcommittee ('a group of able men and women, holding positions of responsibility') investigated. The secretary of the committee met the principal of the college and other members of staff, the applicant, and representatives of the Inner London Education Authority (the employers). She then reported to the subcommittee. Between May 1971 and February 1972 the subcommittee received representations in writing and orally from all concerned. They gave each side a full opportunity of meeting everything that was said on the other side. They discussed the case at length between themselves. 'It must', said Lord Denning, 'have taken many hours.' The subcommittee agreed to recommend that unlawful discrimination had taken place. The full conciliation committee met and came to the same opinion. In March 1972, after attempts at conciliation, the education officer of ILEA rejected the opinion and required the matter to be further investigated by the Race Relations Board.

The Race Relations Board referred the matter to their employment committee of seven members to each of whom was sent a file containing a record (over 100 pages) of the proceedings before the conciliation committee. In June 1972 the employment committee met and decided to reinvestigate the matter themselves. The reinvestigation was made in this way. In August 1972 Mrs C, a conciliation officer, wrote to the ILEA with a summary of the applicant's complaint. On 17 November 1972 they replied in detail and attached a statement which covered sixteen pages. On 24 November, Mrs C wrote to the applicant setting out several points which might be regarded as adversely affecting his case, and asking him to tell her by 8 December whether he wished to reply in writing or to appear personally. The applicant did not reply by that date nor before 13 December when the employment committee met. Meanwhile on 4 December 1972 Mrs C prepared a report for the Board headed 'Clearly Predictable Case – Full papers to Mota Singh' (who was a member of the employment committee and a barrister). There followed a short summary of the complaint and the answer in one and a half pages and a recommendation 'That the committee form an opinion of no unlawful discrimination'.

43. [1975] 1 WLR 1686.

At the meeting of the employment committee on 13 December, Mota Singh sent his apologies for inability to attend and said he agreed with the recommendation. Four of the six members of the committee present had not had all the papers. The chairman said he agreed with Mota Singh and the other members agreed. On 10 January 1973 the employment committee reconsidered the matter with Mota Singh present and confirmed its previous opinion.

In all this story the matter which most troubled the Court of Appeal was that four members of the employment committee were not in a position to form an opinion of their own because they were not in possession of all the information. But, said Lord Denning, of the employment committee of seven members, 'It is impossible to suppose that all of them need sit to determine a matter, or that all of those who sit should have read all the papers or heard all the evidence . . . In my opinion the applicant's complaint had been fully investigated in accordance with the statute. He has been most fairly treated. And the Race Relations Board formed an opinion which was manifestly correct, that there had been no unlawful discrimination against him.' The applicant's case was dismissed.

The members of the Court of Appeal were clearly most reluctant to interfere with the decision of the Race Relations Board. And, no doubt, this reluctance is often justifiable. But in this case the disparities between the ways in which the conciliation committee and the employment committee proceeded were so glaring that the propriety of the employment committee's actions was surely in question. The conciliation subcommittee had seen all the parties and had investigated the matter at great length. The employment committee saw none of those concerned, were presented with a prejudicial recommendation by an officer who had seen none of those concerned, and came to a conclusion although four of its seven members had not seen all the papers. How in the light of all this could Lord Denning conclude that the opinion of the Race Relations Board was 'manifestly correct'? How could he conclude that the applicant had been 'most fairly treated'?

The CRE cases
The Commission for Racial Equality (CRE) was established by the Race Relations Act 1976 to replace the Race Relations Board and the Community Relations Commission. The statutory duties of the CRE are (a) to work towards the elimination of discrimination, (b) to promote equality of opportunity, and good relations, between persons of different racial groups generally, and (c) to keep under

review the working of the Act. By section 48 the CRE are empowered to conduct formal investigations for any purpose connected with the carrying out of those duties. Section 49(1) provides that the CRE shall not embark on a formal investigation unless the requirements of the section have been complied with. Subsection (2) requires the CRE to draw up terms of reference for an investigation. Subsection (3) requires the CRE to give general notice of the holding of an investigation unless the terms of reference confine it to activities of persons named in them but in such a case the CRE must give those persons notice. Subsection (4) provides that where the terms of reference confine the investigation to activities of persons named in them and the CRE in course of it propose to investigate any unlawful discriminatory act which they believe a person so named may have done, the CRE must (a) inform that person of their belief and of their proposal to investigate the act and (b) offer him an opportunity of making oral or written representations with regard to it. A person so named may be represented by counsel or a solicitor or another person. Section 50(1) empowers the CRE to obtain information from any person by serving a notice on him. But under subsection (2) a notice may be served only where (a) the Secretary of State so orders or (b) the terms of reference state that the CRE believe a person named in them may have done or be doing unlawful discriminatory acts and confine the investigation to those acts. Section 58(2) provides that if in the course of a formal investigation the CRE become satisfied that a person is committing or has committed any unlawful discriminatory acts, the CRE may serve on him a non-discrimination notice. Subsection (5) of section 58 provides that the CRE shall not serve a non-discrimination notice on any person unless the CRE have first (a) given him notice that they are 'minded' to issue such a notice, specifying the grounds on which they contemplate doing so, (b) offered him an opportunity to make representations in the matter, and (c) taken account of any such representations. Section 59(1) enables any person served with a non-discrimination notice to appeal to an industrial tribunal or county court. Subsection (2) provides that where the tribunal or court considers a requirement in the notice to be unreasonable because it is based on an incorrect finding of fact or for any other reason, the tribunal or court shall quash the requirement.

Several attempts have been made in the courts to frustrate investigations instituted by the CRE. As the CRE reported in 1983:

There have been legal challenges over investigations on such *highly technical procedural matters* as whether terms of reference are too wide; whether the Commission can investigate named persons without a belief that they are acting unlawfully; whether it is reasonable to embark on an investigation; whether natural justice applies as well as the statutory requirements to hear representations; whether the right to make representations under s.49(4) of the Act applies during the course of an investigation if the Commission forms a belief as to unlawful acts; whether it is reasonable to change from a strategic investigation to one based on a belief that unlawful acts have occurred . . . None of these matters actually touch on the fundamental question whether discrimination has occurred and what should be done about it . . . Yet, all this has happened in a system which was itself designed to give the person investigated every opportunity to make representation.[44]

Three decisions in particular have seriously diminished the scope of investigations by the CRE. In July 1978 the CRE informed a company, under section 49(4) of the Act, of their proposal to investigate and the company submitted eleven pages of representations under that subsection. The CRE, having become satisfied that an unlawful discriminatory act had been committed, told the company, in accordance with section 58, that they were 'minded' to serve a non-discrimination notice and sent a letter containing nine pages of detailed findings on allegations against the company. The company replied by submitting forty pages of further detailed representations. Subsequently the CRE served the non-discrimination notice itemizing the unlawful acts they had found. The company exercised its statutory right of appeal to an industrial tribunal which ordered the CRE to give particulars of every fact found by the CRE in the course of their investigation. The CRE argued that the whole of the lengthy administrative inquiry by the CRE should not be reopened on appeal, especially as the company had had two opportunities of making representations; and that the appeal should be limited to the reasonableness of the requirements in the non-discrimination notice. In February 1982 the Court of Appeal upheld the company's interpretation of the Act. Lord Denning MR, after outlining the facts, said: 'Such is the long procedure which has taken place already. Even so we have only got

44. Commission for Racial Equality: *The Race Relations Act 1976 – Time for a Change*? (July 1983). See also G. Appleby and E. Ellis, 'Formal Investigations by the CRE and EOC' in [1984] Public Law 236, to which I am indebted.

to this preliminary question: should particulars be ordered or not by the industrial tribunal? The appeal itself to the tribunal is a long way off.' And he concluded: 'I am very sorry for the Commission, but they have been caught up in a spider's web spun by Parliament from which there is little hope of their escaping.'[45]

The second case involved Hillingdon London Borough Council whose area includes Heathrow Airport.[46] In consequence the Council has the responsibility under the Housing (Homeless Persons) Act 1977 of providing accommodation for immigrant families who have made no prior arrangements. A Kenyan Asian family arrived and the Council classed them as intentionally homeless and so not entitled to be rehoused. The chairman of the Council's housing committee arranged for them to be taken by taxi and dumped outside the Foreign Office in support of his view that the responsibility should rest on the central government. At about the same time the Council housed a white family who had just arrived from Rhodesia. Because of this disparate treatment, the CRE told the Council they were embarking on a formal investigation and drew up terms of reference. The Council brought an action to quash the investigation.

Lord Diplock (with whom the other Law Lords concurred) held that it was a condition precedent to the drawing up of the terms of reference that the CRE should form the belief, and should so state in the terms of reference that the named persons (here the Council) might have done or might be doing unlawful discriminatory acts of a kind specified in the terms of reference. The terms of reference drawn up by the CRE stated a belief that the Council might have done or might be doing certain unlawful discriminatory acts in relation to the public or sections of the public as were in need of housing through homelessness. Since that form of words might also include acts done in relation to persons other than ethnic minority families arriving at Heathrow as immigrants, the House of Lords held that, as the CRE had admitted that they had formed no belief as to those other persons, the terms of reference were too wide and so invalid. The fact that the Council knew what the CRE intended to investigate and that the CRE had made this explicit to the Council in a draft press release was not thought to be relevant except as indicating the limits of the CRE's belief.

The most recent of this group of cases was *Commission for Racial Equality v. Prestige Group PLC.*[47] In September 1978 the CRE

45. *CRE v. Amari Plastics Ltd* [1982] 2 All ER 499.
46. *R. v. CRE ex parte Hillingdon LBC* [1982] AC 779.
47. [1984] 1 WLR 335.

informed the respondent company that they had decided to embark upon a formal investigation of the company to inquire into the employment of different racial groups by the company and its subsidiaries, with particular reference to the promotion of equality of opportunity between such persons as regards recruitment, access to promotion, transfer, training and any other benefits, facilities, services, and terms and conditions of employment. At this time the CRE had no belief that the company might have committed an act of discrimination. In July 1981 the CRE, having considered information obtained in the course of their formal investigation, gave notice to the company that the CRE were 'minded' to conclude that the company had committed certain specified unlawful discriminatory acts. The company made representations but in November 1981 the CRE decided that the company had committed such acts and served the company with a non-discriminatory notice. After the Lords' decision in *Hillingdon* in June 1982, the company applied to the courts for judicial review claiming that the CRE's entire formal investigation had been ultra vires and void.

The House of Lords held that on the true construction of sections 49(4) and 50(2)(b) of the Act of 1976, the 'condition precedent' – the belief that the named person (here the company) might be discriminating unlawfully – had to exist in these circumstances as in *Hillingdon* and that this entailed the holding of the preliminary investigation under section 49(4). Since there had originally been no such belief and so no investigation, the non-discrimination notice was ultra vires and void. The CRE argued that in *Hillingdon* the terms of reference did contain a statement of belief whereas in *Prestige* they did not; and that any invalidity was cured by the subsequent formation by the CRE of such a belief. But Lord Diplock (with whom the other Law Lords concurred) said that the CRE could not lawfully continue the formal investigation, once they had subsequently formed such a belief, without first holding the preliminary inquiry.

Lord Denning MR further castigated the CRE in *Mandla v. Dowell Lee*.[48] This was the case where a headmaster refused to admit a Sikh as a pupil unless he cut his hair and ceased to wear a turban. The question was whether Sikhs were a 'racial group' defined by reference to 'ethnic origins' within the meaning of the Race Relations Act 1976. The CRE, said Lord Denning, 'pursued the headmaster relentlessly'. And he expressed 'some regret that the

48. [1982] 3 WLR 932.

CRE thought it right to take up this case against the headmaster
. . . The statutes . . . should not be used so as to interfere with the
discretion of schools and colleges in the proper management of
their affairs.' And Kerr LJ thought that all the CRE had achieved
in this case was 'to create racial discord where there was none
before' and referred to notes of an interview between the
headmaster and an official of the CRE which he said read in part
'more like an inquisition than an interview' and which he regarded
as harassment of the headmaster.. Oliver LJ suggested that the
machinery of the Act had operated against the headmaster as 'an
engine of oppression'. The House of Lords overruled the Court of
Appeal, found that Sikhs were a racial group and that there had
been unlawful discrimination. Lord Fraser said that he thought the
Court of Appeal's strictures on the CRE and its officials were
'entirely unjustified'. Lord Templeman agreed that the CRE had
not acted oppressively. Lords Edmund-Davies, Roskill and
Brandon concurred in their decision.[49]

Immigration and deportation

Before 1962 a Commonwealth citizen was entitled to enter the
United Kingdom, but the Commonwealth Immigrants Act of that
year empowered an immigration officer to refuse admissison or to
admit only on conditions (including limitation of length of stay). That
power was not to be exercised if the applicant satisfied the
immigration officer that he or she was ordinarily resident in the
United Kingdom and had been so resident at any time within the
previous two years, or was the wife, or child under sixteen, of a resident. The power of immigration officers to examine any intending
immigrant lapsed twenty-four hours after the immigrant landed.

In *Re H.K.*[50] where the age of a child, said to be under sixteen,
was doubted by an immigration officer, the Divisional Court
refused an application for habeas corpus and upheld the officer's
refusal to admit. The court said they could review the decision if
it had been come to 'unfairly', but that was not so in this case. This
indicated that the court took a limited view of its functions. In *Re
A*.[51] the doubt was whether the child was the plaintiff's son and the
Court of Appeal refused to interfere so long as the immigration
officers acted 'honestly and fairly'. However, in *Ex parte*

49. [1983] 2 WLR 620.
50. [1967] 2 QB 617.
51. [1968] 2 All ER 145.

Amrik Singh[52] where the immigration officer refused permission because he suspected that the applicant was not a genuine visitor for a short period (as he claimed to be), the Divisional Court sent the matter back to the immigration authorities to be reconsidered.

In *Ex parte Ahsan*[53] eleven Pakistanis landed clandestinely (but not illegally) and were arrested shortly afterwards. The question was whether, in an application for habeas corpus, the onus lay on them to prove that their landing had taken place more than twenty-four hours earlier or on the authorities to prove it had taken place within that period. The Divisional Court held that it was the latter. and ordered the release of those arrested. But in *Re Wazid Hassan*[54] the Divisional Court held that, on an application for habeas corpus, it was for the detained person to show that his detention as an illegal immigrant was unlawful.

The most important of these cases under the Act of 1962 was *DPP v. Bhagwan*[55] Here again the immigrant landed clandestinely. Some two years later he was arrested and charged with conspiring to evade the control on immigration imposed by the Act of 1962. It was argued on his behalf that, as he had not acted illegally by landing as he did, the charge disclosed no offence known to the law. This gave rise to discussion about the limits of conspiracy and of *Shaw's* case.[56] The House of Lords gave judgment, unanimously, for the immigrant.

The practical importance of this decision for immigrants was much reduced by the Commonwealth Immigrants Act 1968, which made clandestine landings an offence, and the law was further tightened by the Immigration Act 1971, which declared an 'illegal entrant' to be anyone who had entered the United Kingdom in breach of the immigration laws. In this sense the Act of 1971 was retroactive.[57] But in *R. v. Miah*,[58] the House of Lords refused to apply penal provisions of that Act retroactively so as to render a person liable to criminal proceedings for acts which were not criminal when he committed them.

Since 1969, there has been a right of appeal in some circumstances from the decision of an immigration officer to an adjudicator and to an Immigration Appeal Tribunal. Even so, the courts

52. [1968] 3 All ER 163.
53. [1969] 2 QB 222.
54. [1976] 1 WLR 971.
55. [1972] AC 60.
56. See below, pp. 152–3.
57. See *R. v. Governor of Pentonville Prison ex parte Azam* [1974] AC 18.
58. [1974] 1 WLR 683.

will intervene if they consider that the adjudicator, or the tribunal, has made an error in law or has acted in breach of the rules of natural justice. Probably in these immigration cases the courts would be reluctant to overrule the appellate authorities, but where a student, who had entered the United Kingdom on a twelve-month study permit, was first refused an extension and then subsequently, after various errors in the Home Office, refused leave to appeal, the Court of Appeal overruled the tribunal and allowed her to stay.[59] Similarly, when the Home Office tried to insist that an immigrant, who claimed she had an unrestricted right to enter the United Kingdom, must apply for the necessary certificate in India and not in the United Kingdom, the Court of Appeal upheld her right to make application in the United Kingdom.[60]

Section 14 of the Immigration Act 1971 gives a right of appeal to an immigrant who has a limited leave to remain in the United Kingdom but is refused an extension by the Secretary of State. In *Ex parte Subramanian*,[61] the Court of Appeal held that the application for an extension must be made before and not after the limited leave has expired. If this were done the applicant might stay until the appeal was decided. But in *Suthendran v. Immigration Appeal Tribunal*[62] the House of Lords by a majority held that if an immigrant applies for an extension before his limited leave has expired but the Secretary of State does not give his decision until after the date of expiration, then the immigrant can no longer appeal because he no longer 'has' a limited leave to remain. This absurdly pedantic and literal interpretation means that the immigrant may be deprived of his right to appeal by the Secretary of State deliberately or carelessly failing to decide before the date of expiration.[63]

With those cases may be contrasted two concerning other applicants for admission. Robert Soblen, a citizen of the USA, was convicted of conspiracy to obtain and hand over information valuable to the Soviet Union. While on bail he fled to Israel whence he was removed and put on a flight, in the custody of a United States marshal, which was due to stop at London en route for New York. About twenty minutes out of London he inflicted severe wounds on

59. *R. v. Secretary of State for the Home Department ex parte Mehta* [1975] 1 WLR 322.
60. *R. v. Secretary of State for the Home Department ex parte Phansopkar* [1975] 3 WLR 322.
61. [1976] 3 WLR 630.
62. [1976] 3 WLR 725.
63. Now SI 1976 No. 1572 provides a partial remedy.

himself with a knife and on arrival at London was put in an ambulance and taken to hospital. From there, having been refused political asylum, he applied for a writ of habeas corpus claiming that he was being wrongly detained. Everything turned on whether he had been given leave to land. Attempts had been made when his aircraft landed to serve him with a notice refusing him leave but he was too ill to receive it. Nevertheless the Court of Appeal held that he had been refused leave. In the lower court, the Lord Chief Justice said that he was in no way concerned with whether or not Soblen was, as he contended, innocent of the charges of which he had been convicted and this view was repeated in the Court of Appeal.[64] But the suspicion remained that the deportation order would not have been upheld but for the diplomatic relations between the countries concerned. Shortly before he was due to be flown out of the United Kingdom en route for New York, Soblen took an overdose of drugs and died.

Aliens are normally allowed to enter the country if they come 'for the purpose of full-time study at a recognized educational establishment' and until 25 July 1968 the Hubbard College of Scientology was so recognized. On that date the Minister of Health told the House of Commons that scientology was 'so objectionable that it would be right to take all steps . . . to curb its growth', and that 'foreign nationals already in the United Kingdom for study at a Scientology establishment' would not be granted extension of stay. The plaintiffs were refused leave to extend their stay and brought an action claiming that the Home Secretary was bound to consider their applications on their merits and not merely follow the general statement of policy. By a majority the Court of Appeal dismissed their action. Lord Denning put strong emphasis on the power of the Home Secretary to refuse to admit any alien, without giving any reason. All that was necessary was that the exclusion was for 'an authorized purpose'. He said:

I think the Minister can exercise his power for any purpose which he considers to be for the public good or to be in the interests of the people of this country.[65]

64. *R. v. Secretary of State for Home Affairs ex parte Soblen* [1963] 1 QB 829.
65. *Schmidt v. Secretary of State for Home Affairs* [1969] 2 Ch.149. In *Van Duyn v. Home Office* [1975] 2 WLR 760 the Court of Justice of the European Communities held that the United Kingdom was entitled to exclude a scientologist on the ground of public policy under the terms of the EEC Treaty.

In effect, in this and other cases, the courts refuse to review the exercise of the minister's discretion. As they express the principle, it is virtually impossible for a plaintiff to show that the minister has acted for an unauthorized purpose.

In several habeas corpus cases concerning immigrants it was held that the onus of proof was on the applicant to show that he should be released, and not on the detaining authority to justify detention. In *R v. Secretary of State for the Home Department ex parte Hussain*[66] and *ex parte Choudhary*[67] the Court of Appeal held that although the applicant had set up a prima facie case that he had permission to remain in the United Kingdom indefinitely, if the court was satisfied that the Secretary of State had reasonable grounds for concluding that the applicant was in the country illegally, the court would not intervene by enquiring further into the truth or otherwise of the factual basis on which the Secretary of State founded his opinion. Where, on the other hand, a detention order issued by an immigration officer contained a material error, it was held that the court was entitled to go behind the wording and see whether in fact there were good grounds for detention.[68]

In *Zamir v. Secretary of State for the Home Department*[69] the applicant for habeas corpus was a Pakistani on whose behalf in December 1972 (he was then aged fifteen) an entry certificate was sought so that he might join his father who had been settled in England since 1962. The certificate was eventually granted, in November 1975, on the basis that the applicant was unmarried and dependent on his father. In February 1976 he married in Pakistan. In March 1976 he arrived at Heathrow airport in London, was asked no questions and volunteered no information. He was granted leave to enter for an indefinite period. In August 1978 he was questioned by the immigration authorities and in October 1978 he was detained as an illegal immigrant with a view to his removal from the United Kingdom.

In the House of Lords, Lord Wilberforce, with whom the other Law Lords agreed, said that an applicant for entry to the United Kingdom owed a positive duty of candour on all material facts which denoted a change of circumstances since the issue of the entry clearance. Lord Wilberforce managed to suggest that perhaps the

66. [1978] 1 WLR 700.
67. [1978] 1 WLR 1177.
68. *R. v. Secretary of State for the Home Department ex parte Iqbal* [1979] 1 All ER 675.
69. [1980] 2 All ER 768.

applicant had obtained entry clearance on the basis of a forged birth certificate, though he admitted that this matter had 'not been adjudicated on'. It was, said Lord Wilberforce, for the applicant to show that his detention was unlawful. But this the applicant could not do unless he could show either that there were no grounds on which the immigration officer could legally have detained him or that no reasonable person could have decided as the immigration officer did. To prove these negatives is, of course, virtually impossible. For immigrants the great writ of habeas corpus, which is supposed to stand between the imprisoned individual and the powers of the State, had been effectively neutralized by the judiciary.

Within three years, the House of Lords in a remarkable turnabout reversed its own decision in *Zamir*. The appellant Bohar Singh Khera was born in India in 1956. In 1972 his father was granted leave to enter the United Kingdom for settlement and applied for entry certificates for the appellant and the appellant's mother. In August 1972 they were interviewed by the entry clearance officer in New Delhi. On 5 June 1973, unknown to the UK immigration authorities, the appellant married in India. In December 1974, the appellant and his mother were granted entry certificates. They arrived in the UK in January 1975 and were granted indefinite leave to enter. In November 1978, the appellant's wife applied to join her husband together with two children of the marriage. Enquiries were made, the marriage came to light, and in November 1978 an immigration officer made an order detaining the appellant as an illegal entrant, pending summary removal. The appellant applied to the court for a declaration that he was lawfully in the United Kingdom and had indefinite leave to enter and remain.

It was argued on behalf of the immigration authorities that on one occasion, after the appellant had reached the age of eighteen, he had falsely told a medical officer of the immigration authorities that he was not married and so was guilty of deception on a fact which was material because, as with Zamir, only if he were unmarried and dependent on his father, was he entitled to be admitted for settlement.

The appellant denied that he had made this statement and it appeared that the immigration officer who made the order detaining him had not relied on this evidence and that there was no other evidence outstanding against the appellant.

Lord Fraser who, with Lord Wilberforce, had also participated in *Zamir* remarked that the notice of the immigration officer's decision began: 'Having considered all the information available to me, I am satisfied that there are reasonable grounds to conclude that you are an illegal entrant' and he, with Lords Bridge and Scarman, held that this indicated the immigration officer had applied the wrong test. The officer was entitled to order the detention and removal of a person who had entered the country by virtue of an ex facie valid permission only if that person *was* an illegal entrant and in these cases the degree of probability required that this was so on the evidence was high. The Law Lords also agreed that there was no positive duty of candour although silence was capable of amounting to deception.[70]

Why did the Law Lords reverse their own decision so soon and so completely? The *Zamir* decision was badly regarded by several diverse groups, especially on the ruling of a positive duty of candour. This was seen as unfair and impracticable not only by those who advised immigrants in the UK and abroad, but also by the Home Office and by the lawyers who habitually were concerned with such cases. The apparent reversal of the burden of proof on habeas corpus offended many, including (one suspects) some of the Law Lords themselves. It was recognized that deception took place on a considerable scale but the standard set by Lord Wilberforce was unduly high. In *Khera*, the House of Lords was, save for Lords Wilberforce and Fraser, differently composed and included Lords Scarman, Bridge and Templeman, a more liberal trio than those they replaced. This is reinforced by the history of the cases. On 6 May 1982 an appeal committee consisting of Lords Fraser, Roskill and Brandon dismissed a petition on behalf of Khera for leave to appeal to the House of Lords. On 17 June 1982, Khawaja (whose case was weaker) was given leave by Lords Fraser, Scarman and Bridge. As a result the Khera petition was reheard and leave given. This suggests a crucial change of mind by Lord Fraser between those two dates. And finally, the decision in *Zamir* was being taken to the European Commission on Human Rights and there may have been a wish to avoid yet another decision in Strasbourg critical of the United Kingdom.

The courts continue to puzzle their way through immigration law. Where a citizen of Sri Lanka, wishing to join his wife who had entered the UK for nurse's training, applied for entry as a visitor and said he was unmarried because he thought he would not have

70. *R. v. Secretary of State for the Home Department ex parte Khera* [1983] 2 WLR 321; and see *Ali v. Secretary of State for the Home Department* [1984] 1 All ER 1009 and *R. v. The Same ex parte Awa*, *The Times*, 12 March 1983. (The *Khera* decision is also cited as *ex parte Khawaja*.)

been granted leave if the truth were known, he was treated by the immigration authorities as an illegal entrant, but the Court of Appeal held that his false statement was not a material fact and did not vitiate his right to enter.[71] Where another Sri Lanka citizen was refused entry because the immigration officer was not satisfied that she had sufficient financial support or that she intended to leave when her studies were completed, the House of Lords remitted the matter to the Immigration Appeal Tribunal for reconsideration as there was a discretion to admit her for a short period notwithstanding those doubts.[72] Again, where an over-stayer was convicted by justices and recommended for deportation, the House of Lords held that as he remained in ignorance of a fact constituting a necessary element of the offence he was not guilty of the offence.[73]

The number of cases under the Immigration Act 1971 is very large and the great majority are decided by the Immigration Appeal Tribunal or in the High Court. Sometimes the Court of Appeal and the Law Lords (especially before the *Khera* decision) have been less generous. In *ex parte Margueritte*[74] an immigrant entered as a visitor in 1974, overstayed, and married in 1978 when, his wife being already settled in the UK, he was granted indefinite leave to stay. In 1979 he applied for registration as a citizen of the UK and Colonies for which he would need to have been 'ordinarily resident' for at least five years. The Court of Appeal refused to allow him to count the years before 1978. In *ex parte Kotecha*,[75] an orphan aged sixteen who lived in India was refused entry clearance to enable him to live with his elder brother in the UK. He appealed and in the meantime his elder brother was appointed in India as his legal guardian, one of his sisters had come to the UK, another brother had settled in Tanzania, and his grandmother in India had died. The Court of Appeal held that the appellate authorities had no power to admit evidence of these later events. Lord Lane CJ gave as his reason: 'Were the situation to be otherwise . . . it would mean a never-ending system of appeal, each court up the line being obliged to review the facts in the lights of events as they stood, not at the time of the original decision but as they stood at each

71. *R. v. Home Secretary ex parte Jayakody* [1982] 1 WLR 405 (the Home Secretary supported this appeal).
72. *R. v. Immigration Appeal Tribunal ex parte Alexander* [1982] 1 WLR 1076.
73. *Grant v. Borg* [1982] 1 WLR 638.
74. *R. v. Home Secretary ex parte Margueritte* [1982] 3 WLR 754.
75. *R. v. Immigration Appeal Tribunal ex parte Kotecha* [1983] 1 WLR 487.

stage of the appellate system, and the system would become even more unmanageable than some people believe it to be at present.'

In *ex parte Coomasaru*,[76] an immigrant from Sri Lanka in May 1975 had his passport stamped on entry as employed by the Sri Lanka High Commission owing to a mistake by the immigration officer which was in no way induced by the immigrant. He was in fact employed as subwarden of the Sri Lankan Students' Welfare Centre. He went abroad in April or May 1978 and returned in May 1978 when he was first refused admission but in June 1978 was granted leave to enter for twelve months subject to the restriction that he took no employment save as subwarden of the Centre, a job he no longer held. He contended that in May 1978 he was already 'settled in the UK'. But the Court of Appeal decided against him and ruled that he could not take advantage of the mistake that had been made.

The impression one receives on reading these and many other immigration cases is that the statutory and other provisions are often not clear and that consequently the courts frequently have a large measure of discretion how to interpret them. In these circumstances applicants for judicial review, and their legal advisers, must feel that they are taking part in a lottery, or in a game of roulette where the place the ball finally settles is largely a matter of chance.

Contempt of court, restrictions on publications, and the maintenance of secrecy

A recent report stated that the law relating to contempt of court had developed over the centuries as a means whereby the courts might act to prevent or punish conduct which tended to obstruct, prejudice or abuse the administration of justice.[77] Such conduct may take place, in relation to any particular case, before, during or after the trial. Most obviously, if the court makes an order which is disregarded, that is contempt, as happened when trade unions were fined for failing to obey orders of the National Industrial Relations Court; or as happens in matrimonial cases where parties

76. *R. v. Immigration Appeal Tribunal ex parte Coomasaru* [1983] 1 WLR 14.
77. Report of the Committee on Contempt of Court (Cmnd 5794) para. 1; and see discussion paper Cmnd 7145; and see 948 HC Deb. col. 1340-50 (25 April 1978).

disobey orders not to molest or invade the privacy of other parties.

But, less usually, there may be positive disruption as when, in 1970, a group of Welsh students invaded a court in the Royal Courts of Justice in London and broke up the hearing of a case by striding into the well of the court, shouting slogans, scattering pamphlets and singing. They did this to demonstrate for the preservation of the Welsh language, and those who refused to apologize to the judge were instantly committed by him to three months' imprisonment. On appeal they were bound over for twelve months to be of good behaviour. The members of the Court of Appeal emphasized that the right to protest must be executed within the law. But their judgments also establish, despite statutory law which seemed, as applicable to these students, to require that their sentences should be suspended, that the High Court still had power at common law to commit instantly to prison for such contempt.[78]

Clearly the position of an accused person may be adversely and unfairly affected if, before his trial is concluded, publicity about him appears in the press. This may well create prejudice, not least in the mind of any member of the jury. So for a newspaper to describe an accused person of having had an unedifying career as brothel-keeper, procurer and property racketeer is a serious contempt of court – and when this happened in 1967 *The Sunday Times* was fined £5000.[79]

In an earlier case, two journalists who gave evidence to a tribunal of enquiry investigating breaches of security by an Admiralty clerk refused to disclose the sources of information which they had published. This tribunal was by statute in a similar position, in relation to contempt, as the High Court, and the Court of Appeal upheld sentences of six and three months' imprisonment.[80]

These and other cases are now overshadowed by the decision of the House of Lords in the 'thalidomide' case.[81] The story is long and complicated but, put briefly, between 1959 and 1961 a company made and marketed under licence a drug containing thalidomide, as a result of which about 450 children were born with gross deformities. In 1968 and subsequently actions were begun by the issue of writs against the company and some of these were settled

78. *Morris v. Crown Office* [1970] 2 QB 114.
79. *R. v. Thomson Newspapers* [1968] 1 WLR 1.
80. *A-G v. Mulholland* [1963] 2 QB 477.
81. *A-G v. Times Newspapers* [1974] AC 273.

out of court. For others, negotiations continued and in September 1972 *The Sunday Times* published the first of a series of articles to draw attention to the plight of the children. The company complained to the Attorney-General that the article was a contempt of court because some actions were still pending. The editor justified the articles and at the same time sent to the Attorney and to the company for comment a second article in draft (for which he claimed complete factual accuracy) on the testing, manufacture and marketing of the drug. The Attorney-General asked the courts to grant an injunction to prevent the publication of this second article on the ground that it was a contempt. The Divisional Court granted the injunction but the Court of Appeal refused it. The House of Lords allowed the company's appeal and granted the injunction.

Essentially, the view of the Court of Appeal[82] was that in the unique circumstances of a national tragedy where the public interest required that the issues should be discussed, where the legal proceedings had been dormant for years, and where there appeared no possibility of any action coming to trial, the public interest in fair comment outweighed the possible prejudice to a party. The House of Lords decided against *The Sunday Times* on the ground that the second article might be prejudicial to a subsequent trial. The public interest in proper discussion in the circumstances of this case and the weakness of the parents' situation, unless they could be championed by the press, appeared to carry very little weight with their Lordships whose decision was unnecessary in law and deplorable in practice.

The issue was then taken to the European Court of Human Rights on the ground that the injunction violated Article 10 of the European Convention which protects the right to freedom of expression. The court concluded, by eleven votes to nine, that the injunction did not correspond to a social need sufficiently pressing to outweigh the public interest in freedom of expression and therefore was not 'necessary in a democratic society' for maintaining the authority of the judiciary; and accordingly, was in violation of Article 10.

In response to this finding, the government introduced a bill which became the Contempt of Court Act 1981. Section 5 provided:

> A publication made as or as part of a discussion in good faith of public affairs or other matters of general public interest is not to

82. [1973] 1 QB 710

be treated as a contempt of court under the strict liability rule if the risk of impediment or prejudice to particular legal proceedings is merely incidental to the discussion.

The Act also provided in section 2 that the strict liability rule – which meant liability although there was no intention to interfere with the course of justice – applied only to a publication which created a substantial risk that the course of justice would be seriously impeded or prejudiced.

On 15 October 1980 the *Daily Mail* published an article by Mr Malcolm Muggeridge entitled 'The vision of life that wins my vote' in support of an independent 'pro-life' candidate at a Parliamentary bye-election. She was supported by the Society for the Protection of Unborn Children and took as a main plank in her campaign the stopping of the practice that she asserted was developing in some British hospitals of killing new-born handicapped babies.

The date of publication was also the third day of the trial in the Crown Court at Leicester of a well known paediatrician on a charge of murdering a three-day-old mongoloid baby by giving instructions that it should be treated with a drug which caused it to die of starvation.

The newspaper article made no mention of the trial but it contained the words, 'Today the chances of such a baby surviving would be very small indeed. Someone would surely recommend letting her die of starvation or otherwise disposing of her.'

Lord Diplock said that 'substantial' and 'seriously' in section 2 were intended to exclude a risk that was only remote; that the article was clearly capable of prejudicing the jury against the accused; and that it satisfied the criterion in that section. He held, however, that section 5 applied, that the risk of prejudice was merely incidental to the public discussion about the rights and wrongs of the alleged practice of letting deformed babies die, and that the prosecution for contempt therefore failed. The other Law Lords agreed.[83]

However Lord Diplock also commented that the article in this case was 'nearly in all respects the antithesis of the article which the House of Lords had held to be a contempt of court in *Attorney-General v. Times Newspapers Ltd*' (the thalidomide case). In that case, he said, the whole subject of the article was the pending civil actions against the drugs company and the whole purpose of the

83. *A-G v. English* [1982] 3 WLR 278.

article was to put pressure on the company in the lawful conduct of their defence in those actions.

Lord Diplock's words make clear that, in his opinion, section 5 of the Contempt of Court Act 1981 does not bring English law into conformity with the European Convention. But indeed his judgment seems to go further. His finding that the article was clearly capable of creating a substantial risk that the course of justice would be seriously impeded or prejudiced reflects a poor view of the independence, fair-mindedness, and intelligence of jurors. Moreover, Lord Diplock's emphasis on 'the whole purpose' of the article in the thalidomide case suggests that, in his view, the limitations in the Act on the strict liability rule might not in any event have availed *The Sunday Times*. Those limitations, including section 5, apply only to unintentional contempts, while 'whole purpose' suggests intention. In the result the Contempt of Court Act 1981, as interpreted by Lord Diplock, may well have made further inroads on the freedom of the press and of publications generally. It is not surprising that The Times Newspapers have taken another complaint to the European Commission of Human Rights on the ground that the Government have failed to bring UK law into conformity with the finding of the European Court.[84]

Quite apart from the provisions of the Official Secrets Acts, political restrictions have been imposed on former ministers on the extent to which they reveal what took place when they were in government. This applies most strongly to former cabinet ministers who have normally been required to submit to the Secretary to the Cabinet drafts of their proposed publications. R. H. S. Crossman kept a diary during the six years from 1964 to 1970 when he was a member of the cabinet. Thereafter he began to collate his records and had completed and handed to his publishers the first volume before his death in April 1974. On 10 May 1974, one of the publishers, who was also a literary executor of Mr Crossman, sent a copy of the typescript of this volume (which dealt with the period 1964-6) to the Cabinet Secretary asking for 'a reasonably quick reading' as publication was planned for that autumn. On 22 June the Secretary said that he could not agree to publication of this volume. He said there were two complementary principles. The first was the collective responsibility of the cabinet and the need to

---

84. The Act also extends the power to prevent or postpone press reporting of cases in the courts; effectively prevents research into the jury system; and extends contempt provisions more completely over appellate courts.

maintain secrecy to ensure completely frank discussion within the cabinet and its committees. The second was the personal responsibility of individual ministers. Further correspondence followed and *The Sunday Times* published some extracts from the diaries not all of which had been 'cleared' by the Cabinet Secretary. Then, in June 1975, the Attorney-General brought two actions for injunctions to prevent the publication of the first volume and of further extracts by *The Sunday Times*. The Attorney-General argued that the courts should forbid publication as being contrary to the public interest. He also argued that there was a principle of law that no one should profit from the wrongful publication of information received in confidence. This principle has been recognized as a ground for restraining the unfair use of commercial secrets transmitted in confidence. And in *Argyll v. Argyll*[85] the same principle was applied to domestic secrets passing between husband and wife during marriage. On the basis of the decision in that case, the Lord Chief Justice concluded that when a cabinet minister received information in confidence the improper publication of such information could be restrained by the courts. In particular, he said,

> The expression of individual opinions by cabinet ministers in the course of cabinet discussions are matters of confidence, the publication of which can be restrained by the court when this is clearly necessary in the public interest.

This was a new principle or, at least, the considerable extension of an older principle. When the Lord Chief Justice came to apply this to the case before him, he decided that in view of the lapse of time (nearly ten years since the end of the period covered by the first volume of the diaries) he would not issue the injunctions asked for because he could not believe that publication would inhibit free discussion of the cabinet in 1975.[86]

In the event, therefore, the first volume of the Crossman diaries

85. [1967] Ch. 302. In *Fraser v. Evans* [1969] 1 QB 349 the confidential report of the plaintiff, who was a public relations consultant to the Greek government, came into the hands of *The Sunday Times*. The Court of Appeal refused to issue an injunction to prevent its publication on the ground that the person to whom the confidential duty was owed (i.e. the Greek government) was not seeking the protection of the court.

86. *A-G v. Jonathan Cape Ltd*; *A-G v. Times Newspapers Ltd* [1975] 3 All ER 484.

was published. But more important was the establishment of the new rule of law that the courts have jurisdiction to determine when the public interest requires that ministers shall not be permitted to disclose information. I am not suggesting that there should be no constraints on such publication. But hitherto the constraints, if they have not been imposed by the Official Secrets Acts, have been political. The principle established by this case enables the courts to determine what is in the public interest on a matter which is at the heart of the political system.

In *Francome v. Mirror Group Newspapers*[87] the plaintiffs were man and wife, he being the champion National Hunt jockey. Unknown persons tapped telephone conversations to and from the plaintiffs' home and offered the tapes for sale to the *Daily Mirror*, alleging that they revealed breaches by the jockey of the rules of racing. The plaintiffs brought an action for breach of confidence against the *Daily Mirror*, and the Court of Appeal, pending trial, made an order that the newspaper be restrained from publishing any article based on the tapes, that there be a speedy trial and that the newspaper disclose the identity of the unknown persons. On appeal, this order was varied so that disclosure of the identity was not required at this stage.

Ten days later, a differently composed Court of Appeal considered a case where the plaintiff company marketed an electronic computerized instrument known as the Lion Intoximeter 3000, and 60 per cent of their sales were to police authorities for measuring intoxication by alcohol. Two of their former employees leaked copies of the plaintiffs' internal correspondence to the *Daily Express* and the plaintiffs sought an injunction to prevent publication. A conflict of public interests arose because the allegation was that the instrument was not accurate. The court allowed the publication of some of the documents.[88]

Such cases of breach of confidence or of copyright frequently give rise to such conflicts and the courts determine whether the private rights or the public interests should prevail. In *Francome* Sir John Donaldson MR said:

The 'media' . . . are an essential foundation of any democracy. In exposing crime, antisocial behaviour and hypocrisy and in campaigning for reform and propagating the views of minorities,

87. [1984] 1 WLR 892.
88. *Lion Laboratories v. Evans*, [1984] 3 WLR 539.

they perform an invaluable function. However, they are peculiarly vulnerable to the error of confusing the public interest with their own interest. Usually these interests march hand in hand, but not always. In the instant case, pending a trial, it is impossible to see what public interest would be served by publishing the contents of the tapes which would not equally be served by giving them to the police or to the Jockey Club. Any wider publication could only serve the interests of the *Daily Mirror*.

Official secrets may be protected by the courts under a rule which provides that the Crown may claim that certain documents should not be disclosed to a party engaged in litigation on the ground that the public interest would be harmed by their production. In the leading case of *Duncan v. Cammell, Laird*[89] the plaintiffs were the legal representatives or dependants of some of the ninety-nine men who lost their lives when the submarine *Thetis* sank during tests in Liverpool Bay. The defendants were those who had built the submarine. The plaintiffs called for the disclosure of plans, specifications and other documents relating to the construction of the submarine and the First Lord of the Admiralty objected. The objection was upheld by the House of Lords. That the rule applied to a great variety of cases is shown by the decision of the Court of Appeal in *Wednesbury Corporation v. Ministry of Housing and Local Government*[90] when an objection was upheld to the disclosure of departmental briefs for the guidance of, and correspondence with, ministerial inspectors who had held a local enquiry into a proposal by the Local Government Commission that five local authorities should be extinguished and included in larger county boroughs.

As a result of these and other cases, it had come to be assumed that the affidavit of the minister concerned which claimed non-disclosure, so long as it was properly executed, could not be challenged in the courts. If he said that disclosure was not in the public interest, that was the end of the matter. But in *Conway v. Rimmer*,[91] the House of Lords held that there might be a clash between the public interest that harm should not be done to the nation or the public service by the disclosure of certain documents, and the public interest in the proper administration of justice. If this

89. [1942] AC 624.
90. [1965] 1 WLR 261.
91. [1968] AC 910. For a recent example, see *Burmah Oil Co. Ltd v. Bank of England* [1980] AC 1198.

were so the court could inspect the documents and might override the minister's claim – though if the minister's reasons were beyond the competence of the court to assess, the minister's view would have to prevail. The action in the case was brought by a former probationary police constable against his former superintendent for malicious prosecution and the documents included reports made by the defendant on the plaintiff. In the light of the later decision on the Crossman diaries, Lord Reid's comments at one point in his judgment are interesting and left no doubt where his sympathies lay in the perennial conflict between the secretiveness of governments and people's wish to know what is being done in their name:

> Virtually everyone agrees that cabinet minutes and the like ought not to be disclosed until such time as they are only of historical interest. But I do not think that many people would give as the reason that premature disclosure would prevent candour in the cabinet. To my mind the most important reason is that such disclosure would create or fan ill-informed or captious public or political criticism. The business of government is difficult enough as it is, and no government could contemplate with equanimity the inner workings of the government machine being exposed to the gaze of those ready to criticize without adequate knowledge of the background and perhaps with some axe to grind.

One result of this decision may have been that the Crown's claim to non-disclosure is less frequently made than in the past. Recent cases involving disclosures of documents held by Customs and Excise have been decided in opposite directions[92] but one decision of more public interest is disturbing. Under the Gaming Act 1968, certificates of consent have to be obtained from the Gaming Board for the running of bingo halls. R applied and the Gaming Board made certain enquiries from the police. The assistant chief constable of Sussex replied in a letter, a copy of which came into the possession of R, who laid an information against him alleging criminal libel. As a result the chief constable of Sussex and the secretary of the Gaming Board were both summoned to produce this letter. The Home Secretary objected to its disclosure. The House of Lords held

that the public interest required that the letters should not be

---

92. See *Norwich Pharmacal v. Customs & Excise* [1974] AC 133 and *A. Crompton Ltd. v. Customs & Excise (No. 2)* [1974] AC 405.

produced, since, if the information given to the Board was liable to be disclosed, it might be withheld and they would thereby be hampered in the discharge of the duty imposed on them by statute to identify and exclude persons of dubious character and reputation from the privilege of obtaining a licence to conduct a gaming establishment.

The argument of the House of Lords was based widely on the public interest, not on the particular position of the Crown. Lord Reid said: 'It must always be open to any person interested to raise the question' of the public interest and it was said that Parliament in passing the Gaming Act must have expected that the Gaming Board would be obliged to receive certain documents which no one would contemplate they had to divulge.[93] The problem in all this is, of course, that such decisions make it extremely difficult, often impossible, for a private citizen to challenge a 'confidential' report made about him by the police or other public authority. The 'proper functioning of the public service' can be bought at too high a price.

A similar reflection inevitably arises from considerations of the grounds given by Lord Denning MR for the decision of the Court of Appeal in *Home Office v. Harman* (1981).[94] Harriet Harman, a solicitor and legal officer of the National Council for Civil Liberties, was acting for a convicted prisoner in his action against the Home Office arising out of his treatment in prison in an experimental 'control unit'. She sought certain documents from the Home Office the disclosure of which was refused on the ground of public interest. But a judge ordered their disclosure. In the action brought by the prisoner against the Home Office, several of these documents were read out in court. Subsequently Ms Harman allowed a journalist to see them. The Home Office brought an action against her for contempt on the ground that documents are disclosed only for the purposes of the specific litigation and that she had no right to show them to a journalist even though they had been made public in court.

In words reminiscent of Lord Reid in *Conway v. Rimmer* (see above) Lord Denning said:

It was in the public interest that these documents should be kept confidential. They should not be exposed to the ravages of outsiders. I regard the use made by the journalists in this case of

93. *R. v. Lewes JJ ex parte Home Secretary* [1973] AC 388.
94. [1981] 2 WLR 310.

these documents to be highly detrimental to the good ordering of our society . . . The danger of disclosure is that critics – of one political colour or another – will seize on this confidential information so as to seek changes in governmental policy, or to condemn it. So the machinery of government will be hampered or even thwarted.

The Court of Appeal upheld the decision of the judge at first instance that Ms Harman was guilty of contempt. The court was obviously influenced by the fact that the journalist had used the documents to write an article condemning the Home Office for what he called 'internal bureaucratic intrigue' surrounding the setting up of the control units.

Ms Harman appealed to the House of Lords which upheld the Court of Appeal but only by the decisions of three Law Lords against two. Lord Diplock, who was joined in the majority by Lords Keith and Roskill, began with a stylistic mannerism of which some of the senior judiciary are apparently fond.[95] He insisted that the case was *not* about freedom of speech, freedom of the press, openness of justice or documents coming into 'the public domain'; nor did it call for consideration of any of those human rights and fundamental freedoms contained in the European Convention on Human Rights. To Lord Diplock the case was only about 'an aspect of the law of discovery of documents in civil actions in the High Court', and he saw discovery as 'an inroad' upon the right of the individual 'to keep his own documents to himself'. So seen, the obligation not to use a disclosed document for any purpose other than of the litigation did *not* terminate at the moment the document was read out in court. Lord Keith spoke similarly of discovery constituting 'a very serious invasion of the privacy and confidentiality of a litigant's affairs'.

Lord Scarman, joined by Lord Simon in the minority, took a broader view by reference to the European Convention and American law. And he noted that the Home Office took no steps to prevent the documents from being made public once the judge had ordered their disclosure. The Home Office had not appealed against that order or renewed their objection at the trial. So once the documents were read out in open court, in Lord Scarman's opinion, the obligation binding the litigant and his solicitor ceased.

95. [1982] 2 WLR 338; cp. Lord Wilberforce in *British Steel Corporation v. Granada Television* [1980] 3 WLR at 821: 'This case does not touch upon the freedom of the press even at its periphery.'

The majority seemed to be unmoved by the manifest absurdities of the position they took up (though Lord Roskill was more hesitant than his colleagues). The journalist could have obtained a transcript of the proceedings in court and so have had legitimate access to the documents. Moreover, only the litigant and his solicitor could be bound by the limitations imposed. Anyone could have taken a shorthand note of the documents when they were read out in court and used the information so acquired as he wished.

Two connected facts seem to have been most influential in the minds of the majority. The first was that these were government documents and governments must not be unduly embarrassed in such circumstances. And the second was the use made by the journalist in attacking the activities of a government department. None of the majority was so explicit as Lord Denning in the Court of Appeal but Lord Keith noted: 'It would be unrealistic not to recognize that (Ms Harman) must have been activated by a desire to advance some aspect of the causes espoused by the National Council for Civil Liberties, which employed her as a legal officer.' It must be very doubtful whether any action for contempt would have been brought by the Home Office had the journalist's article not been critical of the Department.

After the decision, Ms Harman, *The Guardian* newspaper and the National Council for Civil Liberties applied to the European Commission of Human Rights which has accepted the complaint against the Convention.

This conflict between the public interest in the proper administration of justice and the protection of documents from disclosure has been the subject of more and more litigation in recent years. In *Neilson v. Laugharne*[96] the plaintiff's house was searched by the police while he was on holiday on suspicion of drug offences but nothing was found. During the search the police noticed that his electricity meter appeared to have been tampered with and, on his return, he was arrested but not charged. He complained to the chief constable who instituted the complaints procedure under the Police Act 1964, which resulted in a decision that there were no grounds for proceedings against the police officers involved. The plaintiff commenced proceedings against the chief constable who refused to disclose statements made during the course of the enquiry into the complaints on the ground that they were covered

96. [1981] 2 WLR 537; and see *Hehir v. Commissioner of Police forMetropolis* [1982] 1 WLR 715.

by legal professional privilege. The Court of Appeal upheld the refusal. Lord Denning MR said, 'Legal aid is being used by complaining persons to harass innocent folk who have only been doing their duty. The complainants make all sorts of allegations – often quite unjustifiable – and then use legal machinery to try to manufacture a case. We should come down firmly against such tactics. We should refuse to order production.' Oliver LJ rested his decision on the ground that disclosures would inhibit the proper conduct of the enquiry procedure and that the public interest required that the documents should be protected as a class.

The facts in *Williams v. Home Office*[97] are set out above.[98] The prisoner sought documents from the Home Office some of which were refused on the ground that they came within the class of documents relating to the formulation of government policy and that their production would inhibit freedom of expression between Ministers and inhibit officials from giving full advice to Ministers. McNeill J ordered the disclosure of some of these documents and, citing the authority of Law Lords in an earlier case, rejected the argument about the need to preserve candour between Ministers and public servants. But in *Air Canada v. Secretary of State for Trade (No. 2)*[99] a group of airlines which wished to challenge the defendant's approval of substantial increases in landing charges at Heathrow airport were refused disclosure of documents concerned with the formulation of government policy. Three members of the House of Lords upheld this refusal on the ground that the plaintiffs had to show that the information sought was likely to help their case or damage their adversary's in the sense that there was a reasonable probability and not just a mere speculative belief that it would do so; and that the plaintiffs had failed to establish this. The other two Law Lords, while agreeing in the result, held that the court should consider disclosures whenever this was necessary for a just determination of the case.

In the Court of Appeal, Lord Denning MR had referred to *Williams v. Home Office*, and to the judge's overruling of the Department's objections to disclosure. Lord Denning said:

He thought that there was a safeguard in that they could only be used for the purpose of the action . . . His decision was claimed

97. [1981] 1 All ER 1151.
98. See p. 121.
99. [1983] 1 All ER 910; see also *Campbell v. Tameside Metropolitan BC* [1982] 3 WLR 74.

by the advocates of 'open government' to be a 'legal milestone'. But the safeguard proved to be no safeguard at all. The documents were used by a journalist to make severe criticisms of ministers and of higher civil servants who could not answer back. When this was brought to our attention, I said, 'The "legal milestone" will have to be taken up and set back a bit,' see *Home Office v. Harman*. That case is a good illustration of the need for keeping high-level documents secret. Once they are let out of the bag, untold mischief may be done. It is no use relying on safeguards. The documents must not be let out of the bag at all. I trust that today we are setting back the 'legal milestone' to the place where it was before.[100]

Many of these questions were reviewed in *British Steel Corporation v. Granada Television Ltd* (1980).[101] An employee of BSC, without the permission of BSC, supplied Granada with confidential documents, the property of BSC. These documents were used by Granada in a televised interview with the chairman of BSC. Subsequently BSC sought an order from the courts requiring Granada to tell BSC who had supplied the information. Granada argued that they should not be obliged to do so, principally because it was desirable in the public interest that press and television journalists should be entitled to protect their sources of information. In the Court of Appeal, Lord Denning MR, who with his colleagues upheld the Vice-Chancellor in ordering disclosure of the name, recognized the interest of journalists. But he found against Granada because he decided that in the circumstances they had not acted 'with a due sense of responsibility'. A majority of the Law Lords agreed with the Court of Appeal. Lord Wilberforce noted that Granada had not disputed that to supply the information was a wrongful act in law. He agreed that journalists had an interest in protecting their sources but the court had to decide, in the particular circumstances, whether that interest was outweighed by other interests to which the law attached importance. He held that BSC had suffered 'a grievous wrong' and to deny them the opportunity of a remedy against their employee would be 'a significant denial of justice'.

Lord Salmon alone dissented. He emphasized that BSC was losing large sums of taxpayers' money and that the employee considered it to be his public duty to reveal the information in the

100. [1983] 1 All ER 161.
101. [1980] 3 WLR 774.

documents. Lord Salmon thought that Granada were right to consider that they had a public duty to disclose any information which exposed the faults and mistakes of BSC. He concluded:

> There are no circumstances in this case which have ever before deprived or ever should deprive the press of its immunity against revealing its sources of information. The freedom of the press depends upon this immunity. Were it to disappear so would the sources from which its information is obtained; and the public be deprived of much of the information to which the public of a free nation is entitled.

The general attitude of the courts shown by these cases is to be strongly protective of the institutions and processes of government.[102] But to this there is one curious exception.

I have already referred obliquely to the Official Secrets Acts.[103] The principal Act was passed in 1911 with very little Parliamentary discussion. Section 1 is concerned with spying but the words are wide enough to cover lesser activities such as demonstrations in 'prohibited places'.[104] Section 2 is so wide that it has been called a catch-all section. It creates offences where almost all that needs to be proved is the unauthorized communication or receipt of official information.[105] In 1971 the section was used to prosecute the editor and a journalist of the *Sunday Telegraph* for publishing material from a report on the Nigerian civil war.[106] The defendants were acquitted after the judge, in his summing-up to the jury, had suggested that section 2 had reached retirement age and should be pensioned off.

In a recent case, when two journalists interviewed a former soldier about the operations of army intelligence seven and more years before, all three were charged under sections 1 and 2. But the judge expressed his view that the use of section 1 in a case not concerned with spying was oppressive and those charges were dropped. The accused were convicted on less serious charges under

102. In *A-G v. Lundin* (1982) 75 Cr. App. Rep. 90 a journalist who refused to reveal the source of his information (which had resulted in the exposure of illegality and corruption at Ladbroke's casinos) was found not guilty of contempt because to reveal the source would have served no useful purpose.

103. See above, pp. 116, 118.

104. *Chandler v. DPP* (see below, pp. 156–7).

105. See the report of the departmental committee on section 2 (the Franks Report) Cmnd 5104 of 1972; and Cmnd 7285 of 1978.

106. *R. v. Cairns, Aitken and Roberts*; and see J. Aitken, *Officially Secret* (1971).

section 2 but none of them was sent to prison. The whole proceedings reflected judicial dissatisfaction for prosecutions under the Official Secrets Acts.[107] Yet one is left with serious doubts whether the Court of Appeal or the House of Lords would have taken a similar view. These cases are a reminder that not all judges act the same way on all occasions.

With the decision of the House of Lords in the thalidomide case and of the Court of Appeal and the House of Lords in the *Granada* case may be contrasted that of the majority of Court of Appeal in *Schering Chemicals Ltd v. Falkman Ltd* (1981)[108] where the court upheld the granting of an injunction restraining Thames Television Ltd from showing a film about the Primodos drug used in pregnancy testing. Two actions by mothers of deformed children claiming compensation against the manufacturers were due to start some nine months later. This was not a decision on contempt of court but on whether there had been breach of confidence by the producer of the film in respect of confidential information. Shaw LJ, for the majority, said: 'The law of England was indeed, as Blackstone declared, a law of liberty; but the freedoms it recognized did not include a licence for the mercenary betrayal of business confidences.' Lord Denning MR, dissenting, said that he stood as ever for the freedom of the press, including television, except where that freedom was abused as, he said, it was in the *Granada* case. Even if there were abuse in this present case, it was not such as to warrant an injunction operating as a prior restraint.

When the Bill that became the Contempt of Court Act 1981 was being considered in the House of Lords, Lord Scarman proposed an amendment that would have permitted disclosure orders only in the interests of national security or the prevention of crime and disorder. This was not accepted but in the House of Commons a new section 10 was added which provided:

No court may require a person to disclose, nor is any person guilty of contempt of court for refusing to disclose, the source of information contained in a publication for which he is

---

107. *R. v. Aubrey, Berry and Campbell*. See Andrew Nicol, 'Official Secrets and Jury Vetting' in the *Criminal Law Review*, May 1979, p. 281. The soldier John Berry had given the information because he was disturbed at the deportation of Agee and Hosenball (see above, p. 85). This was also the case where 'Colonel B' made his appearance and where jury vetting was first, in recent times, disclosed (see above, p. 87). See Crispin Aubrey, *Who's Watching You?* (1981).

108. [1982] QBI.

responsible, unless it be established to the satisfaction of the court that disclosure is necessary in the interests of justice or national security or for the prevention of disorder of crime.

The addition of the phrase 'in the interests of justice' means that almost certainly the decision in *BSC v. Granada* is unaffected. Section 10 was considered in *Secretary of State for Defence v. Guardian Newspapers Ltd.* (1984). A copy of a 'secret' document from the Ministry of Defence was passed anonymously to the editor of the *Guardian* who published it. The Secretary of State asked for the return of the original believing that this could lead to the identification of the informant and claimed that the copyright in the document was vested in the Crown. This was an attempt to evade the effect of section 10 by basing the claim on proprietary rights. The House of Lords held that section 10 applied to all judicial proceedings but, by a majority of three to two, decided in favour of the Ministry on the ground that there was sufficient evidence to show that immediate delivery up of the copy was necessary in the interests of national security. The minority thought the evidence insufficient.[109] Had the 'proprietary rights' argument been accepted the protection given by section 10 would have been greatly diminished. But the case shows how difficult it is to overcome Crown claims of 'national security'.[110]

109. [1984] 3 WLR 986.
110. Compare *In re the Council of Civil Service Unions* (1984) above, p. 86.

5. The control of discretionary powers

The earlier cases

During the inter-war period, the courts showed little reluctance in overruling the decisions of Ministers and local authorities especially where, as in slum clearance and compulsory purchase cases, property rights were interfered with. The exercise of statutory powers was closely scrutinized and any procedural or substantive defect was generally found to be sufficient to nullify a decision. Typical of this attitude was that of Swift J in *Re Bowman*:

> When an owner of property against whom an order has been made under the Act comes into this court and complains that there has been some irregularity in the proceedings, and that he is not liable to have his property taken away, it is right, I think, that his case should be entertained sympathetically and that a statute under which he is being deprived of his rights to property should be construed strictly against the local authority and favourably towards the interest of the applicant, in as much as he for the benefit of the community is undoubtedly suffering a substantial loss, which in my view must not be inflicted upon him unless it is quite clear that Parliament has intended that it shall.[1]

Similarly in *Errington v. Minister of Health*,[2] Maugham LJ said:

> It seems to me a matter of the highest possible importance that where a quasi-judicial function is being exercised, under such circumstances as it had to be exercised here, with the result of depriving people of their property, especially if it is done without

---

1. [1932] 2 KB 621; and see *Carltona v. Commissioners of Works* [1943] 2 All ER 560, *Point of Ayr Collieries v. Lloyd George* [1943] 2 All ER 546, *Robinson v. Minister of Town and Country Planning* [1947] KB 702, *Franklin v. Minister of Town and Country Planning* [1948] AC 87.
2. [1935] 1 KB 249.

compensation, the persons concerned should be satisfied that nothing unfair has been done in the matter, and that *ex parte* statements have not been heard before the decision has been given without any chance for the persons concerned to refute those statements.

Decisions such as these show that the courts inclined to the view that in a conflict between the common law property right of an individual and the statutory powers of a local authority to interfere with those rights, the benefit of any doubt in statute was to be given to the individual – and that this was particularly so if the statute gave less than full compensation to the individual. This is, indeed, often said to be a presumption to which judges should have regard in interpretating statutes. The idea that Parliament, in this field, was 'interfering' with the common law died hard.

The changes in attitudes

But during 1939-45 and for some years after the war, there was a marked change in judicial attitudes. The classic judgment was that in *Associated Provincial Picture Theatres Ltd v. Wednesbury Corporation*[3] where Lord Greene MR indicated the strict limits on the powers of the courts to set aside an administrative decision where the public authority acted within its jurisdiction. Such an authority must act in good faith, use the powers for the purpose for which they were given, take into account relevant matters and disregard the irrelevant, and must not act in a way so unreasonable that no reasonable authority could have so acted. But it was no part of the courts' function to replace the discretionary decision of the public authority with one of its own.

The highest point in this reluctance to intervene with governmental activities was reached in the mid-1950s when the House of Lords interpreted a statutory provision, which limited the courts' jurisdiction to review a compulsory purchase order on land, so broadly that even fraud by public servants was held not to entitle the owner to bring an action.[4]

From the early 1960s, the courts reverted to their former attitude and have become increasingly willing to review govern-

3. [1948] 1 KB 223.
4. *Smith v. East Elloe RDC* [1956] AC 736.

mental activities on a variety of grounds; the reluctance of the 1940s and 1950s has disappeared. Indeed, most recently, the senior members of the judiciary seem to have become enthusiastically interventionist.

This recent approach of the courts is well exemplified in *Prest v. Secretary of State for Wales*[5] which concerned a compulsory purchase order on land required by the Welsh Water Authority for new sewage works. The land was owned by Sir Brandon Rhys Williams, described by Lord Denning MR as 'a doughty fighter . . . under attack in his own homeland . . . he and his forebears have been in those parts for over 300 years.' Sir Brandon offered one of two alternative sites which were discussed at a long public enquiry in 1977. The cost of constructing the sewage plant at one of those two alternatives sites would be £230,000 more, at the other £320,000 more, than at the site preferred by the Water Authority. Lord Denning urged the Authority not to insist on their site but to accept one of Sir Brandon's alternatives. The Court of Appeal quashed the compulsory purchase order on the ground that the Secretary of State had not properly considered the relative costs of acquiring the sites. Watkins LJ repeated the usual principle:

> The onus of showing that a compulsory purchase order has been properly confirmed rests squarely on the acquiring authority and, if he seeks to support his own decision, on the Secretary of State. The taking of a person's land against his will is a serious invasion of his proprietary rights. The use of statutory authority for the destruction of those rights requires to be most carefully scrutinized. The courts must be vigilant to see to it that authority is not abused. It must not be used unless it is clear that the Secretary of State has allowed those rights to be violated by a decision based upon the right legal principles, adequate evidence and proper consideration of the factor which sways his mind into confirmation of the order sought.

The growth of interventionism

The earlier distinction between those matters which fell within ministerial or local authority discretion and those which were within the competence of the courts to adjudicate has become increasingly

5. (1983) 81 LGR 193.

blurred. Certainly the courts today are much less reluctant to intervene in this area than they were. Thus in *Padfield v. Minister of Agriculture, Fisheries and Food*[6] milk producers from the south east asked the minister to appoint a committee of investigation, alleging that the price they were paid by the Milk Marketing Board was too low having regard to transport costs. The relevant statute empowered the minister to set up such a committee but in this case he refused to do so on the ground that the complaint was unsuitable for investigation because it raised wide issues; that if the committee upheld the complaint he would be expected to make an order to give effect to the committee's recommendations; and that the complaint should be dealt with by the Board rather than by the committee of investigation. A majority of the House of Lords found these reasons insufficient and ordered the minister to set up the committee. They agreed that he had a discretion under the statute whether or not to do so but said that he was not justified in refusing if the result was to frustrate the policy of the Act of Parliament. Lord Morris of Borth-y-Gest disagreed. In his view, the court could intervene only if the minister (a) failed or refused to apply his mind to or to consider the question whether to refer a complaint to the committee or (b) misinterpreted the law or proceeded on an erroneous view of the law or (c) based his decision on some wholly extraneous consideration or (d) failed to have regard to matters which he should have taken into account. And he held that none of these was the case.

The view taken by the majority was surprising as the decision of the minister not to intervene was clearly one of policy with which the courts are usually reluctant to interfere.[7]

The decision of the House of Lords in *Anisminic Ltd v. Foreign Compensation Commission*[8] shows how, on occasions, the courts will resist the strongest efforts of the government to exclude them from reviewing executive discretion. The Foreign Compensation Commission was empowered by statute to deal with claims to compensation under agreements with foreign governments. The plaintiffs owned property in Egypt which they

6. [1968] AC 997. Contrast *British Oxygen v. Minister of Technology* [1971] AC 610 where the House of Lords refused to interfere with a ministerial discretion about investment grants.
7. See, for example, *Bushell v. Secretary of State for the Environment* [1980] 3 WLR 22.
8. [1969] 2 AC 147.

lost at the time of the Suez crisis in 1956. The Commission made a provisional determination that the plaintiffs had failed to establish a claim according to the rules laid down under the statute. The statute provided that: 'The determination by the Commission of any application made to them under this Act shall not be called in question in any court of law.'

Despite these last words the plaintiffs applied to the courts for an order declaring that the Commission had misconstrued the rules. The House of Lords, not for the first or for the last time, held that 'determination' should not be construed as including everything which purported to be a determination but was not, and so the court was not precluded from deciding that the order of the Commission was a nullity. Looking at the way the Commission had construed the rules, the House decided that the determination was a nullity.

Lord Morris of Borth-y-Gest again dissented. He agreed that the courts could intervene if the question was whether or not the Commission had acted within its powers or its jurisdiction. But 'what is forbidden is to question the correctness of a decision or determination which it was within the area of their jurisdiction to make.'

This distinction has a long and respectable history. If an Act of Parliament says that A (who may be a minister or a commission or a local authority or an individual) shall be the person to settle certain specified questions and that there shall be neither appeal to nor review by any other body or person (including the courts), then A's decisions are unchallengeable so long as (a) it is A, not another, who decides, (b) A decides those specified questions and not others and (c) A does not act in bad faith or with similar impropriety. The *Anisminic* decision goes much further than this and says in effect that A's decision can be set aside by the courts if they disagree with his interpretation of the rules which he is required to apply. In a later case Lord Denning MR said,

So fine is the distinction that in truth the High Court has a choice before it whether to interfere with an inferior court on a point of law. If it chooses to interfere, it can formulate its decision in the words: 'The court below had no jurisdiction to decide this point wrongly as it did.' If it does not choose to interfere, it can say: 'The court had jurisdiction to decide it wrongly, and did so.' Softly be it stated, but that is the reason for the difference between the decision of the Court of Appeal in *Anisminic* . . . and the House of Lords.[9]

As Lord Diplock said in *Re Racal Communications Ltd*, 'The breakthrough made by *Anisminic* was that, as respected administrative tribunals and authorities, the old distinction between errors of law which went to jurisdiction and those which did not was for practical purposes abolished'. In *Racal* the House of Lords held that where a statute provided that the decision of a High Court judge should 'not be appealable', it could not be reviewed or appealed from.

This extreme case of judicial interference with the powers of public authorities may be contrasted with the attitude of the Court of Appeal in *Secretary of State for Employment v. ASLEF*[10] and *Others (No. 2)*.[11] The Secretary of State exercised his powers to apply to the NIRC under the Industrial Relations Act 1971 for an order requiring a ballot of trade union members to be held. This power existed where, as the statute provided, it appeared to him that there were reasons for doubting whether the trade union members, in taking part in industrial action, were acting in accordance with their own wishes. The trade union appealed against the order given by the NIRC. Lord Denning first considered how far the words 'if it appears to the Secretary of State' put his decision beyond judicial challenge. He said:

In this case I would think that, if the minister does not act in good faith, or if he acts on extraneous considerations which ought not to influence him, or if he plainly misdirects himself in fact or in law, it may well be that a court would interfere; but when he honestly takes a view of the facts or the law which could reasonably be entertained, then his decision is not to be set aside simply because thereafter someone thinks that his view was wrong . . . Of course it is to be remembered here that we are concerned with a grave threat to the national economy. The steps that are proposed do not imperil the liberty, livelihood or property of any man. The issue is simply: should a ballot be held of the railwaymen to ascertain their views?

9. *Pearlman v. Harrow School* [1978] 3 WLR 736, a decision of the Court of Appeal criticized by Lord Diplock in *Re Racal Communications Ltd* [1981] AC 374.
10. Associated Society of Locomotive Engineers and Firemen.
11. [1972] 2 QB 455. The 'others' included the other railway unions.

Lord Denning then turned to the claim that the minister had acted improperly.

> It is said that it must 'appear' to the minister that there are 'reasons' for doubting whether the workers are behind their leaders: and that the minister has given no reasons. We have been referred to several recent cases, of which *Padfield v. Minister of Agriculture, Fisheries and Food* is the best example, in which the courts have stressed that in the ordinary way a minister should give reasons, and if he gives none the court may infer that he had no good reasons. Whilst I would apply that proposition completely in most cases, and particularly in cases which affect life, liberty or property, I do not think that it applies in all cases.

Lord Denning concluded that the proposition did not apply in this case and that there were reasons which a reasonable minister could entertain and so there was no ground on which the court could interfere with the minister's decision to ask for a ballot order. He was supported by the other members of the Court of Appeal. In the event the union leaders were wholly justified, as the result of the ballot showed, in their claim that there were no reasons for doubting that the industrial action was in accordance with the wishes of the workers.

Two cases exemplify greater willingness of the courts to control ministerial discretion. In *Secretary of State for Education and Science v. Tameside Metropolitan Borough Council*[12] the minister acted under section 68 of the Education Act 1944 which provided:

> If the Secretary of State is satisfied . . . that any local education authority . . . have acted or are proposing to act unreasonably . . . he may . . . give such directions . . . as appear to him to be expedient.

In March 1975 the Labour-controlled Tameside Council put forward proposals to the Secretary of State for the reorganization of secondary education along comprehensive lines to come into effect in September 1976. The proposals were approved in November 1975. The council made many of the necessary arrangements for the changeover and told pupils which schools they would be going to.

At the local elections in May 1976, the Conservatives won control

12. [1976] 3 WLR 641.

of the council and on 7 June told the Secretary of State that they proposed not to implement the plans for the conversion of the five grammar schools into comprehensives and sixth-form colleges. On 11 June the Secretary of State gave the council a direction under section 68, requiring them to implement their predecessors' plans, and on 18 June the Divisional Court ordered the council to comply. On 26 July the Court of Appeal overruled the Divisional Court and on 2 August, moving with impressive speed, Lords Wilberforce, Diplock, Salmon, Russell and Dilhorne upheld the Court of Appeal.

The basis of their Lordships' decisions was that the minister could give a valid direction only if he was satisfied that no reasonable local authority could have decided as the Conservative majority did; and that he could not have been so satisfied.

The second case was that of Laker Airways. Under the Civil Aviation Act 1971, the Civil Aviation Authority was empowered to grant licences to those wishing to operate air transport lines. The Authority granted a licence to Mr Freddy Laker for the period from 1973 to 1982 to operate a cheap passenger service known as 'Skytrain' between the United Kingdom and the USA. The Conservative government supported the project but in February 1976 the Labour government (which had previously supported Mr Laker), through its Secretary of State for Trade in a White Paper, announced a change of civil aviation policy.

The Act of 1971 empowered the Secretary of State to 'give guidance' to the Authority with respect to their statutory functions. The White Paper purported to contain such guidance which, in accordance with the Act, was approved by a resolution of each House of Parliament. The crucial phrase in the White Paper guidance was that the Authority should not license more than one British airline to serve the same route, with British Airways as the preferred airline to the USA. That prevented Skytrain from coming into operation.

The Court of Appeal held that the power of the Secretary of State to give guidance to the Authority did not extend to such a discretion. Said Lord Denning MR:

> 'Guidance' could only be used to explain, amplify or supplement the general objectives or provisions of the Act. If the Secretary of State went beyond the bounds of 'guidance' he exceeded his powers; and the Civil Aviation Authority was under no obligation to obey him.

So Mr Laker succeeded in his action.[13]

These two cases while comparable are also dissimilar. In both cases two public authorities were in conflict. In *Laker's* case the minister was seeking to require the Civil Aviation Authority to follow his policy but he chose a way of doing this which the Court of Appeal considered not to be within his powers. In *Tameside* the central department and the local authority were in direct conflict over a matter of administrative feasibility. The minister did not believe that Tameside Council could properly implement the change within the limited time available.

The decision in *Tameside* may be contrasted with *ASLEF (No. 2)*[14] where the trade union's complaint that the minister had no reason to believe that the members were not behind their leaders was not supported by the court. In *Tameside* the minister had sound administrative reasons for believing that the local authority was acting unreasonably but it was held that merely to have such reasons was insufficient. A remarkable feature of this decision of the House of Lords was that it was based on almost no judicial authority at all. One of their Lordships referred to *ASLEF (No. 2)*, and to one other decision. The other three referred to none. Yet this is hardly an area where judicial pronouncements have been lacking. It concerns the whole matter of judicial control over ministerial discretion.

Professor de Smith[15] wrote that Parliament might purport to restrict judicial review by conferring powers in subjective terms, the public authority being entitled to act when it 'is satisfied' or when 'it appears' to it that, or when 'in its opinion', a prescribed state of affairs exists. Then the courts interpret such phrases so as to give themselves more or less control as they wish. This depends on the judges' views of the merits of the case before them or (I would add) the direction their political inclinations lead them – what I call below their 'view of the public interest'.[16] If trade unions are being restricted by ministerial action (as in *ASLEF [No. 2]*) then statutory limitations on ministers' powers will be interpreted loosely. If ministers appear to the courts to be acting in a way which is arbitrary or unfair (as in *Padfield* and *Tameside* and *Laker*) then the limitations will be insisted on. Little attempt is made to treat like situations in a like manner or to act consistently within a framework of judicial analysis. And one is often left with a feeling

13. *Laker Airways Ltd v. Department of Trade* [1977] 2 WLR 234.
14. See above, p. 134.
15. *Judicial Review of Administrative Action* (3rd edn, pp. 318-20).
16. See chapter 9, below.

that in this area of the law judges rely almost entirely on their own sense of justice or on their own personal conception of what is best.

Another case in which the courts appeared to be in conflict with ministers was *Gouriet v. Union of Post Office Workers*,[17] in which the plaintiff sought an order from the court to restrain the defendant trade union from breaking the law by refusing to handle mail to South Africa. Usually, a person, like the plaintiff, who suffers no special damage from a breach of the law, must ask the Attorney-General either to institute proceedings or to give his consent (in a relator action) to the plaintiff's proceeding. In this case the Attorney-General refused to do either. One question that arose in the Court of Appeal was whether this decision was subject to judicial review. Lord Denning said:

> The Attorney-General tells us that when he refuses his consent, his refusal is final. It cannot be overridden by the courts. He is answerable to Parliament, and to Parliament alone. He declines even to give his reasons for his refusal. This is, to my mind, a direct challenge to the rule of law . . . Suppose that he refused his consent for corrupt motives, or in bad faith . . . or for party-political reasons, and not in the interests of the public at large . . . or because he considered that the information was laid by a pressure group, of which he disapproved . . . These instances are, of course, entirely hypothetical. I would not suggest for one moment that they existed here. But the possibility of them convinces me that his discretion to refuse is not absolute or unfettered. It can be reviewed by the courts. If he takes into account matters which he ought not to take into account, or fails to take into account the matters which he ought to take into account, then his decision can be overridden by the courts. Not directly, but indirectly. If he misdirects himself in coming to his decision, the court can say: 'Very well then. If you do not give your consent, or your reasons, we will hear the complaint of this citizen without it.'

But in this Lord Denning was in a minority, both the other Lord Justices (Lawton and Ormrod) holding that the Attorney-General's exercise of his discretion to refuse his consent to the bringing of relator proceedings in his name could not be reviewed or questioned by the courts.

17. [1977] 2 WLR 310 (CA); [1978] AC 435 (HL).

In the House of Lords Lord Wilberforce said:

The distinction between public rights, which the Attorney can and the individual (absent special interest) cannot, seek to enforce, and private rights is fundamental in our law. To break it, as Mr Gouriet's counsel invited their Lordships to do, was not a development of the law, but a destruction of one of its pillars.

So Mr Gouriet could not bring his action, the Attorney-General being the only person entitled to represent the public in a court of justice.

Clauses seeking to exclude the court's jurisdiction are sometimes accompanied by provisions which entitle an aggrieved person, on limited grounds, to apply to the High Court for an order which would quash the decision made by the public authority. This application is required to be made within six weeks of the decision. The reason for the short period is that the decision – particularly to acquire land compulsorily – should not be capable of being reversed except immediately. *Smith v. East Elloe RDC* (see above, p. 130) fell within this provision and some doubt was thrown on this decision by that in *Anisminic*. But in *R. v. Environmental Secretary ex parte Ostler*[18] the Court of Appeal held that the strict rule still applied.

In *Ostler* the aggrieved person was a corn merchant who discovered too late, but without any failure on his part, that a secret agreement about a road scheme had been arrived at under which two local companies withdrew objections to the scheme on being given a 'guarantee' by an official of the government department concerned that the scheme would be amended subsequently – with the result that the merchant's premises and business would be injuriously affected. Because the agreement was secret, the merchant failed to object within six weeks. The court was told that 80 per cent of the land had been acquired and 90 per cent of the buildings had been demolished. Said Lord Denning MR: 'It would be contrary to the public interest that the demolition should be held up or delayed by further evidence or enquiries.' Ostler failed in his action.

These decisions in *East Elloe* and *Ostler* operated harshly against the individual but the courts are caught in a dilemma not of their own making. Clearly, decisions taken by public authorities which will result in public works, such as building houses or improving

18. [1976] 23 WLR 288.

roads, cannot be capable of being reversed after a period of years. So the period for challenge is short. But under the present law it is often impossible for the courts to give damages to an individual who has suffered irreversible loss in these circumstances. The remedy for that lies with Parliament.

The extent to which the senior judiciary now considers itself entitled to control administrative authorities is shown by Lord Diplock's speech in *O'Reilly v. Mackman* (1982).[19] The decision dealt with the procedure for seeking remedies for the infringement of rights protected by public law, the facts being concerned with the rights of prisoners to challenge the findings of disciplinary boards of visitors. Lord Diplock found that the development of judicial control began in recent times with the 'rediscovery' in *R. v. Northumberland Compensation Appeal Tribunal ex parte Shaw*[20] of the power of the High Court to review a decision where it was apparent upon the face of the written determination of the administrative authority that it had made a mistake as to the applicable law. When the Tribunals and Inquiries Act 1958 required tribunals to give reasons, this principle was enlarged in application. Then came the *Anisminic* case which, according to Lord Diplock, 'liberated English public law from the fetters that the courts had theretofore imposed upon themselves . . . by drawing esoteric distinctions between errors of law committed by such tribunals that went to their jurisdiction and errors of law committed by them within jurisdiction.' So also *Ridge v. Baldwin* destroyed the relevance of arguments drawing subtle distinctions between decisions that were quasi-judicial and those that were administrative. Another landmark decision was *Padfield*[21] which enabled Lord Diplock to claim, with a degree of comprehensive certainty that would astonish anyone with any knowledge of continental legal systems, that by 1977 we had 'a developed system of administrative law'. This was the date when the present simplified procedure for judicial review was introduced.

As a consequence of government policy, many of the challenges to the exercise of ministerial discretion in recent years have been instituted by Labour local authorities. These have been largely unsuccessful. In *ex parte Norwich City Council*,[22] the local authority

19. [1982] 3 WLR 1096.
20. [1952] 1 KB 338.
21. For these three cases see pp. 132–3, 163–4.
22. *Secretary of State for the Environment ex parte Norwich City Council* [1982] 2 WLR 580.

were not proceeding with the sale of council houses as expeditiously as the minister wished. Under the Housing Act 1980 he was empowered to 'do all such things as appear to him necessary or expedient' to enable tenants 'to exercise the right to buy'. The minister decided to use his powers of intervention. He was upheld by the Court of Appeal. Given the statutory provisions, it is difficult to see how the court could have decided otherwise.

The introduction of the new block grant system for local authorities under the Local Government, Planning and Land Act 1980 resulted in one hiccough for the minister when the Divisional Court held that he had not listened to further representations when he should have done.[23] This decision is in line with those, like *Padfield*,[24] where the courts have been willing to limit ministerial discretion on various grounds, some of them relatively new at least in their present application. In *Ridge v. Baldwin* (1964)[25] the requirement of 'fairness' in administration received a broader interpretation and now the principle was beginning to be accepted that not to listen to representations might amount to a voluntary and improper fettering of ministerial discretion.[26] Attempts in the Court of Appeal to set aside ministerial decisions on other aspects of the new block grant on more technical and precise grounds failed.[27] The lesson seems to be that a plaintiff has a better chance of attacking the exercise of ministerial power if he can show that in some general way, especially procedural and not substantive, the minister has not played the game according to the newly enlarged rules of natural justice.

Hackney LBC tried another line of attack which was repulsed when the Divisional Court held that there was no requirement for the Secretary of State when issuing guidance to a local authority as to the level of its expenditure to have regard to whether or not the authority would by restricting its expenditure in such a way render itself unable reasonably to discharge any of its statutory duties.[28]

23. *R. v. Secretary of State for the Environment ex parte Brent LBC* [1982] 2 WLR 693.

24. See above, p. 132.

25. [1964] AC 49

26. *R. v. Secretary of State for the Environment and Cheshire County Council ex parte Halton BC* [1984] JPL 97.

27 . *R. v. Secretary of State for the Environment ex parte Hackney LBC and Camden LBC* [1984] 1 All ER 956.

28. *R. v. Secretary of State for the Environment ex parte Hackney LBC, The Times*, 26 March 1984.

The decision in *Lambeth LBC v. Secretary of State for Social Services*[29] where Woolf J struck down the minister's decision to use his statutory powers to suspend the members of an area health authority and to appoint commissioners in their place was strongly interventionist. The power of the minister arises under the National Health Service Act 1977 if he considers that by reason of an emergency it is necessary for a specified period to transfer functions from one body to another. The disagreement between the minister and the area health authority was caused by the overspending by the authority and its unwillingness to make economies. The court held that such a power could not be used, where there was no particular crisis and no specified power, so as to control the authority's financial affairs. The minister had a separate power, which he did not use, to issue directions to the authority. Woolf J referred to the *Tameside* decision[30] and to *ASLEF (No. 2)*.[31] 'There can be no question', he said, 'of my substituting my view of the facts for that of the Secretary of State.' He seems nevertheless to have come very close to substituting his view of the statutory power and the discretions within it for that of the minister.

Mr Louis Blom-Cooper QC, appeared for the applicants in that case. He has told us that the minister relied on the legal advice from within the Department when he issued his directive to the area health authority and put in the commissioners. 'Long, and refreshingly frank, affidavits were addressed in evidence which revealed the faulty advice given to the minister. The drafters of the affidavits had forgotten the lesson that the mother whale gave to her offspring: "It is only when you begin to spout that you get harpooned!"'[32]

The Fares Fair litigation

The decision of the House of Lords in *R. v. Greater London Council ex parte Bromley London Borough Council* (1981),[33] confirming that of the Court of Appeal, has been widely regarded as a political

29. (1981) 79 LGR 61.
30. See p. 135–6.
31. See p. 134–5.
32. 'Lawyers and Public Administration' in [1984] *Public Law*, pp. 225–6. The decision in this case was given on 25 February 1980. On 20 March 1980 the National Health Service (Invalid Direction) Act 1980 was enacted to reverse the decision.
33. [1983] 1 AC 768.

decision, no doubt because it gave a ruling in an acutely political controversy. Both the ruling itself and the judicial reasoning adopted by the Court of Appeal and the House of Lords exemplify what is meant by the politics of the judiciary. The case is of great importance and interest because it illuminates the weaknesses inherent in the role of the judiciary when required to adjudicate in such matters.

In July 1981, the GLC passed a resolution implementing a commitment in the election manifesto of the Labour Party to reduce fares charged by the London Transport Executive (LTE) by 25 per cent and to meet this cost (some £69m) issued a supplementary precept for rates of 6.1p in the £ to all London boroughs. In addition this policy resulted in the GLC losing some £50m of rate support grant from the government. Bromley London Borough Council applied to .the High Court to quash the supplementary rate as ultra vires.

Under the Transport (London) Act 1969, the GLC was placed (by section 1) under the general duty to develop policies, and to encourage, organize and, where appropriate, to carry out measures, which would promote the provision of integrated, efficient and economic transport facilities and services for Greater London. The LTE consisted of persons appointed by the GLC with the function of implementing the policies of the GLC (section 4). The GLC was empowered by the Act to make grants to the LTE for any purpose (section 3) and the GLC intended in this way to reimburse the LTE for the revenue lost by the fares reduction and so enable the LTE to balance its books, this being an obligation placed on the LTE 'so far as practicable'. Subject to that obligation, the LTE was under a duty to exercise and perform its functions, in accordance with principles laid down or approved by the GLC, in such manner as, and with due regard to efficiency, economy and safety of operation, to provide or secure the provision of such public passenger transport services as best met the needs for the time being of Greater London (section 5). If the LTE accounts showed a deficit, the GLC was required to take such action as appeared necessary and appropriate to enable the LTE to balance its books (section 7(6)). Additionally, the GLC was empowered to give the LTE general directions, and the approval of the GLC was required for the general level and structure of fares to be charged by the LTE (section 11).

The Divisional Court of the Queen's Bench Division which first heard the action refused Bromley's application but the Court of

Appeal and the House of Lords upheld it and quashed the precept and so the scheme.

The five Law Lords were Wilberforce, Diplock, Keith, Scarman, and Brandon. All agreed that the GLC's power to make grants to the LTE included a large degree of discretion to supplement revenue received by the LTE from fares, including anticipated or prospective revenue deficits. But they put limitations on this discretion. All except Lord Diplock founded their decision on the ground that the LTE was under a general duty to run its operations on ordinary business principles and that this had been breached by the reduction of fares without regard to those principles. All except Lord Diplock (and in this he positively disagreed) held that the GLC had to have regard, when making a grant, to the LTE's obligation to run its operations so far as practicable, on a break-even basis; so the GLC could make grants to the LTE only to make good unavoidable losses and not to further a particular social policy. All except Lord Keith also held that the GLC was under a fiduciary duty to its ratepayers which they had breached by the scheme, Lord Diplock particularly emphasizing the loss of rate support grant, and that they had acted thriftlessly.

Much argument centred on the proper meanings to be attached to particular words such as 'economic' and on the recent history of transport legislation. But the concept of the fiduciary duty said to be owed by the GLC to its ratepayers was most widely emphasized by their Lordships. It is a judge-made concept and wholly imprecise. Lord Scarman, for example, rejected the GLC's interpretation of the 1969 Act on the ground that it 'would make mincemeat of the fiduciary duty owed to the ratepayers'. If Parliament had intended to depart from the break-even basis, he argued, this would have been enacted expressly in Part 1 of the Act where the general duties of the policy-maker, the GLC, were set; and added: 'But section 1(1) says nothing to suggest the exclusion of the fiduciary duty to the ratepayers.' The answer is, of course, that 'Parliament' never thought about the fiduciary duty at all. And this for the very good reason that the only relevant decision on the fiduciary duty – *Prescott v. Birmingham*[34] – had been immediately negatived by Parliament[35] in its application to the power of local transport authorities to fix the level of fares.

The doctrine of the fiduciary duty, being judge-made, is capable

34. [1955] Ch. 210.
35. By Public Service Vehicles (Travel Concessions) Act 1955.

of extended application as the courts please. In this case, the Law Lords chose to say that the GLC had not adequately taken into account the interests of the ratepayers and that the interests of the users of public transport had been unduly preferred.[36] Such an argument can logically be applied whenever public authorities spend the ratepayers' (or the taxpayers') money to further some statutory purpose. Particular public expenditure can always be criticized on the ground that it is excessive or wrongly directed, whether on defence or education or the building of motorways or any other public service. The constitutional reply is that public authorities, being directly or indirectly elected, are the representatives of the public interest and that their function is precisely that of making such decisions. The criticism is then seen as being political and if the electors of Greater London disapprove of what is done in their name by their representatives, the remedy lies in their hands at the next election. Nor is this merely constitutional or political theory, divorced from reality, for without doubt the election in 1985 for the GLC would have turned very largely on this issue and on the view taken of the controversial Labour administration at County Hall during its four years in office. It is surely no more the function of the judiciary to tell the GLC where the public interest lay in its spending of public money than it is the function of the judiciary to make similar judgments about spending by the Departments of the central government. The application of the doctrine of the fiduciary duty in this case was gross interference by the judiciary in the exercise of political responsibility of an elected local authority.

There remains, however, the much more substantial argument that the GLC had exceeded its statutory powers as laid down in the Transport (London) Act 1969.

We may take Lord Wilberforce's argument as typical of the Lords' approach. He emphasized sections 5 and 7 as 'critical'. Section 5 provided that, subject always to section 7(3), it was the general duty of the LTE to exercise and perform their functions with due regard to efficiency, economy and safety of operation. He said that those last three sets of words 'point rather more clearly than does section 1 in the direction of running on business-like or commercial lines'. And, he said, the word 'economy' prevented the LTE from conducting its undertakings on other than economic

---

36. Cx. *Pickwell v. Camden LBC* [1983] 1 All ER 602 (see below, p. 221); *R. v. Greenwich BC ex parte Cedar Transport*, *The Times*, 3 August 1983.

considerations. He called the initial words of section 5 important as drawing attention to the 'paramount' financing provisions of section 7(3).

This section 7(3) required the LTE so to perform their functions as to ensure so far as practicable that at the end of each accounting period the aggregate of the net balance of the consolidated revenue account of the LTE and of their general reserve was such as might be approved by the GLC; and that if, at the end of any accounting period, the aggregate showed a deficit, the amount properly available to meet changes to revenue account in the next following accounting period should exceed those charges by at least the amount of that deficit. In order words the LTE was to balance its books taking one year with the next. Further, under section 7(6), the GLC was required to have regard to section 7(3) and, where there was a deficit, the GLC was to take such action as appeared to the GLC necessary and appropriate to enable the LTE to comply with the requirements of section 7(3). As Lord Wilberforce said, the GLC might direct fares to be raised or services to be adjusted; or might make a grant to the LTE. Lord Wilberforce read this as meaning that the GLC could not exercise its powers 'unless and until' the LTE had carried out its duty. 'It appears to me clear', he said, 'that neither the LTE in making its proposals, nor the GLC in accepting them, could have power totally to disregard any responsibility for ensuring, so far as practicable, that outgoings are met by revenue, and that the LTE runs its business on economic lines.'

The alternative view is that 'revenue account' did not mean internally generated revenue only but included GLC grants. This is reinforced if the intention of Parliament in passing the Act was that deficits on internally generated revenue would most likely be incurred, not merely casually, but deliberately as a consequence of treating transport as a social service. This view argued that section 7 was meant as an accounting section only and contained only a prohibition against annual accumulated deficits. The GLC was meant to be the dominant authority (see section 1), with the LTE as its instrument, and the power of the GLC to make grants to the LTE 'for any purpose' was strong evidence of this.

Lord Wilberforce answered this alternative view in these words:

There is indeed, and has been for some years, discussion on the political level as to whether, and to what extent, public transport, particularly in capital cities, should be regarded, and financed, as a social service, out of taxation whether national or local. We cannot take any position in this argument; we must recognize that it exists. But I am unable to see, however carefully I re-read the 1969 Act, that Parliament had in that year taken any clear stance on it.

The other Law Lords (Lord Diplock excepted) also placed great reliance on section 7(3) and correspondingly less on sections 1 and 3.

Before we discuss this decision further, there is an aftermath to consider. The Law Lords' speeches in *Bromley* were delivered on 17 December 1981. Almost immediately commercial ratepayers on Merseyside sought to quash a similar scheme. Following the May 1981 elections, the new Labour majority on Merseyside County Council set about implementing its own manifesto which had promised no reduction in transport services but a reduction in fares. The precept required an additional supplementary rate of 6p in the £. The Merseyside authorities operated under the Transport Act 1968 which, though similar, was not the same in its provisions as the Transport (London) Act 1969. Thus the County Council as Transport Authority and its subordinate, the Transport Executive, had to have regard to the promotion of 'a properly integrated and efficient system of public transport to meet the needs of that area with due regard to the town planning and traffic and parking policies' of the other councils. Also the Transport Authority was expressly empowered to require the Executive to provide a service at a cost the Executive considered to be too high, so long as the Transport Authority provided the necessary additional cost. Woolf J also found that the Authority had properly considered the interest of the ratepayers and that the financial duties were not overriding. Further, there was no automatic loss of rate support grant as a result of introducing the scheme. On these and other grounds the judge distinguished *Bromley v. GLC*.

As a result of the decision in *Bromley v. GLC* the fares were doubled and Camden London Borough contemplated taking legal proceedings to challenge their validity. Legal advice from learned leading counsel on both sides was contradictory, and at one stage the Attorney-General advised the Minister of Transport that if the GLC should adopt a certain budgetary policy he thought the courts would accept it. He then made this advice public, thus instituting a free legal aid service of a novel kind.

The reality was that the decision in *Bromley v. GLC* was one which no one wished to be bound by. It seemed to suggest that the GLC and the LTE must try to break even, a course which was certainly feasible if fares were sufficiently increased and services sufficiently reduced, but which was politically as unacceptable to the government as it was anathema to the GLC.[37]

The GLC, bloody but unbowed, next produced a new scheme. This directed the LTE to reduce fares by 25 per cent and involved a grant to be made to the LTE to meet the resulting deficit on revenue account. The LTE objected to the direction on the ground that it failed to have regard to the LTE's financial duty under section 7(3) to break even so far as is practicable.[38]

Kerr LJ said that some of the public comments on *Bromley v. GLC* gave the misleading impression that the judgments in the Court of Appeal and the House of Lords were designed to thwart the wishes of the majority on the GLC for political motives. 'Such reactions,' he said, 'whether based on ignorance or whatever, can only be described as utter rubbish . . . It is to be hoped that nothing like that will happen again.'

All three judges in the Divisional Court (the others were Glidewell J and Nolan J) found the speeches of the Law Lords in *Bromley v. GLC* not easy to understand and impossible to reduce to agreed principles. As Mr George Cunningham MP said in the House of Commons on 22 December 1981, referring to those speeches:

Each of the five judgments rambles over the territory in what can only be called a head-scratching way, making it impossible for the consumer of the judgment to know at the end just what the law is held to be, except negatively, and then only negatively on a few points. When one puts the five judgments together, the effect is chaos.[39]

The Divisional Court upheld the scheme adopted by the GLC but the ground on which they did so seemed to be no more than that 'since the LTE could exercise its function to balance its revenue account by a grant from the GLC, a policy that reduced fares by means of such a grant was not unlawful'. Those words are taken from the headnote in the Law Reports and seem a fair if wholly

37. In order to enable the GLC to finance concessionary fares out of transport funds, the Travel Concessions (London) Act 1982 had to be passed very rapidly.
38. *R. v. LTE ex parte GLC* [1983] 1 QB 484.
39. 15 HC Deb. col. 905.

circular summary. To this was added the proviso that the GLC had not acted arbitrarily and had considered both its duties to the ratepayers and the statutory duties imposed by the 1969 Act on it and on the LTE.[40] This reinforces the view that what upset the Court of Appeal and the House of Lords in *Bromley v. GLC* was, above all, the way in which the Labour majority went about implementing their election promises rather than their statutory powers to do so. Local authorities would be well advised in future to preface all their decisions with the words: 'Having had regard to all relevant matters and having disregarded all irrelevant matters, and having considered the interests of all those likely to be affected, *resolved that*' etc.

When all this has been said, it is still very difficult to see how the Divisional Court in *R. v. LTE ex parte GLC* managed to come down in favour of the GLC in the face of the unanimous decision of the Law Lords. That decision was based primarily not on procedural defects but on interpretations of the words of the statute and on the notion of the fiduciary duty. The new scheme, upheld by the Divisional Court in the later case, was made under the same statute and did not appreciably hold a different balance between ratepayers and transport users. The decision of the Divisional Court bears the marks of a rescue operation, seeking to save some sanity for transport policy in London and for the right of statutory authorities to exercise statutory powers within the statutory terms given to them.

40. See now Transport Act 1983.

6. The uses of conspiracy

Introduction

I have already noted the importance of the crime and the tort of conspiracy in relation to trade unions, particularly in the late nineteenth and early twentieth centuries. More recently, criminal conspiracy has acquired a new significance in other fields.

The essence of the crime of conspiracy at common law is an agreement between two or more persons to commit an unlawful act. The crime is the agreement and its execution or non-execution is irrelevant. Moreover the agreement may be inferred: 'A nod or a wink may amount to conspiracy.' But also it is not necessary that the conspirators should ever have met or known each other so long as there was evidence that they were acting in concert. Men may be selected at random from an extensive picket or well-known individuals selected out of thousands who are demonstrating.[1] A single person may be charged with conspiracy 'with persons unknown'.

Moreover the unlawfulness of the act which the conspirators agree to commit is not limited to criminal acts. It extends widely to civil wrongs also, such as trespass on property and beyond that to an ill-defined area where it seems sufficient that the act is immoral or even a matter of public concern.[2] It follows therefore that a person may be convicted of conspiracy to commit an act for which he could not be prosecuted if he acted alone. The charge of conspiracy may also be used to avoid the necessity of some procedural requirement which attaches to the substantive act. Thus for some crimes – such as prosecutions under the Official Secrets Acts – the leave of the Attorney-General must be obtained.

1. See generally Geoff Robertson, *Whose Conspiracy*? (NCCL, 1974); Robert Hazell, *Conspiracy and Civil Liberties* (Occasional Papers on Social Administration, 1974).
2. See below pp. 152–6. This vagueness means that the definition of the crime is for the court to determine.

But conspiracy to commit an offence under those Acts does not require leave. Again, proceedings for certain specific offences – for example under the Obscene Publications Act 1959 – may be prohibited by statute but the prohibition does not cover conspiracy to commit those offences.

For various technical reasons, the rules of evidence apply much less strictly to proof of conspiracy, and it is common for prosecutors to add a charge of conspiracy to charges on the connected substantive offences. This enables the prosecution to indulge in 'plea bargaining', that is, in offering to drop the conspiracy charge if the accused will plead guilty to one or more of the substantive charges. Judges have objected to the adding of the conspiracy charges but in the case of the Shrewsbury pickets the Court of Appeal advanced a dangerous and prejudicial view. 'It is not desirable', said Lord Justice James, 'to include a charge of conspiracy which adds nothing to an effective charge of a substantive offence. But where charges of substantive offences do not adequately represent *the overall criminality* it may be appropriate and right to include a charge of conspiracy.'[3] But how can this notion of 'the overall criminality' be determined?

As has been said, 'a conspiracy count puts the whole lifestyle of the accused on trial'[4] and this can very easily and adversely affect the minds of the jury with matters which are irrelevant to the charges.

Finally, and importantly, the penalties for conspiracy are in effect unlimited. The substantive offence may carry a maximum penalty of a few months' imprisonment. But if the accused is convicted of conspiracy to commit that offence he may be sentenced to many years' imprisonment. Trade unionists in the nineteenth century were frequently punished in this way. And most recently there has been a revival of the charge of conspiracy to intimidate so that one of the convicted Shrewsbury pickets was sentenced to three years' imprisonment on that charge whereas the maximum penalty for intimidation itself was three months.

The decision whether to prosecute, and if so on what charges, is normally a matter for the police or the Director of Public Prosecutions. In this sense the use of conspiracy in recent years is not the responsibility of the judges. But the extent of their willingness to encourage the development of the common law in this area is strongly influential on decisions about prosecutions and in the success of prosecutions, so we must consider what has been

3. *R. v. Jones* [1974] ICR 310 (my italics).
4. Robertson, *op.cit.*, p. 42.

their attitude to the political and social aspects of this crime.

The Criminal Law Act 1977 created a *statutory* offence of conspiracy limited to agreements to commit criminal offences and also provided that the penalty for such conspiracy should be related to the penalty for those criminal offences. The Act abolished the offence of conspiracy at common law except for conduct which tended to corrupt public morals or to outrage public decency but which would not be an offence if carried out by a single person otherwise than in pursuance of an agreement.

Moral behaviour

The Street Offences Act 1959 made it an offence, punishable by fine and, after more than one previous conviction, by imprisonment, for a prostitute to loiter or solicit in a street or public place for the purposes of prostitution. The effect of this statute was to prevent prostitutes soliciting in public. The accused published a booklet, the *Ladies Directory*, in which prostitutes inserted advertisements which they paid for. He was charged with, first, conspiracy to corrupt public morals; secondly, living on the earnings of prostitution; and thirdly, publishing an obscene article. His conviction on all three counts was upheld by the House of Lords.

With one dissentient the Law Lords held, against the vigorous denial by counsel for the accused, that there was an offence known to the common law of conspiracy to corrupt public morals. Viscount Simonds said:

I entertain no doubt that there remains in the courts of law a residual power to enforce the supreme and fundamental purpose of the law, to conserve not only the safety and order but also the moral welfare of the State, and that it is their duty to guard it against attacks which may be the more insidious because they are novel and unprepared for. That is the broad head (call it public policy if you wish) within which the present indictment falls. It matters little what label is given to the offending act. To one of your Lordships it may appear an affront to public decency, to another considering that it may succeed in its obvious intention of provoking libidinous desires, it will seem a corruption of public morals. Yet others may deem it aptly described as the creation of a public mischief or the undermining of public conduct. The same act will not in all ages be regarded in the same way. The law must be related to the changing standards of life, not yielding to every shifting impulse of the popular will but having regard to fundamental assessments of human values and the purposes of society. Today a denial of the fundamental Christian doctrine, which in past centuries would have been regarded by the ecclesiastical courts as heresy and by the common law as blasphemy, will no longer be an offence if the decencies of controversy are observed. When Lord Mansfield, speaking long after the Star Chamber had been abolished, said that the Court of King's Bench was the *custos morum* of the people and had the superintendency of offences *contra bonos mores*, he was asserting, as I now assert, that there is in that court a residual power, where no statute has yet intervened to supersede the common law, to superintend those offences which are prejudicial to the public welfare.[5]

This now famous statement was not universally applauded, many of those who disliked it being of the opinion that Law Lords were not necessarily the most appropriate persons to prescribe codes of moral behaviour (and to make them into rules of law also) for the rest of the community. Lord Reid's djssent was based on an examination of the history of criminal conspiracy (from its origins in the Star Chamber) and on 'the broad general principles which have generally been thought to underlie our system of law and government and in particular our system of criminal law'. He concluded that there was 'no such general offence known to the law as conspiracy to corrupt morals'.

The judgments in the House of Lords were delivered on 4 May 1961. No further prosecutions for conspiracy to corrupt morals were brought until 1965·in which year seventy-seven persons were convicted and this was followed in 1966 by a further forty-five convictions. In 1972, the Lord Chancellor said that most of the thirty-two cases (involving 134 individual convictions) between 1961 and 1971 were for 'blue' films which could not be proceeded against for obscenity unless shown in a private home.[6] So the conspiracy charge was used.

In 1971 three editors of *Oz* were charged with conspiracy to corrupt public morals by producing a magazine containing obscene articles, cartoons, drawings and illustrations; and with contra-

5. *Shaw v. DPP* [1961] 2 WLR 897.
6. See 333 HL Deb. col. 1569; and 839 HC Deb. col 263-4, 427-8. See also *The Law Commission*, Working Paper no. 57, pp. 35-9.

vening the Obscene Publications Act 1964 and the Post Office Act 1953. On the conspiracy charge the jury acquitted them, not being satisfied that they intended to corrupt public morals. On other charges they were convicted and sentenced to imprisonment of fifteen, twelve and nine months. On appeal these convictions were quashed except for that relating to the Post Office Act the sentence for which was automatically suspended. The appeals succeeded because it was held that the judge had misdirected the jury about the meaning of obscene in the Obscene Publications Act.[7] It was particularly in relation to this case that Mr Robertson drew attention, as I have already mentioned,[8] to the fact that the addition of a conspiracy charge enables the whole lifestyle of the accused to be brought before the court and the jury so that the case becomes politically charged in the sense that the accused can be subjected by prosecution counsel to such allegations as advocating dropping out of society, living off the state, and regarding sex as something to be worshipped for itself.

The next year saw the prosecution of another magazine, *International Times*. Three directors were convicted of conspiracy (1) to corrupt public morals and (2) to outrage public decency, because they had published advertisements inviting readers to meet the advertisers for the purpose of homosexual practices. The House of Lords (with one dissentient) upheld the convictions on the first count, on the grounds either that the *Shaw* case was rightly decided, or that even if it were wrongly decided it should stand until altered by Act of Parliament. The Lords (with one dissentient) allowed the appeal on the second count, two of them on the ground that the offence of conspiracy to outrage public decency was an offence unknown to the law, and two of them on the ground that there had been maldirection by the judge; those latter two and the dissentient agreed that there was an offence of that nature.[9]

Lords Morris and Reid took part in the decisions of both *Shaw* and *Knuller*. Lord Reid had dissented in *Shaw* and had held there was no offence to corrupt public morals; but he was not willing to participate in overruling that decision when the same point arose in *Knuller*. He did, however, hold in *Knuller* that there was no offence of conspiracy to outrage public decency. Lord Morris had been with the majority in *Shaw* when upholding the conviction. And in *Knuller* he was the dissentient to allowing the appeal on the second count.

7. *R. v. Anderson* [1971] 3 WLR 939.
8. See above, p. 151.
9. *R. v. Knuller (Publishing etc.) Ltd* [1972] 3 WLR 143.

In the event therefore the decision in *Knuller* reinforced that in *Shaw*. But Lord Diplock in the former case was strongly critical of *Shaw* saying bluntly of that decision that he thought it was wrong and should not be followed. He said that Viscount Simonds's reasoning in *Shaw* had been anticipated in 1591 in Lambard:[10]

> Is it not meet and just, that when the wicked sort of men have excogitated anything with great labour of wit and cunning, so as it may seem they have drawn a quintessence of mischief, and set the same abroach, to the remedilesse hurt of the good and quiet subject; Is it not meet (I say) that authoritie itself also . . . should straine the line of justice beyond the ordinarie length and wonted measure and thereby take exquisite avengement upon them for it? Yea is it not right necessarie, that the most godly, honourable, wise, and learned persons of the land, should be appealed unto, that may apply new remedies for these new diseases?

It was not, said Lord Diplock, compatible with the development of English constitutional and criminal law over the past century that the House of Lords in its judicial capacity should assume the role of 'the most godly' etc. persons and take 'exquisite avengement' on those whose conduct was regarded as particularly reprehensible when Parliament had not found it necessary to proscribe that conduct and no previous precedent for punishing it could be found. As a result of *Shaw's* case, he said, it would seem that any conduct of any kind which conflicted with widely held prejudices as to what was immoral or indecent, at any rate if at least two persons were in any way concerned with it, might *ex post facto* be held to have been a crime.

In a case in 1973, twenty-one persons were charged with forty-three separate specific offences relating to drugs. And then the forty-fourth count alleged a conspiracy to corrupt public morals in that persons conspired together with other persons unknown to corrupt the morals of such persons as might consume heroin by procuring quantities of heroin and supplying the same to members of the public in, and in the vicinity of Gerrard Street, London, W.1.[11] So it would seem that conspiracy to corrupt public morals may extend, as an offence, beyond the areas of sexual conduct and be used as a net to catch those who may be acquitted on other kinds

10. *Lambard Archeion* (1635 edn) pp. 86, 87.
11. See Hazell, *op. cit.*, p. 33; *New Statesman*, 23 February 1973.

of substantive charges. It should be added that if persons are convicted of a number of substantive offences the penalties can be severe because made cumulative; and that under the Misuse of Drugs Act 1971 the maximum punishment for the more serious offences (of which there are fourteen) is fourteen years' imprisonment. So it cannot be argued that the conspiracy charge is necessary to ensure that the penalties are severe.

The Independent Broadcasting Authority is under a duty to satisfy themselves that, so far as possible, the programmes broadcast do not offend against good taste or decency and are not offensive to public feeling. Mrs Mary Whitehouse sought judicial review of the manner of the exercise of this duty in relation to the showing of the film *Scum* which portrayed life in borstal institutions. Watkins LJ held that the director-general of the IBA had committed a grave error of judgment in failing to refer the film to all the members of the IBA before authorizing its showing. The judge said that, had the decision been his, he would have been opposed to showing the film. Taylor J agreed that the film was shocking but did not accept Mrs Whitehouse's assertion that it was gratuitous exploitation of sadistic violence for its own sake, and he would have permitted transmission. Nevertheless he agreed that the director-general should not have taken it upon himself to make the decision. He thought that Mrs Whitehouse's more general accusations against the IBA were extravagant and unwarranted.[12] The director-general might well have replied that how he exercised his judgement, within the law, was not a matter which the Court had any competence to assess. In this respect it presents a nice contrast to the more ambivalent attitude of the Court of Appeal to the exercise of police judgment.

Demonstrations and protests

In 1961, members of the Committee of 100 who sought to further the aims of the Campaign for Nuclear Disarmament took part in organizing a demonstration at an airfield which was a 'prohibited place' within the meaning of the Official Secrets Act 1911 and which was occupied by the US airforce. The plan was that some people would sit outside the entrances to the airfield while others would sit on the runway to prevent aircraft from taking off. The six

12. *R. v. Independent Broadcasting Authority ex parte Whitehouse, The Times*, 14 April 1984 (this was not a conspiracy case).

accused were charged with conspiring to commit and to incite others to commit a breach of the Official Secrets Act, namely, 'for a purpose prejudicial to the safety or interests of the State' to enter the airfield. Their counsel was not allowed to cross-examine or call evidence as to their belief that their acts would benefit the State or to show that their purpose was not in fact prejudicial to the safety or interests of the State. They were all convicted, five of them being sentenced to eighteen months' and one to twelve months' imprisonment. The Court of Appeal and the House of Lords upheld the conviction and sentences.[13]

The accused were not charged with any substantive offence, such as breach of the Official Secrets Acts (approaching or entering a prohibited place). No doubt, proof of conspiracy was easier.

In July 1972 Peter Hain appeared on charges of conspiracy to interrupt visits of South African sporting teams to Britain. The prosecution was brought by a private individual. He was convicted on one of the four counts, and fined £200. The count concerned his running on to a tennis court in Bristol during a Davis Cup match and distributing anti-apartheid leaflets.[14] It is not clear how far the conviction amounted to trespass (see below) but that was not the basis of the decision. It may be that any action which is 'a matter of public concern' can found an action for conspiracy. If so 'the agreement to commit an unlawful act' which is the definition of conspiracy may have been extended further.[15]

At present, however, another extension is of greater importance because it was created by a decision of the House of Lords as a deliberate statement of new law. The case concerned some students from Sierra Leone who occupied for a few hours part of the premises of the High Commission of Sierra Leone in London. They brandished an imitation gun and locked some ten members of the staff in a room. No blows were struck. Lord Hailsham said, delivering the opinion of the House of Lords, that the students

appear to have been reasonably careful to see that no one was seriously harmed, and their motives were *not necessarily*

13. *Chandler v. DPP* [1962] 3 WLR 694.
14. *Hain v. DPP*, *The Times*, 28 July – 22 August 1972. Robertson, *op.cit.*, p. 16, and Derek Humphry, *The Cricket Conspiracy* (1975).
15. In *Cozens v. Brutus* [1973] AC 854, the House of Lords held that running on to the Centre Court at Wimbledon during a tennis match and distributing anti-apartheid leaflets was not 'insulting behaviour within the meaning of the Public Order Act 1936'.

contemptible. They acted from a genuine sense of grievance. The father of at least one of them was, we were told, under sentence of death at the time of the alleged offence, and all appear to have believed that the government in power in their country, *though recognized by Her Majesty's Government here*, was *arbitrary, tyrannical and unconstitutional* [my italics].

The students were convicted of conspiring with other persons to enter the premises as trespassers.

Sit-ins and occupations, by students and factory workers, had for some time been troubling the courts and the legislators. As forms of protest, these were in varying degrees effective, especially if they received publicity and caused embarrassment. Normally they gave rise to no criminal action and the police were reluctant to intervene in what was seen as a private dispute on private property. From the begining of student activity, however, there had been some who urged the introduction of legislation to enable such demonstrations to be dealt with as criminal.

Lord Hailsham was a Lord Chancellor who chose to sit as a judge more frequently than is usual. On this occasion, he delivered the leading judgment with which two other Law Lords concurred (adding nothing) and the fourth concurred with a brief speech. Lord Hailsham was a highly political Lord Chancellor well known for his flamboyance and overstrained rhetoric. He lumped together in his political speeches:

> The war in Bangladesh, Cyprus, the Middle East, Black September, Black Power, the Angry Brigade, the Kennedy murders, Northern Ireland, bombs in Whitehall and the Old Bailey, the Welsh Language Society, the massacre in the Sudan, the mugging in the Tube, gas strikes, hospital strikes, go-slows, sit-ins, the Icelandic cod war.

The new rule of law he set forth in this case was:

> Trespass or any other form of tort can, if intended, form the element of illegality necessary in conspiracy. But in my view, more is needed. Either (1) execution of the combination must invade the domain of the public, as, for instance, when the trespass involves the invasion of a building such as the embassy of a friendly country or a publicly owned building, or (of course) where it infringes the criminal law as by breaching the statutes

of forcible entry and detainer, the Criminal Damage Act 1891, or the laws affecting criminal assaults to the person. Alternatively (2) a combination to trespass becomes indictable if the execution of the combination necessarily involves and is known and intended to involve the infliction on its victim of something more than purely nominal damage. This must necessarily be the case where the intention is to occupy the premises to the exclusion of the owner's right, either by expelling him altogether . . . or otherwise effectively preventing him from enjoying his property.[16]

By this simple but considerable extension of the existing law, Lord Hailsham brought within the definition of criminal conspiracy, with its vagueness, and with its almost limitless powers of punishment, demonstrations of all kinds which involved either any entry into a public building or any use of property, whether public or private, which interfered (to however small an extent for however short a time) with an owner's enjoyment of any part of his property. Such an owner would be entitled to call on the police to enter the premises and make any arrests they thought appropriate because a criminal offence would be in the course of commission once two or more people appeared to be combining in such a demonstration. This decision is remarkable even for these authoritarian middle decades of the twentieth century. It also provides a very strong weapon for dealing as criminals with those who squat in empty buildings. In the same case, the only other judge to speak (other than to concur) was Lord Cross. He went further even than Lord Hailsham saying that an agreement by several to commit acts, which if done by one would amount only to a civil wrong, might constitute a criminal conspiracy if the public had a sufficient interest. Such vagueness could lead almost anywhere.

The right to protest was further limited in *Hubbard v. Pitt*[17] in 1975. Lord Denning MR said that, some years before, Islington was 'run down in the world', with houses in a dilapidated condition, tenanted by many poor families. Then property developers stepped in, bought up houses, persuaded tenants to leave, did up the houses and sold them at a profit. Now they were occupied by well-to-do families. A group of social workers who deplored this development conducted a campaign. They accused the developers of harassing tenants and trying to make them leave. The social workers

16. *Kamara v. DPP* [1973] 3 WLR 198.
17. [1975] 3 WLR 201.

submitted various demands to local estate agents which, said Lord Denning, if tenants had been subjected to undue pressure, seemed reasonable enough. In the course of the campaign the social workers picketed the offices of Prebble & Co. About four to eight men and women stood on the pavement in front of Prebble's offices for about three hours on Saturday mornings, carrying placards saying 'Tenants Watch Out Prebble's About' and 'If Prebble's In – You're Out', and handing out leaflets. They behaved in an orderly and peaceful manner and with the full knowledge and agreement of the local police. Prebble & Co. brought an action to stop these activities and Forbes J granted an interim injunction from which the defendants appealed. In the Court of Appeal, two of the Lord Justices rejected the appeal on the technical ground that the interim injunction should be continued until the case was fully heard. As these cases are normally decided on the availability or otherwise of interim injunctions, this was an unrealistic view of the matter. Lord Denning, however, dissented from his two brethren, saying:

> Here we have to consider the right to demonstrate and the right to protest on matters of public concern. These are rights which it is in the public interest individuals should possess; and, indeed, that they should exercise without impediment so long as no wrongful act is done. It is often the only means by which grievances can be brought to the knowledge of those in authority – at any rate with such impact as to gain a remedy. Our history is full of warnings against suppression of these rights. Most notable was the demonstration at St Peter's Field, Manchester, in 1819 in support of universal suffrage. The magistrates sought to stop it. At least twelve were killed and hundreds injured. Afterwards the Court of Common Council of London affirmed 'the undoubted right of Englishmen to assemble together for the purpose of deliberating upon public grievances' . . . The courts . . . should not interfere by interlocutory injunctions with the right of free speech; provided that everything is done peaceably and in good order.

This is the voice of freedom under law. But on a technicality it was overridden by the other two members of the Court of Appeal.

The Central Electricity Generating Board was considering possible sites for a nuclear power station in southwest England and were obstructed, first by farmers and later by protestors preventing them from surveying a site. The chief constable refused to remove the protestors since there was no actual or apprehended breach of the peace nor an unlawful assembly. The Board sought an order from the court requiring the chief constable to instruct police officers or agents to act. The Court of Appeal refused the order. Lord Denning MR, while deploring the activities of the protestors, and expressing the hope that the police would help the Board, said it was of the first importance that the police should decide on their own responsibility what action should be taken in any particular situation and that the decision of the chief constable not to intervene was a policy decision with which the courts should not interfere.[18]

In 1974 Lord Diplock said that on five occasions during the previous three years the House of Lords had had to consider 'the protean crime' of conspiracy under one or other of the various shapes it assumed. The one he was considering was *R. v. Withers*[19] in which two husbands and their wives were charged with 'conspiracy to effect a public mischief'. Their actions had been to pretend, for the purposes of their enquiries as an investigating agency, that they were bank employees seeking information from other banks or building societies; and other similar deceptions. The other four cases were *DPP v. Bhagwan*,[20] the *Knuller* and *Kamara* cases and a case argued with *Withers*. Lord Diplock said:

> In each of these five cases what was proved against the defendant at the trial was that he had done something of which the judge and jury strongly disapproved. In each of them what the defendant did was not itself a criminal offence whether done by him alone or in conjunction with other persons – or, if it was, that was not an offence with which he was charged . . . It would be disingenuous to try to conceal my personal conviction that this branch of the criminal law of England is irrational in treating as a criminal offence an agreement to do that which if done is not a crime and that its irrationality becomes injustice if it takes days of legal argument and historical research on appeal to your Lordships' House to discover whether any crime has been committed even though the facts are undisputed.

In *Withers*, the House of Lords concluded that the law knew no such generalized offence as conspiracy to effect a public mischief.

18. *R. v. Chief Constable of Devon & Cornwall ex parte Central Electricity Generating Board* [1981] 3 WLR 967.
19. [9174] 3 WLR 751.
20. [1972] AC 60 (see above, p. 105).

This decision at least stemmed the attempt to spread the tentacles of conspiracy yet further. Viscount Dilhorne said:

> The preferment of charges alleging public mischief appears to have become far more frequent in recent years. Why this is, I do not know. It may be that it is due to a feeling that the conduct of the accused has been so heinous that it ought to be dealt with as criminal and that the best way of bringing it within the criminal sphere is to allege public mischief and trust that the courts will fill the gap, if gap there be, in the law. But if gap there be, it must be left to the legislature to fill.

The increased frequency is due, in part, to that climate of opinion in recent years which shows such animosity to deviations from social and sexual behaviour regarded as normal. It is through such cases that conspiracy has flourished. Thence it has been applied to cases of ordinary criminality.

The animosity seems to be primarily reactionary. That is, there has been in the last twenty years, especially by the younger generation, more disregard for conventional behaviour, more changes of sexual and social *mores*, more rejection of mainstream politics, than in any period since the 1920s. And this development has been more widely spread amongst all social classes than during that earlier period. The animosity has been in reaction to all this.

If the accused in *Withers* had been charged with conspiracy to defraud they might well have been convicted and the convictions upheld by the House of Lords. The prosecution overreached itself in framing the charges as public mischiefs. But if those charges had been upheld, the way would have been opened to almost limitless charges of conspiracy concerning 'immoral' behaviour. It would be most unwise to regard *Withers* as a turning of the tide.[21] Indeed, in *R. v. Soul* (1980)[22] two women were convicted of conspiring to effect a public nuisance, namely to effect the escape of a patient at Broadmoor, detained there by reason of diminished responsibility after a conviction for manslaughter. The limits of public nuisance are so ill-defined that public mischief may be included within its scope.

21. For views of the Law Commission on conspiracy see Working Papers nos. 50, 54, 56, 57, 63.
22. [1980] Crim. LR 233.

7. Students, prisoners and trade union members

Students

In 1718, Dr Richard Bentley, a member of the University of Cambridge, was ordered to appear before the university court. But he refused 'contemptuously' saying the vice-chancellor was not his judge. Whereupon he was deprived of his degrees because of his words. So Dr Bentley went to the ordinary courts who ordered that his degrees be restored to him because the university could deprive him only for a reasonable cause which was not shown in this case.

Dr Bentley had not been given notice that the university court was to hear his case so he could not defend himself and that was a fatal flaw in the proceedings for 'even God himself did not pass sentence upon Adam, before he was called upon to make his defence'.[1]

The courts can generally be appealed to by anyone who considers that a decision has been taken against him which ought to have been taken in accordance with the rules of natural justice but was not. These rules at the least require that a person be told the case against him and be given an opportunity to refute it. If the rules of natural justice are not followed in circumstances where they should be, then the remedy given by the courts will be to quash the decision or to declare that it is invalid. But this remedy may be withheld by the courts even where they are satisfied that the rules of natural justice have not been complied with because the giving of the remedy is said to be at the discretion of the courts. This means that the person complaining may completely establish his complaint and yet the decision may not be quashed because a court does not think he 'deserves' to win. Obviously this ultimate power to withhold the remedy can give rise to feelings of injustice and to accusations that the courts are biased against individuals or particular groups of individuals.

The leading case on the rules of natural justice in recent times

1. *R. v. University of Cambridge* (1723) 1 Str. 237.

concerned the chief constable of the borough of Brighton. In October 1957 he was arrested and charged, together with other persons, with conspiracy to obstruct the course of justice. In February 1958 he was acquitted by the jury but the judge in passing sentence on two police officers who were convicted said that the facts admitted in the course of the trial 'establish that neither of you had that professional and moral leadership which both of you should have had and were entitled to expect from the chief constable'. The judge also remarked on the need for a leader in Brighton's police force 'who will be a new influence and who will set a different example from that which has lately obtained'. Soon after this the watch committee of the borough (the police authority) dismissed the chief constable without giving him a hearing or informing him of the charges against him. The House of Lords held that the dismissal was null and void. Lord Reid said that in cases where there must be something against a man to warrant his dismissal, he could not lawfully be dismissed without first being told what was alleged against him and allowed an opportunity to present his defence or explanation.[2]

When we look at the way the courts have dealt with cases involving students, however, it seems that the narrowest possible interpretation has been applied to the rules of natural justice. In a case from Ceylon, after a student had sat for his final examination for BSc., an allegation was made by a fellow student to the vice-chancellor of the university that the student had had prior knowledge of part of a paper. A commission of enquiry found the allegation substantiated and the student was suspended indefinitely from all examinations of the university. The student went to the courts in Ceylon to have the suspension set aside on the ground that evidence of several witnesses, including that of the fellow student who made the allegation, was taken in his absence, and that he was not aware of this evidence or of the case he had to meet.

The Supreme Court of Ceylon found in his favour because 'the procedure adopted was unfair to the plaintiff in that it deprived him of a reasonable opportunity of testing the truth of the case against him or of presenting his defence and explaining various matters in regard to which adverse inferences were drawn against him'. The decision was reviewed by the judicial committee of the Privy Council. The student did not appear and was not represented, apparently because he could not afford to do so. The Privy Council

2. *Ridge v. Baldwin* [1964] AC 40.

reversed the decision of the Supreme Court of Ceylon. They agreed that the commission of enquiry was bound by the rules of natural justice but held that these did not require the student to be present when witnesses were called. They said that a fair opportunity was given for the student to correct or contradict any relevant statement. The crucial issue was whether the student should have been provided with an opportunity to question the fellow student who made the allegation. As the Privy Council said: 'She was the one essential witness against the plaintiff, and the charge in the end resolved itself into a matter of her word against his.' But the Privy Council concluded that the absence of this opportunity was not an omission sufficient to invalidate the proceedings of the commission. Their Lordships said that this lack of opportunity to question the fellow student 'might have been a more formidable objection if the plaintiff had asked to be allowed to question [her] and his request had been refused . . . There is no ground for supposing that if the plaintiff had made such a request it would not have been granted.'[3]

This was a remarkable position for the Privy Council to take up. The rules of natural justice exist to ensure that proceedings are fair, and it is the responsibility of the authorities conducting the proceedings to see they are fair. To say that because the person alleging unfairness failed to insist on a fair procedure being followed he must suffer the consequences of the unfairness is a singularly crude and inequitable way of absolving those authorities from blame.

An even more remarkable interpretation of the rules of natural justice, as applied to students, concerned a teacher training college. The rules of the college provided, amongst other things, that the director of education for the local authority or his representative should be entitled to attend every meeting of the governing body of the college; and that the principal of the college was empowered to suspend a student for good cause, to report any such action to the chairman of the governing body and to refer the case to a disciplinary committee. This committee consisted of three members each of the governing body, staff and students. All findings of the disciplinary committee were to be referred to the governing body for approval.

Miss W was a student at the college. She, and four other women students, were found one night to have men in their rooms in the hall of residence in breach of the rules of the college. Later that

3. *University of Ceylon v. Fernando* [1960] 1 WLR 223.

morning the principal saw Miss W and told her that it might be better if she left the hall as soon as she could find other accommodation. Six days later, Miss W moved to lodgings in the town.

It appeared that the man had been with her for nearly two months. The story got into the press and Miss W made statements which were reported. Two hundred students at the college signed a petition saying they had on one or more occasions broken the terms of occupancy. Said Lord Denning in later proceedings before the Court of Appeal: 'Many parents were worried lest their own daughters and sons were doing this sort of thing. It was all very bad for the college.'

The principal decided that she would not refer any of the cases to the disciplinary committe and, under the rules, she was the only person who could do so. But the governing body wanted disciplinary action to be taken. So they amended the rules to enable them to refer cases to the disciplinary committee; they then applied the amended rules retrospectively to the students concerned; and they fixed a date for the hearing before the disciplinary committee.

When the disciplinary committee met they were joined by Mr N who was an assistant education officer of the local authority and he stayed with the committee when they considered what their decision should be. The other students were reprimanded and some were required to leave the hall of residence. But Miss W was 'expelled from the college forthwith', and the governing body approved this decision. Miss W thereupon asked the courts to declare that her expulsion was invalid. She argued first that the governing body had no right to change the rules and to refer her case to the disciplinary committee. Apart from what might be regarded as an unfairness in changing the rules so as to enable the principal to be overruled, the difficulty of the amendment was that the governing body had put themselves in the position of appearing as prosecutor and judge. In particular the three members of the governing body who sat on the disciplinary committee would be involved, first, in referring the cases to the committee; second, in hearing the cases in the committee; and third, in approving the recommendation of the committee. To speak mildly, justice would not manifestly appear to be done by such a procedure. But Lord Denning was apparently unmoved by such arguments: 'We have seen the minutes,' he said. 'These show that the governing body, when they decided to refer these cases, were careful not to discuss the merits of any individual case' and with this Lord Denning was satisfied. Nor was he worried about the retrospective aspect. This he said was 'a matter of procedure only'.

What of Mr N's presence with the committee, especially when they were considering their decision? He was no silent spectator of their deliberation.

> Mr N said he considered that Miss W's apparent lack of concern merited more severe treatment than the others. It was a serious offence and Miss W had knowingly flouted the regulations over a long period.

The affidavit in the case shows that he also

> stated that he had been in touch with the Department of Education and Science and they viewed the matter with concern. He also stated that, because of the press report, the college had been made to look fools.

Lord Denning accepted that 'in general no person ought to participate in the deliberations of a judicial or quasi-judicial body unless he was a member of it . . . Nor should he retire with them for their deliberations lest this gives the impression that he is taking part in their deliberations when he is not entitled to do so, for then justice would not be seen to be done.' But Lord Denning thought that the rule that the director of education or his representative was entitled to attend every meeeting of the governing body or its committees 'was wide enough to cover the disciplinary committee'. Moreover, said Lord Denning, 'he only drew attention to the obvious' and 'no harm was done by what he said'.

It is doubtful whether the disciplinary committee was a committee of the governing body. It certainly included persons who were not governors. Moreover the principle that justice must not only be done but must be seen to be done overrides the argument that N did 'no harm'. And did 'the obvious' include N's report of what some official in the department thought? Anyone who has any experience of governing bodies knows how susceptible they are to the view that they are made to look fools. In its effect, N's intervention was highly prejudicial to the question of what punishment should be administered to Miss W.

Even Lord Denning was unhappy about what had happened. He thought that in future 'it would be better for the director of education not to participate' in the disciplinary committee's deliberations and recommended that the rules should be amended accordingly.

In the meantime, of course, Miss W was to be expelled and her career ended. Lord Denning should be allowed the last word:

> Instead of going into lodgings she had this man with her, night after night, in the hall of residence where such a thing was absolutely forbidden. That is a fine example to set to others! And she a girl training to be a teacher! I expect the governors and the staff all thought that she was quite an unsuitable person for it. She would never make a teacher. No parent would knowingly entrust their child to her care.[4]

A different kind of unreality descended on the Court of Appeal in *Herring v. Templeman*.[5] H was a student at a teacher training college. The trust deed of the college provided that the academic board might make recommendations to the principal for the dismissal of students whose standard of work was unsatisfactory; the principal had power to recommend dismissal; and any such recommendation was required to be confirmed by the governing body after considering such representations in writing or in person as the student might wish to make. In this case the academic board sent to the governing body an adverse report on H and this was the only document before the governing body. He was given a copy of this report ten days before the meeting of the governing body, attended the meeting, and was invited to give his reasons why he should not be dismissed. The governing body then accepted the recommendation from the academic body. H asked the courts to set aside his dismissal on the grounds that he should have been accorded a hearing by the academic board before it recommended his dismissal because it took into account extraneous matters going beyond his marks and grades; that he should also have had a hearing by the principal; and that the governing body should not have refused to reopen the academic board's assessment or to allow witnesses to be called or to reveal to H all the evidence, opinions, and reports on which the academic board had based its report.

The Court of Appeal held that there was no obligation on the academic board to give a hearing as it had the power only to make recommendations; that the principal was under no obligation to

4. *Ward v. Bradford Corporation* (1972) 70 LGR 27.
5. [1973] 3 All ER 569; and see *Brighton Corporation v. Parry* (1972) 70 LGR 576.

hold a hearing; and that the governing body had done all it was required to do. Lord Justice Russell, giving the judgment of the court, said that he could see no reason why the academic board should hear the student 'before reaching a conclusion which when reached did not finally determine the student's future, for that matter had still to go to the principal and thereafter, if, but only if, he thought fit, to the governing body'.

It is easy to agree with the Lord Justice that there is not and should not be any obligation for the proceedings before the academic board and the principal to be conducted 'as if the parties were litigants before a court or before a legal arbitrator'. And indeed it is also strongly arguable that there was no obligation on the governing body to reopen the whole issue. But the reality of the proceedings was that the student was unable to present his case at any time when it might have genuinely affected the decision. The principal was (as is usual) the chairman of the academic board and his role would be primarily exercised in that body. It was the decision of the academic board, albeit in the form of a recommendation only, that was in effect conclusive. It would have been highly improbable that the principal would seek to overrule the board and even more improbable that the governing body would overrule the joint recommendations of academic board and principal. If therefore the rules of natural justice were to bite at all they could do so only by requiring a hearing for the student before the board. If the principle were to become established that bodies which recommend but do not decide are not bound by those rules, they would cease to be effective over a very wide range of procedures.

Reference has already been made to the discretionary power which courts exercise in deciding whether or not to give certain remedies. As these are remedies normally sought in cases alleging a breach of the rules of natural justice, this power often is crucial.

Perhaps the most important of this group of cases is *R. v. Aston University Senate ex parte Roffey*.[6] Two students, R and P, were reading for the BSc. They failed an examination in subsidiary subjects in both June and September 1967. The examiners in those subjects and two of the course tutors, one of whom was chairman of the relevant examining boards, met on 19 September, considered the marks (which showed an unprecedented number of failures) and took into account personal and family difficulties. They decided

6. [1969] 2 QB 538.

that six students, including R and P, should be asked to withdraw from the course and letters were sent to them on 20 September. Between that date and 8 December 1967, several bodies considered the matter on several occasions and arrived at divers recommendations: the students' guild, the vice-chancellor, the dean of the faculty of social science, the board of examiners for behavioural science, the board of the faculty of social science, and the senate. 'No doubt,' said Mr Justice Donaldson, 'their interventions were inspired by the most laudable of motives, although their lack of unanimity was in many ways unfortunate.' Eventually on 1 November the senate resolved to confirm the original decision of 19 September. The university council met on 8 December, confirmed the senate's decision, and 'resolved to defend the university against any attack and to issue a public statement'.

P and R applied to the courts, seeking the quashing of the decision to expel them. Mr Justice Donaldson said that the examiners

considered a wide range of extraneous factors, some of which by their very nature, for example personal and family problems, might only have been known to the students themselves. In such circumstances and with so much at stake, common fairness to the students, which is all that natural justice is, and the desire of the examiners to exercise their discretion upon the most solid basis, alike demanded that before a final decision was reached the students should be given an opportunity to be heard orally or in writing, in person or by their representatives as might be most appropriate. It was, in my judgment, the examiners' duty and the students' right that such audience be given. It was not given and there was a breach of the rules of natural justice.

Mr Justice Blain also thought that 'common fairness demanded an opportunity for representation to be made' by or on behalf of P and R, though not necessarily in a personal interview. Lord Parker CJ was 'not prepared to differ from the conclusion that there has been here a breach of the rules of natural justice'.

On the merits of the case, therefore, the students appeared to have successfully established that they had not been treated fairly. But the exercise of discretion was still to come. First R's claim was set aside because he had 'obtained a place at the Regent Street Polytechnic in London and is no longer actively interested in returning to the university'. But P had not been so fortunate and was 'now working in a stationer's shop training for retail management'. He had expressed 'a real wish and need to return to the university'.

But, said Mr Justice Donaldson, the remedies sought

are exceptional in their nature and should not be made available to those who sleep upon their rights. Mr Partridge's complaint is that he was not allowed to resit the whole examination in June 1968, and, if successful, proceed to the pass degree in the 1968-9 academic year, *yet he did not even apply to move this court until July 1968*. By such inaction, in my judgment, he forfeited whatever claims he might otherwise have had to the court's intervention. I would therefore refuse the relief sought. [My italics.]

Mr Justice Blain said that the court did not lightly exercise its discretion to grant the remedies sought, and they would be granted 'only where diligence is shown by an applicant in real need of the remedy'. Moreover, he had formed a view about P which was perhaps decisive. 'This court', he said, 'should not be used for the creation of a real life counterpart to Chekhov's perpetual student.' Lord Parker CJ had no doubt at all that the court, in the exercise of its discretions should not give the relief claimed.

Finally, there was Mr Glynn who sunbathed, without any clothes, on the campus of Keele University, and was photographed there. The picture was sent to the vice-chancellor who wrote him a letter saying that he was fined £10 and 'excluded from residence in any residential accommodation on the university campus from today's date [1 July 1970] and for the whole of the session of 1970/1'. If the fine was not paid by 1 October, he would not be re-admitted to the university at the beginning of the next term. Mr Glynn replied at some length saying that he had had no chance to plead mitigating circumstances or to make any defence. He went abroad at the end of July before a letter from the university of 10 August gave him notice of a hearing of his appeal on 2 September. He did not return until 4 September by which time the vice-chancellor's decision had been confirmed by the appeal committee, Mr Glynn being neither present nor represented. He then sought an injunction in the courts to stop the university excluding him from residence.

The judge said:

I must decide whether in exercising his powers in the present case the vice-chancellor complied with the requirements of natural justice. I regret that I must answer that question without hesitation in the negative. It seems to me that once one accepts that the vice-chancellor was acting in a quasi-judicial capacity, he was clearly bound to give the plaintiff an opportunity of being heard before he reached his decision on the infliction of a penalty, and if so what penalty. In fact he did not do so . . . He ought as a matter of natural justice to have sent for [the plaintiff] before he left Keele, and given him an opportunity to present his own case. With all respect to the vice-chancellor I think he failed in his duty by omitting to send for the plaintiff, and instead, writing him a letter merely announcing his decision.

But again, the discretion. The judge continued:

I have, again after considerable hesitation, reached the conclusion that in this case I ought to exercise my discretion by not granting an injunction. I recognize that this particular discretion should be very sparingly exercised in that sense when there has been some failure in natural justice . . . There is no doubt that the *offence was one of a kind which merited a severe penalty according to any standards current even today* [my italics].

So the injunction was refused.[7]

In *Bentley*'s case,[8] the Chief Justice said:

The vice-chancellor's authority ought to be supported for the sake of keeping peace within the university; but he must act according to law, which I do not think he has done in this case.

Those words were spoken over 250 years ago and they put side by side the two considerations which are most obvious today. Universities, polytechnics, teacher training colleges are regarded by the courts as bodies to which notions of authority and discipline are highly relevant.

Prisoners

Goddard LJ (who became Lord Chief Justice) was a great

7. *Glynn v. Keele University* [1971] 1 WLR 487.
8. See above, p. 163.

disciplinarian and was unlikely to consider that convicted prisoners – or even persons detained without trial under wartime regulations – had any rights. The Prison Rules 1933 were made under the Prison Act 1898 and some detainees brought an action for breach of those Rules against the Home Secretary and prison governors.[9] The Lord Justice said that breach did not confer any rights of action. 'It would be fatal to all discipline in prisons if governors and warders had to perform their duty always with the fear of an action before their eyes.'

A similar case was *ex parte Fry*[10] where a fireman refused to obey an order to clean the uniform of an officer because the order was unlawful. He was punished by his chief fire officer and asked the courts to quash that punishment on the ground that he had not had a fair hearing. Lord Goddard CJ said:

> It seems to me impossible to say that a chief officer of a force which is governed by discipline, such as a fire brigade is, in exercising disciplinary authority over a member of that force, acting judicially or quasi-judicially, any more than a schoolmaster is when he is exercising disciplinary powers over his pupils.

And he equated the fire brigade with the military and the police, denying to all members of those services rights of application to the courts in such circumstances. The Court of Appeal upheld the Lord Chief Justice, basing its refusal on its discretionary power to withhold the remedy. But in *R. v. Hull Prison Board of Visitors ex parte St Germain*[11] the Court of Appeal upheld the right of prisoners to a fair trial before their disciplinary committee when they were charged with offences arising out of a prison riot. Lord Justice Shaw said: 'The courts are in general the ultimate custodians of the rights and liberties of the subject whatever his status and however attenuated those rights and liberties may be as the result of some punitive or other process.'

In *Williams v. Home Office (No. 2)*[12] a convicted person, on parole, brought an action for false imprisonment. He had been kept in a special control unit for 180 days and alleged, amongst other

9. *Arbon v. Anderson* [1943] 1 All ER 154; *Becker v. Home Office* [1972] 2 All ER 679.
10. [1954] 1 WLR 730.
11. [1979] 1 All ER 701: and see [1979] 3 All ER 545; approved by House of Lords in *O'Reilly v. Mackman* [1982] 3 WLR 1096.
12. [1981] 1 All ER 1211. This was the case that gave rise to *Home Office v. Harman* (see pp. 121–2).

things, that this was contrary to Prison Rules. His action failed and the court held that breach of the Rules did not affect the validity of his detention in the control unit. In *Guilfoyle v. Home Office*, a prisoner sought to complain to the European Commission of Human Rights about his treatment. A letter from his solicitor was stopped by the prison Governor from reaching the prisoner but his solicitors lodged a petition with the Commission and the prisoner claimed that, as a party to legal proceedings, he was entitled under Prison Rules to correspond with his legal adviser. The Court of Appeal rejected his claim on the highly artificial ground that the Commission could not make an enforceable adjudication and no individual could directly bring a case before the European Court of Human Rights (but could do so only through the Commission). Lord Denning MR remarked on the prisoner's 'audacity' in seeking to complain to the Commission.[13]

But the rights of prisoners to a fair hearing before the disciplinary boards of visitors were clearly established and a decision of such a board was quashed when it was discovered that prison authorities had not brought to the attention of the board evidence favourable to a prisoner.[14] And in another case[15] convictions against prisoners charged with serious offences against prison discipline were set aside where boards of visitors had refused to grant requests for legal representation and for assistance from a friend or adviser.

Perhaps the most important of this line of cases was *Raymond v. Honey*.[16] A prisoner wrote a letter to his solicitor which the prison Governor decided should not be sent. As a result the prisoner prepared statements for an application to the High Court for leave to commit the Governor and Assistant Governor to prison for contempt of court. The Governor stopped these papers also. The House of Lords held that the stopping of the statements denied the prisoner's right of access to the courts and was a contempt. Following that decision, the High Court ruled that prisoners had a right to unimpeded access to a legal adviser to receive advice and guidance in connection with possible future civil proceedings.[17]

This outburst of liberation received a sharp setback in *R. v.*

13. [1981] 2 WLR 223.
14. *R. v. Blundeston Prison Board of Visitors ex parte Fox-Taylor* [1982] 1 All ER 646.
15. *R. v. Secretary of State for the Home Department ex parte Tarrant* [1984] 2 WLR 613.
16. [1982] 2 WLR 465.
17. *R. v. Secretary of State for the Home Department ex parte Anderson* [1984] 2 WLR 725.

Deputy Governor of Camphill Prison ex parte King[18] where the Court of Appeal refused to allow judicial review of the exercise by a prison Governor of his disciplinary powers which resulted in a prisoner losing fourteen days remission. The ringing principle of Lord Justice Shaw in *St Germain* was replaced by an altogether more modest view of the judicial function. All three members of the Court of Appeal agreed that the Governor had misconstrued a prison rule in coming to his decision to such an extent that the prisoner should not have been found guilty of any offence. But all three decided that the rights of prisoners to challenge the findings of Boards of Visitors should not be extended to the findings of Governors. Lawton LJ proceeded by classification and held that the Governor was acting as a 'manager' for the Home Secretary not as one exercising jurisdiction. And managers were not subject to judicial review. Clearly in the Lord Goddard tradition, Lawton LJ said:

All prisons are likely to have within them a few prisoners intent in disrupting the administration. They are likely to have even more who delude themselves that they are victims of injustice. To allow such men to have access to the High Court whenever they thought that the Governor abused his powers, failed to give them a fair hearing or misconstrued the prison rules would undermine and weaken his authority and make management very difficult indeed.

Browne-Wilkinson LJ admitted there was no logical distinction between the disciplinary functions of prison Governors and those of Boards of Visitors but he was persuaded by the practical repercussions which he found 'frightening'. Griffiths LJ on the other hand, in coming to the same conclusion, thought the courts should act courageously. He said: 'Where logic leads down a path beset with practical difficulties the courts have not been frightened to turn aside and seek the pragmatic solution that will best serve the needs of society.' It would seem that the courts need not take too seriously their position as custodians of the rights and liberties at least of convicted prisoners. They are probably trouble-makers anyway.

18. [1984] 3 All ER 897.

Trade union members

When an individual joins a trade union he agrees to be bound by the rules of the union, present and future, contained in the rule book. The rule book prescribes penalties, such as expulsion from membership and fining, for breach of the rules. Thus there may be a power to expel a member found guilty of 'attempting to injure the union' or of 'conduct detrimental to the union'; or more specifically of failure to pay subscriptions or committing fraud on the union and other such offences. To determine such cases the rule book normally lays down a procedure and entrusts the decision to a disciplinary committee – which the courts call a domestic tribunal.

The ordinary courts over the years have developed principles to decide in what circumstances they will intervene in these proceedings. On the one hand they say that they are not and should not be courts of appeal from such domestic tribunals. Nevertheless they have insisted that a trade union member cannot be expelled from a union unless there is an express rule providing for expulsion; and where there is such a rule, there must be a proper hearing and the rules of natural justice must be followed. Judicial decisions have strictly limited this power of expulsion and strictly insisted on the proper procedure. In some of the leading cases they appear to have gone further.

Thus in *Lee v. Showmen's Guild*[19] the plaintiff was fined by the union for unfair competition in relation to another member. He refused to pay the fine and, in accordance with the rules, was expelled. But the Court of Appeal set aside his expulsion on the ground that his conduct could not be said to have been unfair competition. Denning LJ said:

A man's right to work is just as important to him as, if not more important than, his rights of property. These courts intervene every day to protect rights of property. They must also intervene to protect the right to work.

A few years later the House of Lords decided in *Bonsor v. Musicians' Union*[20] that a wrongfully expelled union member was entitled to the payment of damages from his union for the loss he

19. [1952] 2 QB 329.
20. [1956] AC 104.

had suffered, at least where there had been a breach of the rules in the rule book.

Most of the cases have arisen because of procedural defects on which the courts have been severe. In *Lawlor v. Union of Post Office Workers*[21] expulsions were set aside because there had been no proper hearing and no notification of the offences. In *Taylor v. National Union of Seamen*[22] the fatal defect was that the general secretary of the union took the chair at the meeting which heard the appeal and presented the case against the member, thus improperly doubling the roles of prosecutor and judge. In *Hiles v. Amalgamated Society of Woodworkers*[23] the court held that the appeals committee which reversed a decision in favour of a member had no jurisdiction to hear the case. In *Leary v. National Union of Vehicle Builders*[24] it was held that the member had not had a proper opportunity to meet the charge made against him. In *Edwards v. SOGAT*[25] Lord Denning held that rules which gave the union an unfettered right capriciously and arbitrarily to withdraw temporary membership without regard to the rules of natural justice were invalid. And in *Radford v. NATSOPA*,[26] the court said that had the union rules provided for automatic forfeiture of membership without the necessity for a charge and a hearing, they would have been void; but as they did require this and it was not given, the expulsion was illegal.

In *Shotton v. Hammond*[27] the court found, amongst other things, that the district committee of the union refused to approve S's election as shop steward unless he gave an undertaking to carry out the committee's instructions regardless of whether or not those instructions were authorized by the union's rules. The court in this case went so far as to issue a mandatory injunction ordering the committee to convene a meeting within fourteen days and approve S's election, and ordering the executive committee of the union to ratify this at its next monthly meeting. In *Stevenson v. United Road Transport Union*, the court granted a declaration that the decision of the executive committee of the union to dismiss an official of the union was in breach of the rules of natural justice, *ultra vires*, and void because the official had not been given a fair statement of the

21. [1965] 2 WLR 579.
22. [1967] 1 WLR 532.
23. [1968] 1 Ch. 440.
24. [1971] Ch. 34.
25. [1971] Ch. 354.
26. [1972] ICR 484.
27. *The Times*, 26 October 1976.

charges against him and had not given him a fair hearing.[28]

From all these cases it can be seen that trade unions not infrequently act, in relation to their members, without proper regard for the rules of natural justice.

The contrast with the courts' attitude to the student cases is very great. In the latter, as we have seen, the courts seek assiduously to find some ground on which to disregard breach of the rules of natural justice. In the trade union cases they very rarely allow any such breach to be overlooked. Both groups of cases concern the right to work. Frequently both concern expulsions. The consequences of expulsion in both may be most serious to the livelihood of the individual. When there have been comparable breaches of the rules of natural justice, why is the expulsion of the union member almost always set aside and that of the student almost always upheld? It is right that the courts should protect the individual against a trade union which fails to proceed fairly against him. But why should the protection be denied to a student?

The answer to these questions lies in the general attitudes of the judiciary to which I will return in the final chapter. But in the case of students and trade unionists, it is the attitude of the judiciary to constitutional or public authority that is seen to prevail. Individual members of trade unions are seen as private citizens trying to combat large remote organizations and, moreover, organizations which are not part of the State's authority. And as we have already seen,[29] the judges have never taken kindly to trade unions in their relations with employers or the government. So individuals are apt to be protected by the courts.

On the other hand, students are seen essentially as children and sometimes very unpleasant children – above all, as very undisciplined children. And universities and colleges are institutions of the State and so to be upheld. Both students and trade unions are seen as offering different kinds of challenge to public authority and as such to be controlled. The more liberal attitude in recent years to convicted prisoners can be attributed to strong pressure from specialized campaigning groups and to the impact of the European Court of Human Rights in its judgments against the United Kingdom.[30]

28. [1975] 2 All ER 941.
29. Above, chapter 3.
30. See especially *Ireland v. UK* [1978] 2 EHRR 25; *Golder v. UK* [1975] 1 EHRR 524; *Silver v. UK* (25 March 1983).

Part Three
Policy

The courts hold justly a high, and I think, unequalled pre-eminence in the respect of the world in criminal cases, and in civil cases between man and man, no doubt, they deserve and command the respect and admiration of all classes of the community, but where class issues are involved, it is impossible to pretend that the courts command the same degree of general confidence. On the contrary, they do not, and a very large number of our population have been led to the opinion that they are, unconsciously, no doubt, biased. [Hon. Members: 'No, no', 'Withdraw' and interruption.]

The Secretary of State for the Home Department (Mr W. S. Churchill) on the second reading of the Trade Unions (No. 2) Bill, 1911 (26 HC Deb. col. 1022).

The habits you are trained in, the people with whom you mix, lead to your having a certain class of ideas of such a nature that, when you have to deal with other ideas, you do not give as sound and accurate judgments as you would wish. This is one of the great difficulties at present with Labour. Labour says 'Where are your impartial Judges? They all move in the same circle as the employers, and they are all educated and nursed in the same ideas as the employers. How can a labour man or a trade unionist get impartial justice?' It is very difficult sometimes to be sure that you have put yourself into a thoroughly impartial position between two disputants, one of your own class and one not of your class.

Lord Justice Scrutton in an address delivered to the University of Cambridge Law Society on 18 November 1920 (1 *Cambridge Law Journal*, p. 8).

I know that over 300 years ago Hobart CJ said the 'Public policy is an unruly horse'. It has often been repeated since. So unruly is the horse, it is said (per Burrough J. in Richardson v. Mellish *[1924]) that no judge should ever try to mount it lest it run away with him. I disagree. With a good man in the saddle, the unruly horse can be kept in control. It can jump over obstacles. It can leap the fences put up by fictions and come down on the side of justice . . .*

Lord Denning MR in *Enderby Town Football Club v. Football Association Ltd* [1971] 1 Ch. 591.

So far as this country is concerned, hitherto every judge on his appointment discards all politics and all prejudices. The judges of England have always in the past – and I hope always will – be vigilant in guarding our freedoms. Someone must be trusted. Let it be the judges.

Lord Denning MR in the Richard Dimbleby Lecture, 1980.

The call today is for more 'open government'. It is voiced mainly by newsmen and critics and oppositions. They want to know all about the discussions that go on in the inner circles of government. They feel that policy-making is the concern of everyone. So everyone should be told about it.

Lord Denning MR in *Air Canada v. Secretary of State for Trade (No. 2)* [1983] 1 All ER 161.

8. Judicial creativity

In the first chapter I referred to the importance of the creative function which judges perform both in the development of the common law and in the interpretation of statutes. All the cases in this book are examples, greater or smaller, of this function.

It was common at one time for judges to deny that they had any creative function at all or, more precisely and more positively, to assert that, in the development of the common law, all they did was to declare it. Lord Reid, one of the outstanding Law Lords of this century, has said:

> Those with a taste for fairy tales seem to have thought that in some Aladdin's cave there is hidden the Common Law in all its splendour and that on a judge's appointment there descends on him knowledge of the magic words Open Sesame. Bad decisions are given when the judge has muddled the password and the wrong door opens. But we do not believe in fairy tales any more.[1]

Nowadays, however, the argument still persists in relation to the interpretation of statutes. When a particular interpretation – for example of the Race Relations Acts – is objected to, it is common for the interpretation to be defended on the ground that all the judges can do is to apply the law as made by Parliament and not to improve it.[2]

But if the statute is open to more than one interpretation then the judges are supposed to discover, by looking at the whole of the law on the matter, including the statute itself, what was the intention of Parliament and to interpret accordingly. At this point strong disagreement may arise, even within the court itself. If the court decided that, for example, it was the intention of Parliament to exclude Conservative clubs or dockers' clubs from the operation

1. 'The Judge as Law Maker' in 12 JSPTL 22 (1972).
2. See, for example, Lord Hailsham in a letter to *The Times* on 25 October 1974.

of the Race Relations Act 1968, some critics will say that so widespread an exception, applying to clubs with such extensive membership, is wholly contrary to the spirit and the intention of that statute. And they will go on to say that the courts are showing a restrictive attitude on a matter of social policy and politics.

On the other hand there will be those who say that the Race Relations Acts mark a serious intervention and a considerable regulation of personal relationships. Therefore, they will argue, such regulation should be kept to a minimum and Parliament should be assumed to have intended that the intervention should not be extended beyond the most explicit provision.[3]

A similar division of opinion can be seen where other forms of regulation arise – for example, in the interpretation of the legislation about the control of the use of land. Wherever private rights are regulated, whether of property or of persons, there will be those who say that the regulation should be kept to a minimum and those who say that it must not be so restricted as to weaken its application.

But the difficulty lies deeper than disagreements about the so-called 'intention of Parliament'. First, if particular judges or particular courts consistently interpret certain types of legislation either widely or narrowly they will gain the reputation either of being 'liberal', 'progressive', 'socialist' et cetera, or of being 'restrictive', 'reactionary', 'conservative' et cetera. Secondly, many people will simply disbelieve the judges who say that they are concerned only with ascertaining the intention of Parliament. And this disbelief is strengthened when judges express opinions, in the course of their judgments, which seem to show where their sympathies lie.

Thus Lord Denning found no difficulty in interpreting the rules of Miss Ward's college (which were made under statutory powers) so as to enable the governors to act retrospectively to her disadvantage. But he seems to have taken this view because he was sure her personal behaviour made her unsuitable to be a teacher.[4] Lord Denning's attitude to his function is clearly and frankly revealed in his subsequent comments on that decision. He agreed that there were many irregularities in the manner of Miss Ward's dismissal. 'If I thought it was a wrong decision I would probably have taken [advantage of] those to interfere . . . No injustice was

3. Cp. Lord Diplock in the *Dockers' Club* case; see above, p. 96–7.
4. See above, p. 168.

done to her. She deserved all she got, so to speak . . . I was overriding the irregularities in the procedure . . . or overlooking them in favour of what was in the end a right decision as I regarded it.' And he added: 'I may have been wrong in that case.'[5] Similarly (though these were common law cases) Lord Diplock drew attention to the way the law of conspiracy had developed because 'what was proved against the defendant at the trial was that he had done something of which the judge and jury strongly disapproved' although he had done nothing illegal or, if he had, was not charged with it.[6]

Lord Denning has said:

It is plain that Parliament intended that the Supplementary Benefit Act 1966 should be administered with as little technicality as possible. It should not become the happy hunting ground for lawyers. The courts should hesitate long before interfering by certiorari with the decision of the appeal tribunals . . . The courts should not enter into a meticulous discussion of the meaning of this or that word in the Act. They should leave the tribunals to interpret the Act in a broad reasonable way, according to the spirit and not to the letter: especially as Parliament has given them a way of alleviating any hardship. The courts should only interfere when the decision of the tribunal is unreasonable in the sense that no tribunal acquainted with the ordinary use of language could reasonably reach that decision.[7]

How creative judges should be in either their development of the common law or their interpretation of statutes has long been argued by the judges themselves. Lords Diplock, Devlin and Reid are three most distinguished recent contributors to the debate.[8]

Lord Diplock in 1965 was a Lord Justice of Appeal. He chose to talk about tax law which, he said, he was not interested in reforming – 'It no more lies within the field of morals than does a crossword puzzle.' But judicial decisions interpreting tax law affect all like cases and so the legislative content of such decisions is most

5. In an interview with Terry Coleman in the *Guardian*, 20 December 1978.
6. See above, p. 161.
7. *Ex parte Moore* [1975] 1 WLR 624. Cp. *R. v. Ebbw Vale and Merthyr Tydfil S.B. Appeal Tribunal ex parte Lewis* [1981] 1 WLR 131.
8. Lord Reid on *The Judge as Law Maker* (1972). (See above, p. 181); Lord Devlin on 'Judges and Lawmakers' in 39 MLR 1 (1976); Lord Diplock on 'The Courts as Legislators' (Holdsworth Club, University of Birmingham 1965).

obvious, especially as most cases concern transactions which Parliament had not anticipated or thought about at all. In many such cases Lord Diplock accepted that judges had to adopt a narrow, semantic and literal approach answering the question, what do the words mean? not what did the users of the words intend? But he thought the danger was that the courts tended to apply the same criteria to statutes of a different kind which contained clear indications of general principle or policy which, in his view, ought to qualify the sense in which particular words or phrases were understood.

To Lord Diplock, 'Law is about man's duty to his neighbour.' He saw the fashioning of these rules of human conduct as the proper field of judge-made law and referred with approbation to 'the bold imaginative judgments delivered by a great generation of judges between the 'sixties and the 'nineties of the last century'. This courage and imagination he found lacking in judges of the first half of this century but thought there was evidence of recent change for the better.

Seven years later, in 1972, Lord Reid wrote of 'the real difficulty' about judges making law.

> Everyone agrees that impartiality is the first essential in any judge. And that means not only that he must not appear to favour either party. It also means that he must not take sides on political issues. When public opinion is sharply divided on any question – whether or not the division is on party lines – no judge ought in my view to lean to one side or the other if that can possibly be avoided. But sometimes we get a case where that is very difficult to avoid. Then I think we must play safe. We must decide the case on the preponderance of existing authority.

This caution extended even to those cases where there was 'some freedom to go in one or other direction'. 'We should', continued Lord Reid, 'have regard to common sense, legal principle and public policy in that order,' and he made it clear that the first two criteria were unlikely to leave much scope for the application of the third.

Lord Devlin's position was more elaborate but in the end closer to Lord Reid's than to Lord Diplock's . He distinguished 'activist' from 'dynamic' law-making. The first meant keeping pace with change in the consensus; the second meant generating change in the consensus. And he said that the consensus in a community consisted of those ideas which its members as a whole liked or, if they disliked, would submit to. So he argued that the law had been used cautiously in the field of race relations with some success; but not so cautiously in the field of industrial relations without success. For Lord Devlin the social service which judges rendered was the removal of a sense of injustice and for this both impartiality and the appearance of impartiality were essential. Lord Devlin is clear that the judge should never be a dynamic law-maker.

The discussion about how creative judges should be, how far the approach to statutes should be literal and semantic, or seeking 'the intention' of Parliament, and other variants on the same theme, has been continuing for many years. Yet it has been and is a somewhat unreal discussion. While in certain circumstances and on some specific issues particular judges can be shown, from the record of their decisions, to belong more to the creative or more to the conservative school, it is very doubtful whether either tendency follows from one or other general judicial position. Lord Diplock is not regarded as a more creative judge than was Lord Reid, and Lord Devlin was thought of by some as a more creative judge than either.[9]

All this leads to the conclusion that, as one might expect, judges like the rest of us are not all of a piece, that they are liable to be swayed by emotional prejudices, that their 'inarticulate major premises' are strong and not only inarticulate but sometimes unknown to themselves. The judges seldom give the impression of strong silent men wedded only to a sanctified impartiality. They frequently appear – and speak – as men with weighty, even passionate, views of the nature of society and the content of law and of their partial responsibility for its future development.

Individualistic strains could, of course, exist alongside a consistent attitude to creativity or its opposite. What is lacking however is any clear and consistent relationship between the general pronouncement of judges on this matter of creativity and the way they conduct themselves in court. Lord Simonds was Lord Chancellor in 1951-4 and is often quoted as the exemplar of the conservative view. Thus in one case he said that he would not 'easily be led by an undiscerning zeal for some abstract kind of justice or ignore our first duty, which is established for us by Act of Parliament or the binding authority of precedent'.[10] Yet it was he who in the previous year had discovered that there was an offence

9. Lord Devlin retired from the bench in 1964 at the age of fifty-eight.
10. *Scruttons Ltd v. Midland Silicones* [1962] AC 446.

known to the common law of conspiracy to corrupt public morals, a view which caused no little surprise in legal and political circles.[11]

For a time Lord Simonds and Lord Denning carried on a public dispute, the latter making a strong plea for the creative function. Lord Denning, like Lord Simonds, is a reminder that creativity is neither good nor bad but that thinking makes it so. When he supported the action of the college governors in changing the rules of discipline to enable them to dismiss the woman student who was found to have a man in her room, he was certainly acting 'creatively'.[12] When he sought to protect the rights of demonstrators to protest outside the offices of the estate agents in *Hubbard v. Pitt* he was refusing to be bound by an earlier procedural decision which his colleagues on the bench thought binding on them. And he did so on strong liberal principles. The view taken by Lord Denning can be seen as either creative (refusing to be bound by the earlier decision) or conservative (maintaining the traditional right of individuals to 'free speech', as he put it).

I am arguing that the public position adopted by judges in the controversy about creativity is not consistently reflected in their judgments and that more important are their reactions to the moral, political and social issues in the cases that come before them.

The law reports abound with references to the duty of the courts to abide by the provisions of Acts of Parliament. But that does not help in deciding how to deal with ambiguities or obscurities. In *Chandler v. DPP*[13] Lord Reid said:

> Of course we are bound by the words which Parliament has used in the Act. If those words necessarily lead to that conclusion then it is no answer that it is inconceivable that Parliament can have so intended. The remedy is to amend the Act. But we must be clear that the words of the Act are not reasonably capable of any other interpretation.

The 'conclusion' referred to was that Parliament in passing the Official Secrets Act in 1911 intended that a person who deliberately interfered with vital dispositions of the armed forces should be entitled to submit to a jury that government policy was wrong and that what he did was really in the best interests of the country. Lord Reid continued:

11. *Shaw v. DPP*; see above, pp. 152–3.
12. See above, pp. 165–8.
13. [1962] 3 WLR 694; see above, pp. 156–7.

The question whether it is beneficial to use the armed forces in a particular way or prejudicial to interfere with that use would be a political question – a question of opinion on which anyone actively interested in politics, including jurymen, might consider his own opinion as good as that of anyone else. Our criminal system is not devised to deal with issues of that kind. The question therefore is whether the Act can reasonably be read in such a way as to avoid the raising of such issues.

Lord Reid concluded that it could be read 'in such a way' and that the submissions about government policy were rightly excluded.

The problem in *Charter* (the Conservative Club case) and the *Dockers' Labour Club* case[14] was where to draw the line between 'public' and 'private' in interpreting the Race Relations Act of 1968. In both cases Lord Reid extended the notion of what was private far beyond the domestic sphere. And he said in *Charter*:

I would infer from the Act as a whole that the legislature thought all discrimination on racial grounds deplorable but thought it unwise or unpracticable to attempt to apply legal sanctions in situations of a purely private character.

The three members of the Court of Appeal and one member of the House of Lords disagreed with Lord Reid and with the majority in the Lords. It is difficult to believe that the judges in these cases did not consider the effect their views would have on race relations. It is difficult to believe that such considerations would be regarded as improper by the ordinary layman. It was, after all, what the Act of Parliament was concerned with.

Similarly, are we expected to assume that the House of Lords did not take into account or were ignorant of the effect of their decision in *Rookes v. Barnard*?[15] The realities were referred to by Lord Devlin. He said:

But there is one argument, or at least one consideration, that remains to be noticed. It is that the strike weapon is now so generally sanctioned that it cannot really be regarded as an unlawful weapon of intimidation; and so there must be something wrong with a conclusion that treats it as such. This thought plainly

14. See above, pp. 96–7.
15. See above, p. 62.

influenced quite strongly the judgments in the Court of Appeal
. . . I see the force of this consideration. But your Lordships can,
in my opinion, give effect to it only if you are prepared either to
hobble the common law in all classes of disputes lest its range is
too wide to suit industrial disputes or to give the statute a wider
scope than it was ever intended to have.

The Court of Appeal had held that the tort of intimidation did
not include a threat to break a contract. The Law Lords, including
Lords Devlin and Reid, held that it did. And so a crucial section
of the Act of 1906 received an interpretation nearly sixty years later
which challenged the right to strike and had to be corrected by
another statute.[16] Lord Devlin warned their Lordships of the
dangers of the courts interfering in 'matters of policy' in this branch
of the law although this was certainly the consequence of their
decision. Again, creativity or its opposite is not the issue.

One group of decisions well illustrates the difficulties. We have
seen that in *Shaw v. DPP* (1961)[17] the House of Lords invented a
new crime called 'conspiracy to corrupt public morals'. This was
certainly a creative decision and one which Lord Reid dissented
from in that case. He said:

Notoriously, there are wide differences of opinion today as to
how far the law ought to punish immoral acts which are not done
in the face of the public . . . Parliament is the proper place, and
I am firmly of the opinion the only proper place, to settle that.
When there is sufficient support from public opinion, Parliament
does not hesitate to intervene. Where Parliament fears to tread
it is not for the courts to rush in.

Nine years later the House of Lords in a judgment delivered by
Lord Diplock and concurred in by the other Law Lords (including
Lord Reid) allowed the appeal of Mr Bhagwan[18] who had been
convicted of a conspiracy to evade immigration control although he
had not committed any wrong. The House of Lords could certainly
have followed the lead given in *Shaw*'s case – Lords Morris and
Hodson sat in both cases – but preferred to distinguish it and Lord
Diplock used words which seemed to seek to diminish the
importance of *Shaw*'s case.

16. Trades Disputes Act 1965.
17. See above, pp. 152–3.
18. See above, p. 105.

Then in 1972 came the decision in *Knuller*[19] (the *IT* case). The Court of Appeal followed *Shaw*'s case and upheld the convictions of conspiracy to corrupt public morals. The House of Lords (Lord Diplock dissenting) upheld the Court of Appeal on this count. Lords Morris and Kilbrandon did so on the ground that *Shaw*'s case was rightly decided. Lord Reid (with Lords Morris and Simon) did so on the ground that even if it were wrongly decided it must stand until it was altered by Parliament.

Lord Reid said:

> I dissented in Shaw's case. On reconsideration I still think that the decision was wrong . . . But I think that however wrong or anomalous the decision may be it must stand and apply to cases reasonably analogous unless or until it is altered by Parliament . . . Parliament alone is the proper authority to change the law with regard to the punishment of immoral acts.

It is a logical but curious position to adopt. Lord Reid said in *Shaw*'s case that the House of Lords should not there act creatively but his advice was not regarded. But when the opportunity arose in *Knuller* to reverse the decision in *Shaw*'s case, Lord Reid refused to do so because that also would be to act creatively in an area where the courts should not do so.

Lord Diplock had no such qualms. He said:

> My Lords, this appeal raises two questions of outstanding importance . . . The first is: whether the decision of the majority of this House in *Shaw*'s case upon the count which charged a conspiracy to corrupt public morals was right. I think that it was wrong. The second is: ought it to be followed even if it was wrong. I think that it should not.

Since 1966, the House of Lords has considered itself not bound by its own decisions.[20] But it is reluctant to overrule them as this, it is argued, would introduce more uncertainty into the law. As Lord Reid said elsewhere:

> I would venture the opinion that the typical case for reconsidering an old decision is where some broad issue is involved, and that it should only be in rare cases that we should

19. See above, p. 154.
20. See [1966] 1 WLR 1234.

reconsider questions of construction of statutes or other documents. In very many cases it cannot be said positively that one construction is right and the other wrong . . . Much may depend on one's approach. *If more attention is paid to meticulous examination of the language used in the statute the result may be different from that reached by paying more attention to the apparent object of the statute so as to adopt that meaning of the words under consideration which best accord with it.*[21]

The words I have emphasized indicate how the differences between the more literal and the more creative approaches may lead to different conclusions.

When judges get carried away by their personal convictions of where rightness and justice lie and stray too far from the established rules of the common law or the words of statutes, they create uncertainty. If those convictions are held on issues which are political, broadly or narrowly so, then they will arouse animosity as well as support. And if the political issues are serious and large, as are those of industrial relations, judicial pronouncements begin to lose their authority and their legitimacy.

The considerable conflict that surfaced in late 1979 and early 1980 between the Court of Appeal and the House of Lords over the interpretation of industrial relations law flowed from differing views about the creative function of the judiciary and not from differing views about the undesirability of that law. The Court of Appeal pursued its policy of interpreting the legislation restrictively so as further to control and curtail the activities of trade unionists. But the House of Lords refused to adopt a similar role and began to emphasize the danger to the administration of justice of so positive and so political a stance.[22] At the same time, some of them made no secret of their distaste for the legislation.

The conflict became acute when the Court of Appeal held in *Duport Steels v. Sirs* that the extension of the steel strike to the private sector was not 'in furtherance' of a trade dispute. In view of the recent decision of the House of Lords in *Express Newspapers v. McShane*, the Court of Appeal's interpretation of the phrase was positively perverse, and was a challenge which their Lordships could not ignore. Nor did they. Lord Diplock said:

21. *Jones v. Secretary of State for Social Services* [1972] 1 All ER 145.
22. See above, pp. 70–3.

When the meaning of the statutory words is plain and unambiguous it is not for the judges to invent fancied ambiguities as an excuse for failing to give effect to its plain meaning because they themselves consider that the consequence of doing so would be inexpedient or even unjust or immoral . . . It endangers continued public confidence in the political impartiality of the judiciary, which is essential to the continuance of the rule of law, if judges, under the guise of interpretation, provide their own preferred amendments to statutes which experience of their operation has shown to have had consequences that members of the court before whom the matter comes considers to be injurious to the public interest.

The prose may be convoluted but the meaning is clear. Lord Scarman said:

My basic criticism of all three judgments in the Court of Appeal is that in their desire to do justice the court failed to do justice according to law. Legal systems differ in the width of the discretionary power granted to judges but in developed societies limits are invariably set, beyond which the judges may not go. Justice in such societies is not left to the unguided, even if experienced, sage sitting under the spreading oak tree.

Lord Scarman then distinguished common law where society has been content to allow the judges to formulate and develop the law. Even in this, their 'very own field of creative endeavour', the judges bound themselves by the doctrine of precedents. But in the field of statute law 'the judge must be obedient to the will of Parliament in its enactments'. And in the *Express Newspapers* case Lord Scarman said: 'It would need very clear language to persuade me that Parliament intended to allow the courts to act as some sort of backseat driver in trade disputes.'

This is to put the matter boldly – deliberately so, no doubt, to make the argument stick. In practice, judges are often most reluctant to be creative in the development of the common law though it is precisely there that Lord Denning has been at his most creative during his long judicial life. And judges are often not reluctant at all to interpret statutes in a way which Parliament could not have intended. But I think Lord Scarman is here rebuking Lord Denning for applying his common law instinct for creative developments to statute law where, according to Lord Scarman, it has much less justification.[23] The distinction is a valuable contribution to the debate (which will continue as long as the present system lasts) about the proper limits of judicial creativity.

23. 'The choice', Lord Denning has said on statutory interpretation, 'is a matter of policy for the law: which gives the more sensible result? It is not a semantic or linguistic exercise.' (*R. v. Crown Court Sheffield ex parte Brownlow* [1980] 2 All ER 444 at 451.)

9. The political role

The traditional view

In the traditional view, the function of the judiciary[1] is to decide disputes in accordance with the law and with impartiality. The law is thought of as an established body of principles which prescribes rights and duties. Impartiality means not merely an absence of personal bias or prejudice in the judge but also the exclusion of 'irrelevant' considerations such as his political or religious views. Individual litigants expect to be heard fairly and fully and to receive justice. Essentially, this view rests on an assumption of judicial 'neutrality'.

This neutrality is regarded as more than impartiality between the parties. It means, also, that the judge should not advert to matters which go beyond those necessary for decisions in the case before him. On this view the judge is not to take into account any consequences which might flow from his decision and which are wider than the direct interests of the parties. He must act like a political, economic, and social eunuch, and have no interest in the world outside his court when he comes to judgment.

Where the issues are simple and the dispute limited to the interests of the two parties, the judge may fulfil his traditional function. Divorce, the meaning of a contract between businessmen, a personal claim for injury sustained in a road accident, the buying and selling of a house – for these the traditional view often suffices. But less simple issues can easily emerge. If there are children of the marriage which is to be dissolved, if the purpose of the contract is contrary to public policy, if the accident was caused by dangerous driving, if the seller is a bankrupt, then other persons and even the State itself may be involved. And their interests may have to be taken into account.

Moreover, these are all civil cases. But if the proceedings are for

1. As in the foregoing parts of this book, I am speaking in this part primarily of judges of the High Court, the Court of Appeal and the House of Lords.

alleged crimes, then the state is almost always directly concerned and considerations again arise which go beyond the individuals themselves.

A more sophisticated version of this traditional view sees the judiciary as one of the principal organs of a democratic society without whom government could be carried on only with great difficulty. The essence of their function is the maintenance of law and order and the judges are seen as a mediating influence. Democracy requires that some group of persons acts as an arbiter not only between individuals but also between governmental power and the individual. In criminal matters this governmental power will be exercised through the police to bring a wrongdoer before the court. It will ensure that the order of the court is enforced, that prisons are provided, that fines are paid. But there must be some body, other than the government, which hears the case, makes the decision, and decides the sentence. By this means the daily use, by the government and its agencies, of *force* is legitimated and so made acceptable to society at large.

Judges then, in this view, are an essential part of government but exist to operate as a part of democratic organization. They take their place alongside the other two great institutions of the executive and Parliament, more passive than they, but indispensable. No doubt there is something of a dilemma in the judiciary's position as both upholders of law and order and protectors of the individual against a powerful executive. But this is explained in terms of checks and balances or countervailing power and so what might be an inherent contradiction dissolves in a cloud of words which nevertheless, be it noted, defines the function of the judiciary in *political* terms.

In these terms, therefore, the judiciary may come into conflict with the government (the executive) of the day. Formally, this conflict can arise only where the government acts 'illegally'. But it is the judges who, particularly in their creative and interpretative function, determine whether governments or their agents have so acted. Thus they set limits to the discretionary powers of governments and to the rights of individuals, especially when these two forces conflict. Where and how they set those limits has been the theme of this book.

Governments have extensive powers and, with adequate Parliamentary majorities, can add to them without too much difficulty. This being so, it is well that judges should be willing to ensure that government bodies do not seek to act beyond those powers. And no doubt the existence of the courts and of opportunities to bring before them dubious exercises of governmental power is some deterrent to any public servants who may be inclined to stretch their powers beyond legal limits. So also where statutes lay down procedures to be followed before powers are exercised, the courts should insist that those procedures are followed and may even add their own gloss to ensure that governmental bodies do not act unfairly or in bad faith. How far beyond those elementary propositions of principle the judges should go, how far they should exercise their own wide powers further to control governmental activity, is the crucial political question.

The myth of neutrality

I have said that, traditionally, impartiality is thought of as part of a wider, judicial neutrality. Judges are seen essentially as arbiters in conflicts – whether between individuals or between individuals and the State – and as having no position of their own, no policy even in the widest sense of that word.

In denying such neutrality, I am not concerned merely to argue that judges, like other people, have their own personal political convictions and, with more or less enthusiasm, privately support one or other of the political parties and may vote accordingly. That, no doubt, is true but political partisanship in that sense is not important. What matters is the function they perform and the role they perceive themselves as fulfilling in the political structure.

Neither impartiality nor independence necessarily involves neutrality. Judges are part of the machinery of authority within the State and as such cannot avoid the making of political decisions. What is important is to know the bases on which these decisions are made.

Lord Devlin put this most clearly when he wrote immediately after the industrial dispute of 1972 and when the five dockers had just been released from prison (see above, p. 66). He made a distinction between consensus and non-consensus law, by consensus meaning a result which people generally were 'prepared to put up with'. 'Most law', said Lord Devlin, 'is in fact based on this sort of consensus. It is what gives the law its stability and saves it from change after every swing of the pendulum.' The Industrial Relations Act 1971, continued Lord Devlin, was not based on consensus and he asked what was the position of the courts to such law. Lord Devlin then said:

The question would not need to be asked if in Britain the role of the courts was in accordance with theory. In theory the judiciary is the neutral force between government and the governed. The judge interprets and applies the law without favour to either and its application in a particular case is embodied in an order which is passed to the executive to enforce. It is not the judge's personal order; it is substantially the product of the law and only marginally of the judicial mind. If its enforcement is resisted or evaded, the judge is no more concerned than if he were an arbitrator.

British judges have never practised such detachment. The reason may lie in their origin as servants of the Crown or perhaps in the fact that for a long time the law they administered was what they had made themselves. A mixture of the two has left the High Court with the power to enforce its order in civil cases by treating disobedience as contempt itself.

In the criminal law the judges regard themselves as at least as much concerned as the executive with the preservation of law and order. Then there is what can best be described as the expatiatory power. Whereas under most systems the judgment is formal, brief and to the legal point, the British judge may expatiate on what he is doing and why he is doing it and its consequences; and because of his prestige he is listened to.

These high powers make the British judiciary more than just a neutral arbitral force. On the whole their wise and cautious deployment has enabled the judiciary to use its reputation for impartiality and independence for the public good. But it is imperative that the high powers should not be used except in support of consensus law. If the judges are to do more than decide what the law means, if they are also to speak for it, their voice must be the voice of the community; it must never be taken for the voice of the government or the voice of the majority.

So, he argued, non-consensus law should not be enforceable by the courts and he criticized the way the Industrial Relations Act involved the courts in making orders for the enforcement of strike ballots and cooling-off orders. 'The prestige of the judiciary,' concluded Lord Devlin, 'their reputation for stark impartiality to be kept up in appearance as well as in fact, is not at the disposal of any government: it is an asset that belongs to the whole nation.'[2]

2. *The Sunday Times*, 6 August 1972.

The distinction drawn between consensus and nonconsensus law is not easy to sustain. Every government passes a number of politically controversial statutes – commonly about ten in each session – which contain much that is objected to by a large section of the electorate. Tax provisions, nationalization, housing finance, pay beds, industrial relations, comprehensive schooling, race relations, all these are obvious recent examples. If Lord Devlin means to limit non-consensus legislation only to those measures which people generally are not 'prepared to put up with' then his list will be very short indeed. If he means to extend it to include those major areas of controversy just exemplified then the list will be much longer. Is he saying that the enforcement procedures of the courts should not be used where, for example, council tenants refuse to pay rents, or councillors refuse to pay sums surcharged on them after an auditor's examination, or a member of the National Front refuses to remove a sign from his property which is in breach of the Race Relations Act, or a parent keeps his child away from a comprehensive school, or Welsh students disrupt court proceedings?

Surely Lord Devlin is trying to have it both ways. If the judiciary is more than 'a neutral arbitral force' – and I agree that it is – then it is most obviously so in controversial matters where its 'deployment' of power is highlighted. When the public interest is involved, judges become active and cannot suddenly become coy about enforcing laws – if necessary by their own procedures – which they believe to be politically controversial. Judges are in the business of upholding the law and that means they are part of the machinery for enforcing party political law as much as other 'consensus' legislation. Moreover, Lord Devlin is wrong if he believes that trade union distrust of the judiciary flows from the fact that the enforcement of the order for committal to prison of the dockers was effected by court officials rather than by other public servants. It was the order of the court that mattered, not the method of its enforcement.

Nevertheless, when all this is said, the importance of Lord Devlin's analysis rests in his denial of the neutrality of the judiciary in matters like the criminal law and, I would add, inevitably whenever judges set limits, as they frequently do, to governmental powers and individual rights in circumstances where statutes and common law give guidance which is inadequate or imprecise.

The public interest and its application

At this point the traditional views become inadequate as descriptions of what judges do. The judges determine (where doubts arise) the limits of governmental powers and of individual rights. But as the law has not provided them with full indications of where those limits are to be drawn, they must have regard to some concept on which they can base their judgments.

The higher judiciary comprises some hundred persons, but the truly effective number of policy-makers in the Divisional Court, the Court of Appeal and the House of Lords is fewer than forty. *These judges have by their education and training and the pursuit of their profession as barristers, acquired a strikingly homogeneous collection of attitudes, beliefs and principles, which to them represent the public interest.* They do not always express it as such. But it is the lodestar by which they navigate.

I use 'the public interest' because that is the phrase most used by the judges themselves when they choose to be explicit. Sometimes they speak of 'the interests of the State' but this carries a somewhat narrower meaning and suggests either the interests of the United Kingdom internationally or the interests of good government. 'The national interest' is synonymous, in judicial usage, with State interests. I take 'the public interest' to embrace both these other phrases but also to include the interest of the people at large, especially when contrasted with the interests of sections of the people.

What is or is not in the public interest is a political question which admits of a great variety of answers. On important issues, especially where there are only two or three possible alternative courses of action, personal opinions easily become part of group opinions. Indeed, as conventional rhetoric, political parties always claim that their policies, and not those of their opponents, best serve the public interest. Another truism is that I will be inclined to identify my interests with those of the public. If I am chairman of General Motors I will be inclined to think that what is good for General Motors is good for the nation. But my own interests, as I see them, will not be limited to my obvious economic interests. They may include, for instance, the continuing stability of the society in which I live, or the continuance of those surrounding circumstances which may give my life meaning.

Clearly then what the government proposes to do may, or may not, in my opinion, promote the public interest. To accuse the government of not acting in the public interest is the oldest political criticism.

Judges in the United Kingdom are not beholden politically to the government of the day. And they have longer professional lives than most ministers. They, like civil servants, see governments come like water and go with the wind. They owe no loyalty to ministers, not even that temporary loyalty which civil servants owe. Coke said that Bracton said that the King ought to be under no man but under God and the law.[3] Judges are also lions under the throne but that seat is occupied in their eyes not by the Prime Minister but by the law and by their conception of the public interest. It is to that law and to that conception that they owe allegiance. In that lies their strength and their weakness, their value and their threat.

By allegiance to 'the law' judges mean the whole body of law much of which has its origins in the judge-made common law. 'The law' also means the rule of law and here the allegiance is to the philosophical ideal that we should be ruled by laws and not by men. If that means that power should not be exercised arbitrarily or on the whim of rulers and their officials but should be dependent on and flow from properly constituted authority and from rules written down and approved by some form of representative assembly, it is an admirable and necessary, if partial, safeguard against tyranny. The proposition can hardly be taken further because, in modern industrial society, it is impossible to avoid vesting considerable discretionary power in public officials if only because laws cannot be adequately framed to cover every eventuality.

The judicial conception of the public interest, seen in the cases discussed in this book, is threefold. It concerns first, the interest of the State (including its moral welfare) and the preservation of law and order, broadly interpreted; secondly, the protection of property rights; and thirdly the promotion of certain political views normally associated with the Conservative Party.

First, then, the interests of the State, as the basis of judicial law-making, are most obvious in cases where the country is seen as being in an emergency of national dimensions. The civil liberty cases like *Liversidge v. Anderson, Greene, Halliday* and others (see above, pp. 83–5) are examples, and it is significant that the so-called libertarian principles which are said to lie behind habeas corpus and other such remedies have seldom proved strong enough to prevail over the interests of the State in these circumstances – as Mr Soblen,

3. *Prohibitions del Roy* (1607) 12 Co. Rep. 63.

Mr Hosenball and Mr Zamir discovered (see above, chapter 4). The decisions of the House of Lords in the *Guardian Newspapers* and the *GCHQ* cases show how difficult it is to rebut overriding claims by Ministers that actions are necessary in the interests of national security (see above, pp. 86, 128).

But the interests of the State, or the national interests, are invoked more widely as the basis for judicial policies. The exercise of judicial legerdemain which sprang the five dockers from prison in 1972 was certainly motivated by the imminence of a probable general strike (see above, pp. 65–7). So also the national interest in the administration of justice was appealed to – unconvincingly – by the judges when they decided to stifle further discussion by *The Sunday Times* of the thalidomide scandal (see above, pp. 113–14).

The power of the Crown to claim that documents ought not, in the public interest, to be disclosed, conflicts directly with the political claim that the public has a right to know unless strong evidence is adduced to the contrary. In *Conway v. Rimmer* (see above, pp. 119–20) the House of Lords shifted their interpretation of where the public interest lay a little towards the interest of the public. But Lord Reid swept aside in the grand bureaucratic manner a few democratic rights when he said that the most important reason for preserving secrecy for government documents was that their disclosure might 'create or fan ill-informed or captious public or political criticism' from those 'without adequate knowledge of the background and perhaps with some axe to grind' (see above, p. 120). This undue protectiveness towards governmental institutions was markedly emphasized by the House of Lords in *British Steel Corporation v. Granada Television* (see above, pp. 125–6) and by the House of Lords in *Home Office v. Harman* (see above, pp. 121–2). In the former case Lord Wilberforce made a significant distinction when he said: 'There is a wide difference between what is interesting to the public and what it is in the public interest to make known.' So also, the Lord Chief Justice in the Crossman diaries case (see above, p. 117) may have introduced his judicial colleagues to new and dangerous opportunities for the exercise of their conception of the nature and extent of the public interest and have established a new legal principle of confidentiality under which the views of ministers and former ministers could be suppressed without resort to the Official Secrets Acts. But for that we must wait and see. Nevertheless it seems clear that the courts are poised to develop the principle of confidentiality, in addition to contempt of court, so as to limit still further the freedom of the press, as the *Schering*

Chemicals case (see above, p. 127) shows.

The public interest expressly informs the attitude of the courts to questions of moral behaviour. Lord Denning's 'She would never make a teacher. No parent would willingly entrust their child to her care,' was no doubt a trivial, though revealing, comment (see above, p. 168). But the great periods of the rhetoric of Viscount Simonds, creating a new crime of conspiracy to corrupt public morals, when he claimed that the courts had the power 'to enforce the supreme and fundamental purpose of the law, to conserve not only the safety and order but also the moral welfare of the State' (see above, p. 152) were not trivial at all.

As Lord Devlin has said, in the passage already quoted (see above, p. 196), 'the judges regard themselves as at least as much concerned as the executive with the preservation of law and order.' One of the greatest political myths is that the courts in this country are alert to protect the individual against the power of the State. Sometimes, it is true, they will intervene to help the weakest, as some of the immigration cases show. But minority groups, especially if they demonstrate or protest in ways which cause difficulty or embarrassment, are not likely to find that the courts support their claims to free speech or free assembly. The judges see themselves as occupying a key position in the struggle to enforce the law, and are always conscious of the dangers which they believe will follow if they do not support the powers of the police.

The student cases are excellent examples of the judicial obsession with, as they see it, the necessity to protect and preserve the structures of constitutional authority without undue concern for the rights of those who wish to challenge that authority. Student protest is seen as essentially a problem of law and order.

The judicial attitude has been almost wholly condemnatory, seemingly based on the assumption that if students oppose university or college authorities they must be acting unreasonably. Here the view of the courts seems to have been based, fairly simply, on the public interest in maintaining 'discipline' regarding adult educational institutions rather as if they were public boarding schools. At the same time there is more than a hint that the courts do not wish to be troubled by argumentative students and that the Visitors are more appropriate tribunals.[4]

Demonstrations, if properly organized and controlled by the police, are acceptable by the judiciary as being within the

4. See *Casson v. University of Aston in Birmingham* [1983] 1 All ER 88.

framework of law and order. But individual demonstrators are always likely to be viewed with considerable disfavour by the courts. Although very different in kind, two of the most repressive decisions handed down in recent years were those in *Kamara* (see above, pp. 157–9) and in *Hubbard v. Pitt* (see above, pp. 159–60). Lord Hailsham's extension of the criminal law to cover peaceful sit-ins and occupations as a method of demonstration in the first of these cases, and the Court of Appeal's finding for the estate agents against peaceful demonstrators in the second, mark once more the willingness of the judiciary to extend the rather special judicial conception of where the public interest lies into the areas of political controversy.

In perhaps the most important area of all, that of police powers (see above, pp. 87–94), the judges have left largely unfulfilled their self-styled role as protectors of the individual. The practice of the police in relation to questioning, search and seizure, access to lawyers, the obtaining of confessions, the conduct of identification parades and telephone tapping, has frequently, in recent years, stretched far beyond their powers and infringed not only the spirit of the law but its letter also. Suspects have been held for long periods of time 'helping the police with their enquiries' and solicitors have been positively prevented by the police from seeing their clients. These practices have been generally supported by the judiciary.[5] When on 2 July 1976 Lord Justice Lawton in the Court of Appeal warned customs and police officers against detaining people to help with enquiries and refusing solicitors access to clients, as happened in the case before him, the press treated his statement as remarkable and one legal journalist went so far as to say that the Lord Justice had 'blown the gaff.'[6] The reaction was more revealing than the statement.

The second aspect of the public interest, as seen by the judges, is the protection of private property. Here the tradition stems from the common law so much of which arose specifically for the purpose of settling disputes relating to land and settlements. In public law, the disputes arise because of the power of the State to control the use of land, to acquire land for public purposes or for slum clearance, or in other ways (where the notion of property extends to rights in interests other than land) to limit the activities of

5. It is arguable that the right of access to a lawyer is at present more firmly protected by the courts for convicted prisoners than it is for those arrested but not charged (see above, p. 172–5).

6. See *The Times*, 3 July 1976; and *The Guardian*, 5 July 1976.

personal owners. We have seen (in Chapter 5) how, apart from a brief period during and after the Second World War, the courts have continuously intervened to limit and curtail the powers of governments to interfere with property rights, especially where the holding is large and the owner is a company, not an individual; and that they have been far more assiduous in this than in the protection of civil rights or liberties.

Not only the attitude but the very function of the judiciary in modern society are exemplified and emphasized by the difference in the protection of property rights and of personal human rights. Indeed 'rights' itself has two separate meanings in this context. Property rights are vested in individuals by the operation of the law. Contracts, leases, trusts, wills and settlements are all ways of creating and transferring these rights in law. And the protection of these rights is the primary purpose of a legal system. The law protects legal rights as they are. Its function, and that of the judiciary, is to maintain the existing state of affairs.

Personal – or human – rights are not vested rights but claims. Even where they are presently enjoyed, they have to be continuously insisted on and continuously fought for. Any carelessness in the protection of freedom leads directly to their erosion. Moreover, the enlargement of my freedom, my liberties, means the diminution of power, to however small an extent, enjoyed by some other person or, more likely, some official or institution. When, therefore, the judiciary is asked to defend such personal rights, it is being asked not to protect but to assert, not to strengthen institutions but to weaken them. And this is something which judges are reluctant to do for it is alien to their principal function which is not the enlargement of liberty, but the preservation of legally vested rights.

The attitude of the courts to trade union members who incur the displeasure of union officials is, as we have seen, one of considerable sympathy. When it can be shown that the officials have acted unfairly or improperly, this sympathy is well-placed for it is a most serious matter to deprive a man of his livelihood. Yet the same sympathy is not extended to the same degree to those who claim that their companies have unjustly dismissed them. And the suspicion arises that the courts in protecting the individual trade unionist are motivated more by their dislike of organized trade unions than by their wish to advance the personal rights of individuals.

The third aspect of the public interest is, I have suggested, the promotion of certain political, conservative views. First there are the trade union cases. We have seen (see above, pp. 154–7) that the prevailing view of the senior judiciary in the late nineteenth and early twentieth centuries was, in conflict with much of the governmental view of the time, that the growing power of the trade unions should be strictly controlled by law. The judges were seeking to undo some of the effects of earlier legislation and Lord Halsbury, as Lord Chancellor, led them to some success in this attempt. When, over half a century later, the judges and the unions once more came into conflict, the government had adopted the judicial view which was shown in the picketing cases, *Rookes v. Barnard*, and the culmination in *Heaton*'s case and the imprisonment by the NIRC of the five dockers (see above, pp. 64–7). Nor is the view unpopular. But when the economic consequences of the continued detention of the dockers and the threat of a general strike became clear, then what was in 'the public interest' was seen to have changed dramatically, and the dockers were released. The president of the NIRC imprisoned the dockers expressly in defence of the rule of law when to ignore their challenge would be to 'imperil all law and order', on which 'our whole way of life' was based. A few days later he released them – also, expressly, in defence of the rule of law – having been provided by the House of Lords with a flimsy justification for so doing (see above, p. 66).

So the National Industrial Relations Court in 1972 forced the judiciary to take up a position on the government's side of industrial disputes which divided the country (see above, pp. 195–7). But, especially here, the distinction must be observed between the interests of the government of the day and the judiciary's view of the public interest. Certainly, the two interests coincided for the judges enabled the government to escape from a situation which would probably have brought it down and would have presented the trade union movement with a considerable political victory. The judges, we may assume, were not concerned to save that particular Conservative government. They were concerned, however, both to preserve the authority of governments and to avoid economic chaos. That was where they saw the public interest to lie. The price they paid was the increase in distrust between themselves and the trade union movement. So they may have mistaken the public interest. But that is a political comment about a political choice.

In the conflict between the Court of Appeal and the House of Lords in 1979-80 (see above, pp. 70-3) the difference in views of the law, as I have said, did not reflect any difference about its undesirability. In *NWL Ltd v. Woods* Lord Diplock talked of the possibility of wage demands bringing down 'the fabric of the present economic system'. In *Express Newspapers v. McShane* he said that the consequences of applying the subjective test in interpreting 'furtherance of a trade dispute' 'not surprisingly have tended to stick in judicial gorges',[7] and in *Duport Steels v. Sirs* he said that the immunity given to trade unionists was:

> intrinsically repugnant to anyone who has spent his life in the practice of the law or the administration of justice . . . It involves granting to trade unions a power, which has no other limits than their own self-interest, to inflict by means which are contrary to the general law, untold harm to industrial enterprises unconcerned with the particular dispute, to the employees of such enterprises, to members of the public and to the nation itself . . .[8]

even though the 'immunity' was, as Lord Scarman said, in substance that given by the legislation of 1906.

In the same case Lord Edmund-Davies called the outcome of the statute 'unpalatable to many', and Lord Keith referred to trade unionists as 'privileged persons' who could 'bring about disastrous consequences with legal impunity'.[9]

Similarly, Lord Denning MR in the Court of Appeal said:

> There is evidence of the disastrous effect which the action will have, not only on all the companies in the private sector, but on much of British industry itself . . . our competitors will clap their hands . . . there is a residual discretion in the courts to grant an injunction restraining such action as in this case, where it is such as to cause grave danger to the economy and the life of the country, and puts the whole nation and its welfare at risk.[10]

Why, then, did the House of Lords not support the Court of Appeal? To have done so in *Express Newspapers v. McShane* would not have been difficult. It is not manifestly absurd to interpret 'in furtherance of a trade dispute' as implying an objective test and the gap between Lord Wilberforce's approach and that of Lord Denning (see above, pp. 71–2) is not large. To have supported the

7. [1980] 2 WLR at 97.
8. [1980] 1 All ER at 541; and see Wedderburn's article referred to below at note 43.
9. Ibid. at 548, 550.
10. Ibid. at 535, 536, 538.

Court of Appeal would certainly have brought the judiciary into even sharper confrontation with the trade unions and to have further diminished in certain quarters what Lord Diplock in *Duport Steels* called 'that voluntary respect for the law as laid down and applied by courts of justice'.[11] Lords Keith and Scarman expressed similar fears.

Moreover these decisions were taken at a time when the newly elected Conservative government were embarking on their legislative reforms of trade union law, the Employment Bill being published at the beginning of December 1979. Their Lordships may well have concluded that it would be wiser to leave such highly contentious political matters to the professional politicians. At the same time, some of their Lordships did not hesitate to push the Conservative government in what they saw as the right direction. Their criticism of the powers which the existing legislation gave to trade unionists could hardly have been stronger and Lords Diplock, Salmon and Edmund-Davies in *Duport Steels* made quite clear that they hoped the law would be changed. To the layman it must have seemed that members of the senior judiciary were publicly throwing their weight behind the Conservative government.

The Law Lords were, in these cases, moving sharply and clearly to restrain Lord Denning and the Court of Appeal from developing a policy of restricting trade union activity. The Law Lords saw the need, in the public interest, of avoiding an open conflict between the courts and the trade unions. The disagreement between the Court of Appeal and the House of Lords presented a clear difference of tactics. Both courts were agreed that trade union power should be curbed, and in this their political position was identical. But on the question of how far the courts should intervene, the Law Lords preferred discretion to valour.

The approach of the courts to the Race Relations Acts, as shown in the decisions in *Zesko* and the club cases particularly, proceeds on the basis that this legislation is primarily an interference with the rights of individuals to discriminate and that the public interest is best served by restricting the impact of that legislation as far as possible (see above, pp. 95–7). Despite the natural conservatism of the House of Lords, this does seem to be a more than usually restrictive attitude. The alternative interpretation of the legislation was so clearly available to their Lordships that it is impossible to avoid the conclusion that theirs was a deliberate policy decision.

11. Ibid. at 547.

Lord Diplock perhaps gives the key when he speaks of the Race Relations Act 'however admirable its motives' as restricting liberty. The idea of intervening by legislation in this way with the freedom 'enjoyed at common law to differentiate between one person and another' was clearly offensive to him, as it is indeed to many.

The attitude of the judiciary to immigrants reached a high level of injustice in *Zamir* (see above, p. 108) and *Kotecha* (see above, pp. 112–12). It is hoped that *Khera* (see above, pp. 109–10) marks a change.

Three case studies

If it is agreed that the senior judiciary, especially those who sit in the Court of Appeal and the House of Lords, are required from time to time to decide where the public interest lies (or which of two conflicting public interests should prevail) and that, in this sense, they cannot be neutral but must make political choices, the question is how well they perform this difficult task. It has been part of the argument of this book that they are inevitably, as are the rest of us, to a considerable extent conditioned by their social background, by their experiences and by their professional careers as barristers. But they are also constrained by the system within which they work.

The senior judiciary are, of course, well aware of the importance of their role in government. They are better informed about policy and its development than most of those who are neither ministers nor senior civil servants. Their ears are close to the ground of politics, whether it concerns industrial relations or race relations, immigration policy, police powers or national security. On many matters their policies (or views of where the public interest lies) accord with those of the government of the day because they are part of that consensus. If the political differences between the major political parties were more divergent, and a party of the right or of the left, holding what would now be regarded as extreme views, were elected, the senior judiciary would be faced with critical choices. But this is not, and is not likely to be, the case.

At the same time, the senior judiciary are men of great ability and strong opinions. Their assessment of the public interest does from time to time differ from that of the central Departments and local authorities whose decisions and actions they are called on to judge. And they are not greatly knowledgeable in the processes of administration. Nor, despite their sensibility, are they necessarily fully aware of current developments in policy or administration.

These two factors – the independence of their assessments and their lack of knowledge – explain how, from time to time, they come to decisions that seem eccentric.

Three recent examples are illustrative. The first is the *Bromley v. GLC* litigation over the Fares Fair policy.[12]

It may be, of course, that the Court of Appeal and the Law Lords deliberately intervened to control the collectivist policies of the administration at County Hall because they disapproved of those policies. But in addition and perhaps more significantly, they seem not to have understood what they were doing, because they did not grasp the nature of the problem of London transport. The administrative build-up to the Fares Fair policy had its roots in the mid-1960s; and professional administrators, not only in London, had been grappling with the problems over a long period. It was for that reason that those administrators were stupefied and dismayed by what seemed to them to be arbitrary and wholly unrealistic sets of reasons advanced by the Court of Appeal and the House of Lords for upsetting an attempt to solve the financial, administrative, social and economic problems of London Transport.

The judgments delivered in the Court of Appeal and the House of Lords in *Bromley v. GLC* demonstrate how ill-suited is judicial review to the examination of administrative policies. They show how the narrow approach of the courts to the interpretation of statutes leads to a misunderstanding of the purpose of legislation. When this is combined with the application of a broad principle ('the fiduciary duty') to the examination of the exercise of administrative discretion, the mismatch becomes almost total. We do not know to what extent the members of the two courts sought to inform themselves of the recent developments in transport policy, other than by looking at the legislation of the 1960s. Lord Wilberforce, as we have seen,[13] while recognizing that there existed 'discussion on the political level', concluded that 'the only safe course' was to try to understand 'the contemporary language' by which he meant the words of the Act of 1969. Lord Diplock was again the exception, refusing to accept, in the absence of clear words, that the GLC was prohibited from operating a system of deficit financing deliberately created.

The crisis in urban transport received popular recognition in the publication in 1963 of Colin Buchanan's *Traffic in Towns*. This was

12. See above, pp. 142–9
13. See above, p. 146.

followed in 1966 by the white paper on *Transport Policy*.[14] This emphasized the 'severe discomforts' brought by the growth of road traffic: congestion, the misery of commuter travel, noise, fumes, danger, casualties and the threat to the environment; and the need to plan, as a whole, for the related needs of industry, housing and transport.[15] The paper drew attention to the mutually contradictory objectives of providing adequate services and self-financing. In January 1968, the London Transport Joint Review was published and was followed in July by the white paper *Transport in London*[16] The Review found that the major factor underlying London Transport's recurrent financial deficit was the imbalance between peak and off-peak demand. The Review was somewhat ambiguous about the need for financial viability, but it certainly envisaged some form of grant and emphasized the social benefits of controlling the level of fares while providing proper services. *Transport in London* went further in emphasizing the need of the transport system to take account of 'the social as well as the economic needs of the country'. Subsidization through the local rates was one of the means adopted by the Transport Act 1968 for conurbations outside London and this was intended to enable the transport authorities to achieve, in part, the purpose of developing transport as a social service.

The Transport (London) Act 1969 was seen by ministers as taking this approach further. For the first time in London, the responsibility for transport was given to a directly elected local authority acting through an Executive appointed by itself. Comparison has been made with a nationalized industry operating the day-to-day management under the general directions of a minister. But the control by the GLC over the LTE was much tighter than that of a minister over the coal, gas or electricity authorities. The GLC was not merely empowered but required by section 1 'to develop policies, and to encourage, organize and, where appropriate, carry out measures'. The LTE existed to implement policies of the GLC (section 4(1)) and to act 'in accordance with principles laid down or approved by the GLC' (section 5(1)). Additionally, the GLC might give the LTE general directions in relation to functions which the GLC was under a duty

14. Cmnd. 3057. On the development of transport policy in the 1960s see J. Dignan, 'Policy-making, Local Authorities and the Courts' in 99 *Law Quarterly Review* (1983) 605, to which I am much indebted.
15. Car and motorcycle licences in the London Transport area rose from 1.7m in 1960 to 2.3m in 1966.
16. Cmnd. 3686.

to perform (section 11(1)). There were also other more detailed provisions emphasizing the powers of the GLC. Above all, the GLC's primary duty was to promote 'the provision of integrated, efficient and economic transport facilities and services for Greater London.' Finally, the LTE was required to submit to the GLC for their approval the general level and structure of the fares to be charged and the GLC might 'direct the Executive to submit proposals for an alteration in the Executive's fare arrangements to achieve any object of general policy specified by the Council in the direction' (section 11(3)).

As Dignan has written:[17]

If one examines in this way the detailed legislative history of the 1969 Act and its closely related predecessor, enacted in the previous year, it will be seen that the Labour Government had clearly embarked on a radical new policy for urban transport, one which entailed profound implications for the local state in terms of its functions, its powers and its responsibility. It was not just that the government's novel response to a whole series of interrelated problems represented a substantial break with earlier transport policies; rather, it marked a decisive shift from one kind of legislative framework to another, consistent with . . . a transition from a gesellschaft to a bureaucratic-administrative infrastructure.

Separate from the social and political background which shaped the transport of the late 1960s was an administrative development of significance. It was a period of 'planning, programming and financing'.[18] The approach at this time, not only for public transport, was, first, to determine what was to be achieved; second, to produce a programme for this end; and third, to determine how it was to be financed. This does not mean that the cost was irrelevant. On the contrary, it was an important element in determining what was to be achieved and how it was to be achieved. But finance was used as a tool of measurement. Once it was decided what transport policy, for example, should be and how it was to be implemented, the question of the method of financing (by fares,

17. See note 14 above.
18. I am much indebted to a paper by Mr Stonefrost, then Comptroller of Finance and later Director-General of the GLC, presented to the Oxford University Faculty of Law and SSRC Centre for Socio-legal Studies on 2 March 1983; and to Mr Fitzpatrick, Solicitor to the GLC.

by grants, by taxation) was determined as seemed most appropriate. The principle, beloved of market economists, that the consumer should pay the full cost unless some very special case could be made out for some form of subsidy, was not seen as of great significance. As Mr Stonefrost wrote:

> To hold out a presumption that an undertaking can 'break even' or 'make a profit' when such an assumption is implicity known to be impracticable on current policies in the accounting period in question is to contribute to irresponsibility. Management needs to be set realistic financial possibilities. In public administration in the late 60s debts were cleared on several public services, realistic planning and management targets were established and, if subsidy was known to be necessary, its size and the conditions applying to its availability were set in advance as a necessary precondition to set out and to test management performance.

The House of Lords, like the Court of Appeal, had a clear policy choice in interpreting the 1969 Act.[19] By choosing to set the words of section 7 (dealing with the financial accounting arrangements between the GLC and the LTE and the financial duties of the LTE) over the policy provisions of sections 1 and 5 (the grants section) and by invoking the concept of the fiduciary duty, the courts were able virtually to ignore social and economic factors which had produced the Act. Why did they make this choice?

For the members of the Court of Appeal, one reason seems to have been their annoyance with the way in which the GLC majority group implemented their manifesto commitment. Five days after the election in May 1981 the leader of the GLC instructed the chairman of the LTE to submit proposals for the 25 per cent reduction in fares to a meeting on 1 July. Lord Denning held that the GLC had no power to make resolutions to enforce a 25 per cent cut which 'was a completely uneconomic proposition done for political motives – for which there is no warrant'. Similarly Watkins LJ had 'no doubt whatsoever that the large reduction of fares the LTE was ordered to introduce by the GLC arouse out of a hasty, ill-considered, unlawful and arbitrary use of power . . . and the ratepayers of this great city, who are unlikely to gain anything from it (many of them will in fact be at a loss), will bear the cost of what

19. See above, p. 146.

seems to many to have been an astounding decision.' With a nice touch of judicial arrogance he added: 'Those who come newly to govern people and who act in haste in wielding power to which they are unaccustomed would do well to heed the words of Gladstone . . . "The true test of a man, the test of a class, the true test of a people is power. It is when power is given into their hands that the trial comes."' Oliver LJ also found the procedural hurdle ('perhaps rather a technical one') impossible for the GLC to surmount.

In the House of Lords these arguments hardly featured and were certainly not crucial. There, with all the emphasis on 'economic', on the need for the GLC to act in a 'business-like' manner, the reason for the choice seems to have been primarily the Law Lords' strong preference for the principles of the market economy with a dislike of heavy subsidization for social purposes. Their decisions were in the tradition of individual rather than social, private rather than collective, enterprise. They appeared to think there was something unseemly in a policy change of these dimensions. Lord Keith, referring to the power of the GLC in section 11 to direct the LTE to submit proposals for an alteration in the fare arrangements to achieve 'any object of general policy' specified by the GLC, said that that phrase 'clearly' was 'confined to the field of transport policy'. Such a limitation, very difficult to justify from the language of the Act, shows how far their Lordships were from understanding the statutory intention. Whether or not their Lordships were politically biased, their habits of thought determined their decision.

Bromley v. GLC raises all the questions about the nature, the function, and the limits of judicial review. The whole method of adjudication as presently adopted by the courts is inappropriate to the consideration of political decisions affecting the distribution of costs between the tax and ratepaying public, on the one hand, and the users of public services, on the other. As Mr Stonefrost said, in the paper to which I have referred, as he reflected on the judicial process in this case:

> The process itself was more in the nature of an intellectual marauding over a wide area of hunting territory rather than an ordered, structured, predictable and prepared process. Some issues were dealt with comprehensively and with full intellectual rigour. But others were not and it was not possible to predict on which of many issues a member of the Court might concentrate upon at any one time. The basic judicial process of adversarial advocacy, punctuated courteously but irregularly, unpredictably

and frequently by important court questions and interjections working from a mound of papers within a necessarily highly concentrated but limited time scale, contrasts sharply with an administrative policy decision which may be an important final expression of widespread political struggle and practical pressures over a very long period of time.

The second example is the treatment by the Court of Appeal and the House of Lords of the Commission for Racial Equality.[20]

In *Hillingdon*, Lord Diplock took the view that the terms of reference defined the scope of the investigation and that the terms as drawn were wider than the 'belief' and so invalid; and that this was so even though the CRE had made clear from the beginning that their investigation would be limited to the area of their belief about the treatment of immigrants only.

Lord Diplock's interpretation was clearly not one to which he was driven by the words of section 49(4). He chose a narrow and over-literal meaning and so unnecessarily frustrated the main purpose of the Act. Nor could it be said that the alternative interpretation would have caused injustice to the Council. 'Belief' in this context is understood, even by Lord Diplock, as a very modest state of consciousness. In *Prestige* he said that the CRE 'should in fact have already formed a suspicion that the persons named may have committed some unlawful act of discrimination and had at any rate *some* grounds for so suspecting, albeit that the grounds upon which any such suspicion was based might, at that stage, be no more than tenuous because they had not yet been tested.' If 'belief' may properly be as weak as that, no measurable hardship can come from drawing terms of reference a little widely especially when they do not name any person other than one to whom justifiable suspicion is directed.

As we have seen, it was in *Hillingdon* that Lord Diplock first laid down that 'belief' about a named person was a condition precedent to the drawing up of terms of reference. In *Prestige* he repeated and applied this. 'We have always taken the view', said the CRE in 1983, 'that the CRE is entitled to carry out formal investigations whether there are grounds for suspecting an unlawful act or not,' and they regarded the Court of Appeal's contrary opinion in *Prestige* (which was to be confirmed by the House of Lords) as 'a severe, and in our view wrong, constraint on the discretion of the

20. See above, pp. 99–104.

Commission'.[21] The strategy of the CRE in relation to formal investigations – which had had considerable success – is having to be rethought, as in the view of the CRE they can now only investigate a named organization – 'and all organizations have names' – if they already have reason to believe that it may be discriminating unlawfully.[22]

Here again, Lord Diplock in *Prestige* made his choice. The words of sections 49 and 50 of the Act are fully capable of being interpreted as meaning that a named-person investigation need not be directed to uncovering discrimination, although in such a case the CRE would have no coercive powers. Of course the distinction between a named-person investigation and a general investigation is frequently not clear because the latter is often sparked off by specific complaints.

Again, the judicial interpretation of sections 49(4) was far from obvious. This subsection was, as Lord Denning MR pointed out in *Hillingdon*, a drafting blunder. Lord Hailsham had moved an amendment as a new clause to the Bill to a similar effect with the intention of ensuring that a person named would have the right to be heard *during the course* of a formal investigation. The government rejected his formulation and produced one of their own. But this was tacked on as subsection (4) to the previous clause (now section 49) and so fell under the terms of subsection (1) which requires compliance with subsections (2)-(4) before the CRE could embark on a formal investigation. In *Prestige*, unlike *Hillingdon*, no 'belief' was expressed in the terms of reference, and it was not until the investigation was well advanced that the CRE came to a belief that Prestige were committing discriminatory acts. So, CRE argued, subsection (4) applied only to the start of an investigation when in the terms of reference a belief had been stated about a named person.

Moreover subsection (4) refers to a named person having the right to make representations with regard to 'it' in a context where 'it' could mean the proposal to investigate or the discriminatory act itself. If it were interpreted to mean the latter, then the obligation on the Commission before embarking on the investigation would be limited to offering an opportunity to make representations about the act during the course of the investigation, which is what Lord Hailsham (and we may assume the government) meant.

Both these interpretations were rejected by Lord Diplock

21. See above, p. 101, note 44.
22. CRE *Annual Report* for 1983 at p. 3.

although both of them would have promoted the purposes of the statute without causing injustice.

We have already seen how Lord Diplock, in 1974 in the *Dockers' Club* case, saw legislation seeking to deal with racial discrimination as a restriction on the liberty of the citizen.[23] In these cases involving the CRE his emphasis is the same. As the CRE said in 1983: 'It may be that judges will never be able to accept the fact that Parliament has entrusted the CRE with sweeping investigative powers to work towards the eradication of a great social evil being carried out covertly.'[24] Individual grievances were left, under the Act of 1976, to individuals to redress. The CRE was given 'a major strategic role in enforcing the law in the public interest'.[25] The idea of a public authority invested with the power to investigate, to adjudicate and to decide, while providing persons affected with opportunities to make representations, was too much for the senior judiciary, reared in the tradition of private rights, to accept. Lord Denning MR expressed their horror.

I would draw attention to the immense powers already granted by Parliament to the statutory commissions. They can conduct 'formal investigations' by which they can interrogate employers and educational authorities up to the hilt and compel disclosure of documents on a massive scale. They can take up the cause of any complainant who has a grievance and, in his name, issue a questionnaire to his employers or educational authorities. They can use his name to sue them, and demand full particulars in the course of it. They can compel discovery of documents from them to the same extent as in the High Court. No plea is available to the accused that they are not bound to incriminate themselves. You might think that we were back in the days of the Inquisition. Now we come to the most presumptuous claim of all. They demand to see documents made in confidence, and to compel breaches of good faith – which is owed to persons who are not parties to the proceedings at all. You might think we were back in the days of the General Warrants.

The decision in the *Laker Airways* case[26] provides a third example of the inadequacies of the judiciary when faced with administrative

23. See above, pp. 96–7.
24. See above, p. 101, note 44.
25. The Home Secretary (Mr R. Jenkins) during the second reading debate on the Bill (906 HC Deb. col. 1558, 4 March 1976).
26. See above, p. 136.

processes with which they are unfamiliar.[27] In 1960 the Air Transport Licensing Board was created by statute primarily to decide whether the Board should issue to an airline an 'air service licence' without which the airline could not operate. Under the Act and regulations, the Board was required to hold hearings and the procedure was highly judicialized. There was a right of appeal to the minister from a decision of the Board and he appointed a Commissioner to hear the appeal and to make recommendations which the minister could accept or reject. The minister also had to enter into agreements with foreign states in relation to traffic rights and fare levels. In addition the minister gave general non-statutory guidance to the Board on policy matters. The working relationship so constructed between the Board and minister did not make for rational policy-making and G. R. Baldwin concluded that the Board provided 'an unadventurous blend of the judicial with the managerial and of expertise with independence'.[28]

In 1967 the Select Committee on Nationalised Industries recommended drastic changes.[29] So did the Edwards Committee which in 1969 recommended the setting up of a much stronger agency and favoured the use of written policy guidance from the minister. Such guidance should be set down in 'terms sufficiently clear to be generally understood and if necessary to stand the test of judicial interpretation'. The Labour government published a White Paper[30] which emphasized the need for a new Civil Aviation Authority (CAA), the essential feature of whose status would be the separation between policy formulation (which would be for ministers to determine) and the detailed application of policy (where the CAA would have a wide discretion). This was the Authority set up by the Conservative government under the Civil Aviation Act 1971. As we have seen, the minister was now statutorily empowered to issue written policy guidance and to hear appeals. The first guidance comprised twenty-two pages of general policy. In 1974 the new Labour minister conducted a review of policy to which the CAA submitted detailed reports and in July 1975 he proposed a number of policy changes to be incorporated in the new guidance. One of these changes was that the new policy would in general rule out long-haul scheduled competition. British

27. See G. R. Baldwin, 'A British Independent Regulatory Agency and the "Skytrain" Decision' [1978] *Public Law* 57, to which I am indebted.
28. See note 27 above.
29. HC 673 of 1966-7.
30. Cmnd. 4213 (1969).

Caledonian and British Airways would be given protected spheres of interest and Laker's Skytrain would not be allowed to operate. The new guidance was issued in March 1976.[31]

The crucial question in the litigation was therefore whether the minister's power of 'guidance' entitled him to overrule the CAA. And this, in turn, depended on the purpose of the legislation in relation to the minister's powers generally over the CAA. The Court of Appeal, in the usual judicial manner, based itself on semantics. 'The word "guidance"', said Lord Denning, 'does not denote an order or command.' Roskill LJ said: 'it is not unreasonable to think, in spite of certain dictionary definitions of guidance . . . that the draftsmen intended a different result to follow according to whether it was guidance or a direction that was to be given.' And Lawton LJ said: 'The word "guidance" has the implication of leading, pointing the way, whereas "direction" even today echoes its Latin roots of *regere*, to rule. When the Secretary of State exercises his statutory powers to direct he does indeed rule. He is in command: he is more than a guide.' To all this the answer is that, as the history of the matter shows, it was the minister who was intended to determine policy by his guidance and that competitiveness or monopoly on long-haul routes was essentially a matter of policy.

G. R. Baldwin's summary seems irrefutable.

The judges of the Court of Appeal strove to protect the CAA's discretion and to cut down the Minister's discretion. In doing so they conceived of the CAA as a traditional body with 'quasi-judicial' functions. They saw it as a court giving licences with rights to be protected by legal due process and as a judicial body deserving protection from executive interference. They failed to see the significance of the CAA as a new form of multi-faceted agency of government, attempting to combine judicial and executive methods in a delicately balanced legal framework whilst acting in a politically contentious area. In attempting to preserve for the CAA an independent judicial status the judges sought to achieve the impossible. No one expected the CAA to be fully independent of government, in the manner of a court. As was pointed out in the Court of Appeal, the Government could always control the agency in ways other than by using Guidance. The Court of Appeal decision damaged a system of

31. Cmnd. 6400.

balance based on compromise because the system of control fitted no neat jurisprudential category.

It might be asked 'Why is it that the intentions behind the 1971 Act were not communicated to the judges?' The answer appears to be that the 1971 Act was based on a new conception of the relationship between the independent agency and government, a conception which the judges, with more old fashioned views concerning 'quasi-judicial' tribunals and ministerial powers, were unable to accept. The decisions are explicable perhaps, as the product of a period in which the courts (and some judges in particular) demonstrated a distinct eagerness to increase their review of executive powers and discretion. They were certainly disruptive.

The interaction between judicial and executive power is further illuminated by the policies concerning the illegal entry of immigrants.[32] In June 1973, the House of Lords ruled that the powers to detain and remove illegal entrants contained in the Immigration Act 1971 were retrospective[33] and so deprived many Commonwealth citizens in the UK of their status and made them liable to be detained and deported. On April 1974 the Home Secretary announced that he would not exercise this new judge-made power. In effect he declared an amnesty. The next step by the courts was to declare in 1976 and 1977 that, contrary to previous belief, illegal entrants included those who had secured entry by deception whether by the entrant himself or by someone acting on his behalf with or without his knowledge.[34] The Home Secretary responded in November 1977 by announcing that he would not use the retrospective powers where entry had been obtained by deception. The Home Office policy was that for deception to amount to illegal entry, the deception practised on an immigration officer had to be deliberate, material, and positive (the last meaning a clear failure to disclose information sought or a clearly misleading misrepresentation as to the truth). Failure to volunteer information was not considered to be deception. Then came the *Zamir* decision[35] which conflicted with the Home Office view. The Home

32. See Minutes of Evidence taken before the Home Affairs Committee subcommittee on race relations and immigration (HC 89 of 1980-1).

33. *R. v. Governor of Pentonville Prison ex parte Azam* [1974] AC 18.

34. *Khan v. Secretary of State for the Home Department* [1977] 3 All ER 538; *R. v. Secretary of State for the Home Deparment ex parte Hussain* [1978] 1 WLR 700.

35. See above, pp. 108–9.

Office responded by saying that they intended to interpret the judgment narrowly and that it was unlikely to lead to significant changes of policy or practice. The Home Office would not consider a person to be an illegal entrant unless satisfied that he realized or should have realized that the facts he failed to disclose were material.

The heart of this interaction is that whatever interpretation the courts may give to the definition of 'illegal entrant', it is for the Home Secretary to decide whether to take any action in each case. Every year the Home Office allows a substantial proportion of illegal entrants to remain indefinitely.

The *Zamir* decision was therefore wholly contrary to administrative policy and imposed a far harder line on dealing with immigrants than the Home Office had been practising. Indeed if that decision had had to be followed by deportation in each case, gross and manifest injustice would have resulted and it is significant that in the *Jayakody* case [36] the Home Office supported an appeal by an immigrant on the question of the materiality of the information withheld. Lord Wilberforce's language in *Zamir* showed his own approach.

At the very lowest an intending entrant must not practise a deception . . . deception vitiates the permission to enter . . . an alien seeking entry . . . is seeking a privilege.

We may assume that by the time the House of Lords came to consider *Khera* they had realized that the Home Office policy made more sense and was more just. And so they reversed their decision in *Zamir*. But the whole story demonstrates again how maladroit and clumsy is the approach adopted by the courts when faced with the difficult task of interpreting legislation designed to confer discretionary powers on administrative authorities.

The same comment may be made of the decision in *Padfield*.[37] The reason why the minister was empowered rather than required to refer a complaint to the committee of investigation was to enable him to decide that the complaint was a matter of policy and so appropriate for determination by the Milk Marketing Board and himself. By requiring him to set up the committee and refer the complaint to it, the House of Lords misinterpreted the statute. The result was the the minister referred the complaint to the committee

36. See above, p. 110–11.
37. See above, p. 132.

which recommended certain changes in the scheme. Whereupon the minister rejected the recommendation and the absurdity of the Lord's decision was demonstrated.[38]

These examples show that, under their present procedures, judges are ill-equipped to make political decisions which determine the way in which administrative authorities fulfil their duties. The courts of law are not designed as research centres, and judges in our system are most reluctant to assume an inquisitorial role and to seek to discover all the relevant facts. They rely on the adversarial method and take judicial notice only of those matters and those arguments presented to them. This position is carried to the extreme of not enabling a party to obtain discovery of documents unless he can show their direct relevance to his case.

In *Air Canada v. Secretary of State for Trade (No. 2)*[39] Lord Fraser said:

> In an adversarial system such as exists in the United Kingdom a party is free to withhold information that would help his case if he wishes, perhaps for reasons of delicacy or personal privacy. He cannot be compelled to disclose it against his will. It follows in my opinion that a party who seeks to compel his opponent, or an independent person, to disclose information must show that the information is likely to help his own case.

Lord Wilberforce said: 'There is no independent power in the court to say that . . . it would like to inspect the documents, with a view to possible production, *for its own assistance*' (emphasis added). Lord Edmund-Davies said, 'To urge that, on principle, justice is most likely to be done if free access is had to all relevant documents is pointless, for it carries no weight in our adversarial system of law.' The contrary view was put by Lord Templeman who said, 'The judge must decide whether the public interest in maintaining the confidential nature of the document prevails over the public interest in ensuring that justice is achieved.' So also Lord Scarman said, 'Discovery is one of the few exceptions to the adversarial character of our legal process. It assists parties and the court to discover the truth.' But they agreed with the majority in the event.

If the judiciary were willing to adopt a more inquisitorial role, they could insist that evidence be called on specific matters. The

---

38. See C. Harlow and R. Rawlings, *Law and Administration* (1984), pp. 327-9.
39. [1983] 1 All ER 161.

evidence of those directly concerned in both policy-making and the administrative process would clarify the issues and enable the courts to come to a more complete understanding of the nature of the public interest involved. Counsel can put the general situation before the court but their arguments are likely to be less effective and less well-informed than those of the individuals directly involved, be they politicians or public servants. Expert evidence also can play a most important part in the instruction of the judiciary.

In *Pickwell v. Camden LBC*,[40] a strike by the council's manual workers was settled on terms which were more favourable to those workers than the terms on which a parallel national dispute was settled. And a year later the council added a further cost-of-living increase, negotiated at the national level, and did not absorb it within the extra pay margin. The district auditor asked the court for a declaration that both payments were unlawful. But the court held that the council had not acted unreasonably or considered irrelevant matters or failed to consider relevant matters. The district auditor's calculations were challenged in an affidavit from a professor, expert in the field of pay and employment. Forbes J said: 'Whether the district auditor or Professor Metcalfe be right, the existence of so fundamental a divergence of opinion on a matter so important must cast some doubt on whether it can properly be said that no reasonable authority could possibly have acted as did Camden in this instance.' How far such evidence should be on affidavit and how far by oral testimony (and so open to cross-examination) would be for the court to decide. To this suggestion, two objections may be made. The first is that it would prolong the hearing of cases. This may well be so but if the judiciary are to continue to review decisions of the kind in *Bromley v. GLC*, the *Laker* and the *CRE* cases, they must have relevant evidence before them.

The other objection is more serious. If the judiciary were to adopt a more investigatory role, the danger is that they would be encouraged to encroach even more on policy matters than they do at present. So it would be necessary to curtail the scope of their enquiries.[41] Lord Scarman has said:

When one turns away from the field of legislation to that of

---

40. [1983] 1 All ER 602.
41. See my chapter in P. Archer and A. Martin (eds.), *More Law Reform Now* (1983), pp. 54-9.

executive discretion and decision, co-operation calls for a high degree of judicial restraint. The ambit of executive decision and executive discretion must be defined by statute: and judges must respect it. They will, of course, become the watch-dogs empowered to compel compliance with the conditions to which executive power is subject. But within these limits executive power is not to be curtailed by judicial action unless there be infringements of basic human rights such as liberty or natural justice or unless it can be demonstrated that the power was exercised in such a way as no reasonable person invested with the power could have exercised it. In other words, within the ambit of the power there can be no judicial challenge save to protect human rights or to curb abuse of power.[42]

It has been said that the House of Lords as the upper chamber of the Legislature does nothing in particular and does it very well. It could be said of that House in its judicial capacity that, in the field of public law, it does too much in particular and does it rather badly.

Conclusion

In suggesting that the senior judiciary look to a view of the public interest to inform their attitude to the controversial matters of law and order, of political and economic conflict, of sexual and social *mores*, of personal liberty and property rights, of protest, of governmental confidentiality, of students, of race relations, of immigration and the rest, I mean to absolve them of a conscious and deliberate intention to pursue their own interests or the interests of their class. I believe that in these matters and within the considerable area of decision-making open to them they look to what they regard as the interest of the whole society. However, we are left to consider why it is that their view of that public interest is what it is.

It is common to speak of the judiciary as part of the system of checks and balances which contains and constrains the power of the government; or as one of the three principal institutions of the State, each of which acts to limit the powers of the other two. The image has a pleasing and mechanistic appearance suggesting some

42. In a lecture at the Royal Institute of Public Administration on 4 November 1982.

objective hidden hand which holds the constitution in perpetual equilibrium. The extent to which the image reflects reality is less obvious.

If we limit our examination to the working of the three institutions – Parliament, the government, and the judiciary – in their relationships with each other, then it is clear that each of these groups influences the way in which the others act. And it is clear, in particular, that the judiciary may oppose the government to the extent of declaring its actions invalid or requiring it to pay compensation or even subjecting one of its members or servants to penalties.

If however we look more broadly and more widely we see that this judicial activity of opposing governments is a deviance from the norm, an aberration, which occurs most infrequently and in very special circumstances. The judiciary is not placed constitutionally in opposition to the government but, in the overwhelming mass of circumstances, alongside it.

In our society, as in others, political power, the power of government, is exercised by a relatively small number of people. Senior ministers are most obvious of that number, as are senior civil servants, chairmen of nationalized industries, the chairmen and chief officers of the largest local authorities. Among those who are not members of State institutions should be added a few industrialists and, under Labour governments, a few trade union leaders. And the leading members of Her Majesty's Opposition are also, from time to time, a part of the decision-making process at this highest level. The whole group numbers a few hundred people. They represent established authority.

The rest are outside. Some may be influential as advisers. Others may be very important as professional men and women. But they, along with the population at large, remain outside the governing group. Of course there are many organizations which exercise many different kinds of power within their own sphere. In this narrow sense, we live in a pluralist society. But the political power of governing the country is oligarchic, exercised by a few.

The senior judges are undeniably among those few. The importance of their task, their influence on behaviour, the extent of their powers, the status they enjoy, the extrajudicial uses to which they are put, the circles they move in, the background from which they come, their habits of mind, and the way in which they are regarded by other members of the group confirm beyond question their place within the governing group of established authority. And, like other members of the group, they show themselves alert to protect the social order from threats to its stability or to the existing distribution of political and economic power.

I have said that judges look to what they regard as the interests of the whole society. That, in itself, makes political assumptions of some magnitude. It has long been argued that the concept of the whole society suggests a homogeneity of interest among the different classes within the society which is false. And that this concept is used to persuade the governed that not the government but 'the State' is the highest organization and transcends conflicts in society. It is a short step to say that it is the State which makes the laws, thus enabling those in political power to promote their own interests in the name of the whole abstracted society. Inevitably the judiciary reflects the interests of its own class. Lord Wedderburn has written that 'the eras of judicial "creativity", of new doctrines hostile to trade union interests, have been largely, though not entirely, coterminous with the periods of British social history in which the trade unions have been perceived by middle-class opinion as a threat to the established social order'.[43]

In one analysis, the judiciary is no more than an instrument of the ruling class. Rules are made by the government or, through the common law and statutory interpretation, by the judiciary. These rules are 'the law' and that phrase gives them a supra-political respectability. The rules are what they are because of the nature of the society, because of its cultural and particularly its economic ordering. The government is the political manifestation of the economic forces and the judiciary also subserves those forces. E. P. Thompson summarizes this 'sophisticated, but (ultimately) highly schematic Marxism' which to his surprise, he says, 'seems to spring up in the footsteps of those of us in an older Marxist tradition' in these terms:

> From this standpoint the law is, perhaps more clearly than any other cultural or institutional artifact, by definition a part of a 'superstructure' adapting itself to the necessities of an infrastructure of productive forces and productive relations. As such it is clearly an instrument of the *de facto* ruling class: it both defines these rulers' claims upon resources and labour-power – it says what shall be property and what shall be crime – and it mediates class relations with a set of appropriate rules and

43. See *Industrial Law Journal* (June 1980) at p. 78.

sanctions, all of which, ultimately, confirm and consolidate class power. Hence the rule of law is only another mask for the rule of a class.[44]

The Marxist view depends on the notion of the State as an organization created by and serving to protect and promote the interests of the ruling class.[45] Law is the will of that State which seems to stand outside and above society. This seeming independence of the State and therefore of law helps to obscure the real power relationships which are determined by the economic relationships between classes, helps to legitimate the exercise of that power, and enables the State and the law to appear neutral.

Their (the capitalists') personal rule must at the same time be constituted as an average rule. Their personal power is based on conditions of life which as they develop are common to many individuals, and the continuance of which they, as ruling individuals, have to maintain against others and, at the same time, maintain that they hold good for all. The expression of this will, which is determined by their common interests, is law.[46]

For my purposes the Marxist brush is here much too broad. Nor can I accept the view of law and of judges as no more than superstructure or as adequately defined by that metaphor.

My thesis is that judges in the United Kingdom cannot be politically neutral because they are placed in positions where they are required to make political choices which are sometimes presented to them, and often presented by them, as determinations of where the public interest lies; that their interpretation of what is in the public interest and therefore politically desirable is determined by the kind of people they are and the position they hold in our society; that this position is a part of established authority and so is necessarily conservative and illiberal. From all this flows that view of the public interest which is shown in judicial attitudes such as tenderness towards private property and dislike of trade unions, strong adherence to the maintenance of order, distaste for minority opinions, demonstrations and protests, indifference to the promotion

44. E. P. Thompson, *Whigs and Hunters* (1975), p. 259.
45. For a useful summary see Maureen Cain, 'The Main Themes of Marx's and Engels's Sociology of Law' in 1 *British Journal of Law & Society* 136, to which I am indebted.
46. Marx and Engels, *The German Ideology* (1965 edn), p. 358, quoted by M. Cain, *op. cit.*

of better race relations, support of governmental secrecy, concern for the preservation of the moral and social behaviour to which it is accustomed, and the rest.

Professor Mancini of the University of Bologna has singled out 'the susceptibility of English judges to be analysed as a politically cohesive group' – what I have called their homogeneity – as the factor distinguishing them from judges in Italy, France and Spain. 'What I mean', he says, 'is (a) that English judges seldom make decisions of a nature to challenge a universally received notion of public interest; and (b) that when they happen to do it, their decisions are a result of strictly individual options.' He draws a very sharp contrast: 'the trend towards a more politicized and politically polarized judiciary . . . in Italy, France and Spain . . . has acquired, or is in the process of acquiring, traits so neat and forcible as to rise to the dignity of a major national issue.'[47]

One reason for this continental phenomenon is historical and political: the greater divergence between the right and the left in Italy and France as compared with Britain. But it is made possible by the fact that in those countries judges are appointed in their early or mid-twenties after open competitive examinations. It is therefore possible for men and women with widely different, and, at the time of their examination, unknown political opinions to reach the bench and to remain there, effectively, until retirement. If they display political attitudes of which their superiors disapprove, their promotion may not be speedy. And these superiors continue to be 'politically cohesive'. But to remove the dissidents from office is much more difficult. This split between right and left among the judiciary in those countries is highly significant and wholly without parallel in Britain.

Indeed, the similarities with the position in Britain are to be found among the more rigid regimes of Eastern Europe, South Africa and other countries, capitalist and communist, where the judiciary is manifestly more at one with established authority. In all these countries judges perform similar functions, reflecting their respective societies.

By this I do not mean that the influence exerted directly on the judiciary by the political arm of the State in those countries is paralleled by a similar direct influence in Britain. No doubt, in the great majority of cases before the courts, the judges in those

47. G. F. Mancini, 'Politics and the Judges – the European Perspective' in 43 *Modern Law Review* (1980) 1.

countries act independently of the executive and are prepared to invalidate actions by its members. But in the small number of crucial cases where the offences are political the political influence is more obviously direct. And here political offences means offences which may be drawn in broad terms to include conduct deemed detrimental to State interests. Further, I am speaking of the judiciary only and not of the activities of the political police, or of powers to detain without trial. If I were of a radical turn of mind with a leaning towards iconoclasm and a distrust of those in authority, I would (to put it mildly) find more scope and greater continuity for my activities in Britain than in more totalitarian societies.

But the relative responsiveness of the judiciary to political pressure is not an attribute or a function specific to capitalism or to communism. It would be easy to name a score of countries which are undeniably capitalist and where the judges are as strongly under the influence of the political executive as they are in any communist society. That relative responsiveness reflects the extent to which the judges share the aims and values of the political system, and the extent to which they are its enthusiastic supporters.

It is in this sense that I speak of judges in different countries performing similar functions, reflecting their respective societies, and the political power which operates in them.

Again any analysis which places the judiciary in the United Kingdom in a wholly subservient position to the government misreads history and mistakes the source and nature of the common law. Those who criticize existing institutions in the United Kingdom need always to remember that, in comparison with most other countries, this country enables its citizens to live in comparative freedom. To what extent is this a consequence of our judicial system and of our judges?

That they play some part is undeniable. They will even, on occasion, enforce the law which forbids arrest without reasonable cause or imprisonment without trial, and support the right of free association or, within its limits, of free speech. The idea of the rule of law is not wholly illusory.

Recently an argument has sprung up between two weighty disputants of the left, E. P. Thompson and Perry Anderson, about the meaning and effect of the rule of law.[48] This is not the book in

48. E. P. Thompson, *op.cit.*, pp. 258-69, and the *Bulletin of the Haldane Society*, Spring 1979. Perry Anderson, *Arguments within English Marxism* (1980), especially pp. 197-207.

which to analyze their different positions except to say that Thompson emphasizes how law can be a weapon in the hands of those who are seeking to resist what they see as oppression by established authority; while Anderson emphasizes how despots have typically had comprehensive legal codes and how the distinction between arbitrary power and law is far less obvious than Thompson makes it out to be. My own view is that these two disputants, on this matter of the nature of the rule of law, are not joined in combat because they have failed to define clearly the meaning they attach to the rule of law.

In Britain, laws are rules made by governments, with the authority of Parliament, or by judges. Without these rules governments would not be able to perform their traditional functions. But these laws, which empower governments, by so doing define their powers. And if governments exceed these powers, they may be controlled by the courts and their actions declared unlawful.

What then is meant by 'the rule of law'? The law rules in this sense: that government and all who exercise power as part of established authority are themselves bound by the existing body of laws unless and until they repeal or reform any of those laws. When a government makes a law under Parliamentary authority it makes a rod for its own back as well as for the backs of others. The Declaration of Rights of 1689 declared illegal the suspending or execution of laws by royal authority without the consent of Parliament; and the power to dispense with laws. The exercise of arbitrary power by governments is contrary to the rule of law and the true mark of the despot is that he can, at his own wish and without restraint, set aside the existing laws in any case. Judges are similarly constrained in their law-making function by the doctrine of precedent.

There is another way in which the powers of governments are restricted. As Thompson has observed, if laws are to be plausible as legitimating agents they must not be excessively partial or unjust.

So, because the powers of governments in Britain are limited by law (even though governments may make new laws and change existing laws), there is always the possibility that the exercise of power by governments may be challenged; and because judges, however much they share the values and aims of governments, are not governmental servants, the challenge may be successful.

There is a sense, however far it falls short of what is claimed for it, in which those who exercise legalized force in our society must have regard to the existence of a judiciary which may be prepared to condemn them in some circumstances and will be supported in so doing. Nevertheless, in the event of an attempt by a government to exercise arbitrary and extensive powers, curtailing individual liberty, it cannot be forecast how the judges would react. The political circumstances would be crucial and the judiciary would be divided, as Lords Parker and Gardiner were divided over official torture in Northern Ireland (see above, p. 43). A left-wing attempt would meet with judicial opposition more immediately than a right-wing attempt. And there is little evidence to suggest that the judiciary would be quick to spring to the defence of individual liberty wherever the threat came from.

To whatever extent we seek to define more precisely the function of the judiciary in our society so as to take account of the power of judges to act independently of others, their place as part of the governing group remains unaffected. Nor must we lose sight of two major determinants of the whole. The first is that we in the United Kingdom do live in an increasingly authoritarian society and that this is the outstanding phenomenon of all modern states. I do not mean to belittle the remarkable achievements in authoritarianism of the great systems of government in the past. But modern authoritarianism deals with millions where the tyrants of the past dealt with thousands. And the means of control today are obviously more scientific and much more thorough. It is within such systems that the judges operate; and they operate to help to run these systems. And authoritarianism is always, by its essential nature, conservative and reactionary. It must preserve itself.

Secondly, judges are the product of a class and have the characteristics of that class. Typically coming from middle-class professional families, independent schools, Oxford or Cambridge, they spend twenty to twenty-five years in successful practice at the bar, mostly in London, earning very considerable incomes by the time they reach their forties. This is not the stuff of which reformers are made, still less radicals. There are those who believe that if more grammar or comprehensive schoolboys, graduating at redbrick or new glass universities, became barristers and then judges, the judiciary would be that much less conservative. This is extremely doubtful for two reasons. The years in practice and the middle-aged affluence would remove any aberration in political outlook, if this were necessary. Also, if those changes did not take place, there would be no possibility of their being appointed by the Lord Chancellor, on the advice of the senior judiciary, to the bench.

Ability by itself is not enough. Unorthodoxy in political opinion is a certain disqualification for appointment.

Her Majesty's judges are unlikely to be under great illusions about the functioning of political power in the United Kingdom today. And I think we come close to their definition of the public interest and of the interests of the State if we identify their views with those who insist that in any society, but especially societies in the second half of the twentieth century, stability above all is necessary for the health of the people and is the supreme law.

It follows that governments are normally to be supported but not in every case. Governments represent stability and have a very considerable interest in preserving it. The maintenance of authoritarian structures in all public institutions is wholly in the interest of governments. This is true of all governments of all political complexions, capitalist and communist alike. Whenever governments or their agencies are acting to preserve that stability – call it the Queen's peace, or law and order, or the rule of law, or whatever – the judges will lend their support and will not be over-concerned if to do so requires the invasion of individual liberty.

When, then, is it justifiable, in the opinion of judges, not to support governmental power? From recent cases, certain generalizations can be drawn. First, none of the decisions which conflict with that power falls within that aspect of the judicial view of the public interest which is concerned to maintain law and order, the pre-eminence of which is wholly preserved. Secondly, the courts seem very willing to intervene when the essence of the plaintiff's case is that he is the victim of an exercise of the political policy of ministers, as in *Laker, Tameside, Padfield* and *Anisminic* (see above, chapter 5). Perhaps this is part of that old common law resentment which judges have against statute law. Perhaps it is all that is left of the former tradition of protecting individual liberty.

All those judicial decisions struck down political decisions taken during the period of Labour governments. But, with the exception of the ministerial decision in *Tameside*, it is doubtful whether the political complexion of the government had much to do with those decisions. Much more significant is that these cases and others reflect the emergence of a period of judicial activism or intervention which began in the early 1960s and has been growing in strength ever since. How far this development has been inspired or assisted by the fact that between 1964 and 1979 Labour governments were in office for all but four years is an open question. Perhaps all that can be said is that Labour governments are more likely than

Conservative governments to act in ways which offend the judicial sense of rightness, the judicial view of where the public interest lies.

It is interesting to speculate how far the judges would be willing to push their opposition to the government of the day if convinced that its policies were contrary to the public interest, and how far the government would permit such opposition to continue. Lord Devlin, writing about the *Padfield* decision, wondered, 'whether the courts have moved too far from their base' which, he said, was 'the correction of abuse'. He continued, and here he was also speaking of the *Tameside* decision:

> One may also share to some extent the apprehensions of the Civil Service. All legal history shows that, once the judges get a foothold in the domain of fact, they move to expand. Questions of fact become in a mysterious way questions of law. The fence between error and misconception crumbles with the passage of time. The civil servant may fear the day when he dare not reach a conclusion without asking himself whether a judge will think all the deciding factors as relevant as he does. I do not think that the judiciary should be thrust out of the domain of fact.

Lord Devlin wanted above all to see judicial review 'preserved as a weapon against arbitrary government and I am conscious that its efficacy depends upon the good will of Whitehall'. Because of the power of government to exclude judicial review by statutory provision 'judicial interference with the executive cannot for long very greatly exceed what Whitehall will accept'.[49] Or, as the Prime Minister said in 1977 in the House of Commons: 'We should beware of trying to embroil the judiciary in our affairs, with the corresponding caveat that the judiciary should be very careful about embroiling itself in the legislature.'[50] And in *Duport Steels Ltd v. Sirs* Lord Scarman said: 'If people and Parliament come to think that the judicial power is to be confined by nothing other than the judges's sense of what is right . . . confidence in the judicial system will be replaced by fear of it becoming uncertain and arbitrary in its application. Society will then be ready for Parliament to cut the power of the judges.'

The ultimate, if partial, subservience of the judiciary to the government is spelt out clearly in those words. But the phraseology seems to me greatly to overstate, by implication, the willingness or

49. *The Times*, 27 October 1976.
50. 941 HC Deb. col. 909 (15 December 1977) (Mr Callaghan).

the desire of judges to control 'arbitrary' government. Behind the administrative difficulties which the minister foresaw in *Tameside*, and the consequent harm to groups of pupils, lay the principle of comprehensive schooling. There, as in the cases arising out of legislation concerned with housing and planning, trade unions, and race relations, the judiciary digs its trenches against what it sees as government not in the public interest. But *Padfield, Tameside* and *Laker*, though significant of the modern trend towards greater judicial intervention, are still untypical. They represent the judicial desire not so much to control arbitrariness as to protect the individual against political policies which are seen by the judiciary to be contrary to the public interest. This, of course, is not always possible as Lord Denning reluctantly decided in *Smith v. Inner London Education Authority* (1978) when some parents sought to prevent the Authority from closing St Marylebone Grammar School as part of the change to comprehensive schooling. 'Search as I may,' said Lord Denning, 'and it is not for want of trying, I cannot find any abuse or misuse of power by the education authority . . . It is sad to have to say so, after so much effort has been expended by so many in so good a cause.'[51]

Lord Scarman's plea for the introduction of a Bill of Rights is relevant here.[52] The purposes he has in mind may be wholly admirable being based largely on the Universal Declaration of Human Rights. But others who have also spoken in favour of such a Bill, whose provisions would be entrenched and only repealable or declared inapplicable with the approval of a special (perhaps two-thirds) majority in Parliament, have amongst other things hoped it would prevent the curtailment of freedom of speech in the Race Relations Acts, the educational policies of the Labour government which denied parental choice, the right of entry of factory and health inspectors, and a tax policy, the effect of which would be (it was claimed) to destroy a substantial proportion of independent businesses.[53]

The European Convention of Human Rights, also a candidate for entrenchment in our law, after listing a number of desirable purposes, adds provisos to each in terms like:

No restrictions shall be placed on the exercise of these rights other than such as are prescribed by law and are necessary in a

51. [1978] 1 All ER 411; see also *North Yorkshire County Council v. Secretary of State for Education and Science, The Times*, 20 October 1978.
52. Sir Leslie Scarman, *English Law, the New Dimension* (1975).
53. See the examples collected by M. Zander, *A Bill of Rights?* (1981).

democratic society in the interests of national security or public safety, for the prevention of disorder or crime, for the protection of health or morals or for the protection of the rights and freedom of others. This Article shall not prevent the imposition of lawful restrictions on the exercise of these rights by members of the armed forces, of the police or of the administration of the state.

It is difficult to see how the welfare of the individual would be promoted by the enactment of such provisions if they were to be interpreted by the judiciary of today.

Nevertheless, the approach to an examination of the nature of judicial power through a consideration of human rights had, for the British political system in the mid-1970s, an air of novelty. Liberal thinking among the judiciary has, as we have seen, shown itself only occasionally and then only in minority judgments or dissents. The protection of the public interest in the preservation of a stable society is how the judges see their role.

In other eyes their view of the public interest appears merely as reactionary conservatism. It is not the politics of the extreme right. Its insensitivity is clearly rooted more in unconscious assumptions than in a wish to oppress. But it is demonstrable that on every major social issue which has come before the courts during the last thirty years – concerning industrial relations, political protest, race relations, governmental secrecy, police powers, moral behaviour – the judges have supported the conventional, established, and settled interests. And they have reacted strongly against challenges to those interests. This conservatism does not necessarily follow the day-to-day political policies currently associated with the party of that name. But it is a political philosophy nonetheless.

Many regard the values of the bench and bar in Britain as wholly admirable and the spirit of the common law (as presently expressed) to be a national adornment. The incorruptibility of the English bench and its independence of the government are great virtues. All this is not in issue. When I argue that they regard the interests of the State or the public interest as pre-eminent and that they interpret those interests as meaning that, with very few exceptions, established authority must be upheld and that those exceptions are made only when a more conservative position can be adopted, this does not mean that the judges are acting with impropriety. It means that we live in a highly authoritarian society, fortunate only that we do not live in other societies which are even more authoritarian. We must expect judges, as part of that authority, to act in the interests, as they see them, of the social order.

The judges define the public interest, inevitably, from the viewpoint of their own class. And the public interest, so defined, is by a natural, not an artificial, coincidence, the interest of others in authority, whether in government, in the City or in the church. It includes the maintenance of order, the protection of private property, the promotion of certain general economic aims, the containment of the trade union movement, and the continuance of governments which conduct their business largely in private and on the advice of other members of what I have called the governing group.

Far more than on the judiciary, our freedoms depend on the willingness of the press, politicians and others to publicize the breach of these freedoms and on the continuing vulnerability of ministers, civil servants, the police, other public officials and powerful private interests to accusations that these freedoms are being infringed. In other words, we depend far more on the political climate and on the vigilance of those members of society who for a variety of reasons, some political and some humanitarian, make it their business to seek to hold public authorities within their proper limits. That those limits are also prescribed by law and that judges may be asked to maintain them is not without significance. But the judges are not, as in a different dispensation and under a different social order they might be, the strong, natural defenders of liberty.

Judges are concerned to preserve and to protect the existing order. This does not mean that no judges are capable of moving with the times, of adjusting to changed circumstances. But their function in our society is to do so belatedly. Law and order, the established distribution of power both public and private, the conventional and agreed view amongst those who exercise political and economic power, the fears and prejudices of the middle and upper classes, these are the forces which the judges are expected to uphold and do uphold.

I am not sure what would be the attitude of judges in the ideal society. Perhaps they would not be needed because conflict between governments and the governed would have been removed. But in the societies of our world today they do not stand out as protectors of liberty, of the rights of man, of the unprivileged. With very few notable exceptions, judges in South Africa, in India, in the Soviet Union, in Western Europe, in Chile, and elsewhere have not shown that they are 'no respectors of persons and stand between the subject and any attempted encroachments on his liberty by the executive',[54] nor have they insisted that holders of great economic power, private or public, should use it with moderation. Their view of the public interest, when it has gone beyond the interest of governments, has not been wide enough to embrace the interests of political, ethnic, social or other minorities. Only occasionally, in the United States of America, has the power of the supreme judiciary been exercised in the positive assertion of fundamental values. In both capitalist and communist societies, the judiciary has naturally served the prevailing political and economic forces. Politically, judges are parasitic.

That this is so is not a matter for recrimination. It is idle to criticize institutions for performing the task they were created to perform and have performed for centuries. It is possible to criticize the police if they use excessive force or illegal means in maintaining law and order, but to criticize them for fulfilling their function is absurd. So also with the judiciary. Their principal function is to support the institutions of government as established by law. To expect a judge to advocate radical change, albeit legally, is as absurd as it would be to expect an anarchist to speak up in favour of an authoritarian society. The confusion arises when it is pretended that judges are somehow neutral in the conflicts between those who challenge existing institutions and those who control those institutions. And cynicism replaces confusion whenever it becomes apparent that the latter are using the judges as open allies in those conflicts.

Thus it is usual for judges in political cases to be able to rely on the rules of law for the legitimacy of their decisions. As we have seen, there are innumerable ways – through the development of the common law, the interpretation of statutes, the refusal to use discretionary powers, the claims to residual jurisdiction and the rest – in which the judges can fulfil their political function and do so in the name of the law.

54. Lord Atkin in *Liversidge v. Anderson* (see above, p. 84)

Indexes

General index

Index of cases